WITH ALL
YOUR MIND

WITH ALL YOUR MIND

A Christian Philosophy of Education

MICHAEL L. PETERSON

University of Notre Dame Press
Notre Dame, Indiana

Manufactured in the United States of America

Paperback reprinted in 2005, 2007

Library of Congress Cataloging-in-Publication Data
Peterson, Michael L., 1950–
    With all your mind : a Christian philosophy of education /
Michael L. Peterson.
        p.   cm.
    Includes bibliographical references and index.
    ISBN 10: 0-268-01967-3 (cloth : alk. paper)
    ISBN 13: 978-0-268-01968-6 (pbk. : alk. paper)
    ISBN 10-268-01968-1 (pbk. : alk. paper)
        1. Teaching—Religious aspects—Christianity.
    2. Education—Philosophy. 3. Education—Aims and objectives.
    I. Title.
    LB1027 .2 .P48   2001
    370'.1—dc21

                                                    2001004258

For the love of my life,

REBECCA

Contents

Acknowledgments

A vision for the integral relationship between Christian faith and humane learning has long captivated my thinking. During my undergraduate days, Professors James Hamilton, Paul Denlinger, Roger Kusche, and Cecil Hamann first opened my eyes to this compelling idea. Throughout my career in philosophy, I have continued to refine my ideas in discussion with colleagues: Gerald Miller, Alan Moulton, Kevin Sparks, Daniel Strait, Paul Vincent, and others. They will see traces of our conversations in the following pages.

Many others have also had a hand in the making of this book. Those writers from whom I draw energy and inspiration will soon become apparent. Some persons would not be so apparent unless I named them: Anna McEwan suggested certain features of the book; Morgan Tracy assisted with research; and Trina Erlewein keyed in much of the bibliography. My son Aaron Peterson helped with the bibliography and advised on several computer-related matters. My son Adam Peterson proofread the final manuscript.

My wife, Rebecca, is always a hidden support in all that I do. I loved her before I ever met her. That is, I always cherished the ideal of a beautiful and caring and faithful companion—and I have found it perfectly exemplified in her. I married my high school sweetheart, who has become my lifelong partner and best friend. Love,

deepened by over three decades of commitment, leads me joy-
fully to dedicate this book to her.

Michael L. Peterson
Wilmore, Kentucky

Introduction

This book represents an attempt to think deeply about education from a Christian point of view. Clearly, education is in crisis and needs guidance to find its way. Techniques and theories of education continue to be debated in regard to every level of education, from the earliest grades to doctoral programs. Parents, students, clergy, politicians, trustees, and educators, in both religious and secular settings, add their voices to the discussion. All who are concerned about education are invited to participate in this study, which analyzes representative theories and practical strategies in order to show the power of Christian ideas in this vital area.

Convinced that thinking philosophically about education is our only hope for meaningful progress, I explain basic concepts, work out their implications, and then evaluate their adequacy. The reader will learn a good deal of philosophy while being enabled to grapple with extremely important educational matters.

The theological perspective I bring to the task here is broadly and ecumenically Christian. Defining my perspective as historically orthodox, I am appreciative of the contributions of all valid Christian traditions. It is my hope that this book will serve as a model of how Christians can address important issues out of our deeper unity.

My intention in this writing is neither to present a piece of cutting-edge research nor to give technical treatment to every major issue. I offer it as what I call "digested scholarship"—the careful reflections of a senior scholar, reflections guided by professional expertise and emerging out of long experience, but expressed in a friendly, accessible style.

Although the ways of thinking here apply to both formal and informal education at every stage, I have done most of my thinking about higher education. Long ago, the vision of liberal arts in vital interplay with Christian faith captured my imagination and my heart. Many points I make in the book apply, therefore, to the ongoing consideration of that ideal. I trust that, in the pages to follow, the reader will unmistakably find as much inspiration as information.

CHAPTER ONE

What Is Philosophy of Education?

O n one occasion Aristotle was asked how much educated people were superior to those uneducated: "As much," he replied, "as the living are to the dead."[1] The words of the great teacher remind us of the incredible power of education. All persons, of course, have value and worth regardless of their level of education. But Aristotle's point is that proper education enlivens the mind and shapes the whole person.

Most people in the United States spend at least twelve years of their lives in formal education, and most in other Western countries spend at least eleven years. Many extend their education through college or beyond. The enormous time and energy devoted to education justify careful consideration of its nature and purpose. In the words of Abraham Lincoln, the discussion of education is "the most important subject which we, as a people, can be engaged in."[2]

When we consider education, all sorts of important questions immediately arise: What form should education take? How should education interact with culture? Can morals and values be taught? What is the knowledge most worth having? What relationship should education have to gainful employment? What impact does religious faith have on learning? What impact does learning have on faith? Working through such questions and arriving at clear and consistent answers puts us in the best position to guide the education of our young.

WHY STUDY THEORY?

The most significant questions concerning education are theoretical, not practical. They pertain to how we think in broad terms about education. At the level of theory, we contemplate education in terms of its aims and goals and ideals. Discussions of these matters depend on even more fundamental debates over what the human being is that we are trying to educate, on what truth is, and on what capabilities people have for knowing it. These are abstract and complicated subjects calling for deep thought and reflection.

Yet our culture does not encourage us to be reflective. We are typically more concerned with actions and results than with theory: we are more interested in "how" rather than "why." This obsession with practice has been detrimental to the educational enterprise. Charles Silberman claims that our educational milieu suffers from "mindlessness," charging that it uncritically prizes technique over understanding and elevates methodology over well-defined goals.[3] Modern educators have been so busy devising new instruments for measuring intelligence, exploring effective strategies for teaching computer skills to elementary school children, and offering more efficient ways to complete a college degree that they have seldom stopped to ask why such things are desirable.

Few practicing educators in Western culture address the larger meaning of education. According to Lawrence Cremin, this is painfully true in the United States:

Too few educational leaders in the United States are genuinely preoccupied with educational issues because they have no clear ideas about education. And if we look at the way these leaders have been recruited and trained, there is little that would lead us to expect otherwise. They have too often been managers, facilitators, politicians in the narrowest sense. They have been concerned with building buildings, balancing budgets, and pacifying parents, but they have not been prepared to spark a great public dialogue about the ends and means of education. And in the absence of such dialogue, large segments of the public have had, at best, a limited understanding of the ways and wherefores of popular schooling.[4]

Clearly, many teachers do a good job of teaching. Perhaps they do so instinctively, without really pondering aims of education. But they would greatly enhance their contribution as educators by deliberate reflection on educational theory. Although suggestions occasionally surface about nurturing our educators in the great literature of education, we should pay much more attention to this need. Astoundingly, the business of education continues at a rapid pace without educators or the general populace having clear answers to the most basic questions: What is the purpose of education? What goals do new techniques and methods serve? What kind of person is our educational system supposed to produce? These are theoretical questions that force us to articulate and evaluate our basic commitments.

Our fixation on educational methodology and avoidance of vigorous, open discussion of educational theory has led over time to our unconscious or at least uncritical acceptance of unworthy and confused ideals. Unless we squarely face the tough, foundational questions, we can never get solid answers, and without reliable answers education in America is vulnerable to political and cultural pressures. To be sure, education will always serve some ideals. We must make sure that its ideals are worthy.

Borrowing religious terminology, Neil Postman writes that education inevitably serves various "gods." A god in this sense is a comprehensive story or "narrative" that has sufficient complexity and symbolic power to attract us to organize our lives around it. A great narrative constructs ideals, prescribes rules of conduct, and provides a sense of purpose; it tells us what the universe is like and how to understand our place in it.⁵ "Where there is no vision," Proverbs tells us, "the people perish."⁶ This is true in all areas of life, and it is true in education. Education requires some organizing principle, some dominant vision to give meaning and direction to its pursuit.

The history of education, like the history of civilization itself, contains the record of many gods that failed, many narratives that were not ultimately satisfying. There was once the narrative of the Protestant work ethic, which assured people that hard work and self-denial were sure ways to secure God's favor. In its name, children were educated to avoid idleness and develop self-discipline. There was also the great god of Communism, which promised equal distribution of wealth in a classless society. Under this god, education was to serve the state's ultimate purposes. Obviously, there are many other gods. Some have been discarded on the ash heap of history while others still have their following. A god still in vogue is consumerism, whose story tells us that we are what we possess and that our identity is defined by what we do for a living. Education in service to this god turns out productive economic units that keep the economy growing.

But all of these gods are false ultimates, and education fashioned in the image of a false god is misguided education. What other gods or ideals are being served in our day? In the future, will we also look back on them as failures, untenable ultimates? Wise answers to these questions will come only through our close attention to educational theory.

We need to recover the normal link between educational theory and practice. Theory guides practice by establishing the aims of education and projecting basic ways in which these ends can be reached. To paraphrase Kant, practice without theory is blind. Without theory, responses to problems are arbitrary, shortsighted, and susceptible to hidden agendas. Concrete decisions—about whether to distribute condoms in high schools, whether to add distance learning over the Internet to a college curriculum, and a host of other matters—should stem from a coherent theoretical framework.

Obviously, education is a topic about which responsible people disagree, but unless we engage in reasonable dialogue, there is little hope for salvaging, let alone improving, our rapidly deteriorating public educational system. Where should we start? We cannot make initial progress by debating the conduct of education: curriculum offerings, pedagogical methods, sex education in the lower grades, and other such matters. All such practical strategies and techniques inevitably reflect more abstract goals and objectives. Our differences about the goals of education predictably cause disagreements about practical strategies and techniques, whereas consensus on goals would allow meaningful agreement regarding practice.

Educational goals and objectives, in turn, arise from still more basic philosophical commitments. So, our deliberations must ultimately be rooted in ideas about the nature of reality, knowledge, and humanity itself. This is why it is urgent that we become aware of the various underlying philosophical concepts that shape educational discussions and become skillful in evaluating them. Thus, in the final analysis, no educational practice can proceed intelligently without theory. Every policy and every method, whether we realize it or not, is laden with some concept of what education is all about, and this concept arises from some fundamental philosophical viewpoint. If we seek the broadest possible perspective on education and want to understand the root of so many educational controversies, we must start at the most general, foundational level and work our way to more specific issues. Nothing could be more practical than considering theory first.

Practice has a reciprocal impact on theory. Practice can "test" a theory; it can validate or invalidate educational policies and proposals. A fine-sounding theory may run into difficulties in application and thus cause us to rethink, modify or relinquish our original ideas. Every educational theory has to encounter the hard realities of ordinary life and stand or fall according to its adequacy to human experience. So, there is a proper time for debating the effectiveness and legitimacy of the practical and technical aspects of education. To extend our earlier paraphrase of Kant, theory without practice is empty.

There is a hierarchy to our ideas, from the most abstract and general to the most concrete. Educational policy and practice are logically subordinate to and dependent upon educational theory, and educational theory itself is subordinate to and dependent upon a larger worldview. These relationships are graphically illustrated in figure 1.

FIGURE 1

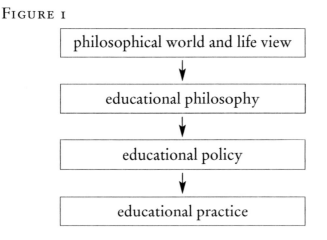

As a rule, the positions one holds concerning issues at lower levels are derived from the higher levels. An educational philosophy affects policy and practice either by generating a specific conclusion or by providing a general way of thinking. So, no educational decisions can have clear direction without reference to some educational philosophy or theory. Furthermore, no educational theory can have a firm basis without an even more general philosophical perspective.

This hierarchical understanding applies to all educational issues. Take, for example, the practice of nondiscrimination in hiring teachers and in dealing with students. This action arises from a general policy that discrimination is wrong. But the reasons why it is wrong may vary according to one's educational philosophy. At the level of educational philosophy, discrimination might be viewed as wrong because it violates the inherent dignity of human beings. This belief in their inherent dignity is likewise anchored in an overall worldview, such as a theistic worldview, which understands persons to be created by a personal deity. Of course, the same practical policy of nondiscrimination could also be rooted in a quite different, non-theistic educational philosophy. Many versions of naturalism consider human beings as political entities in competition for power. A corollary of this may be the belief that in education we should level the playing field in the ongoing power struggle.

At this point we have reached the most universal level of discussion in all educational matters—the level of worldview commitments. The more concrete educational strategies and techniques we employ are necessitated or ruled out or at least made optional within the context of a larger worldview. When we become aware of these conceptual relationships, we are then prepared to be discerning and prudent in our deliberations about educational matters. This preparation requires that we acquaint ourselves with the field of philosophy.

PHILOSOPHY AND EDUCATIONAL THEORY

The term "philosophy" can be used to designate either an inherent tendency in human beings or an academic discipline. Literally, "philosophy" means "the love of wisdom." Human beings have the innate desire to increase their understanding of the world and to find wisdom. Some have the desire more strongly than others, but this desire can be tutored, developed, and refined by an organized course of study. The discipline of philosophy is important, then, because the human quest for wisdom is so important.

The philosophical enterprise is concerned with the analysis and evaluation of beliefs about life's most important questions: the conditions of knowledge, the nature of morality, the structure of society, the existence of God, the meaning of the human venture, and many more. In addition, philosophy sometimes involves the attempt to assemble a set of answers and insights related to such questions into a coherent system of thought known as a "worldview." A worldview provides a total, comprehensive way of looking at everything—knowledge, ethics, humanity, meaning, and even the divine.

Although there are numerous ways of packaging philosophical content into academic courses, one way is to designate relatively discrete "departments" of philosophical inquiry, such as philosophy of science, philosophy of art, philosophy of law, and the like. The various "departmental philosophies," as they are often labeled, investigate the philosophical foundations of specific disciplines, recognizing that these deep commitments shape our thinking about each area. Predictably, thinkers who disagree on fundamental philosophical matters disagree over issues arising within the specific branches of knowledge.

Philosophy of education is one of the many departmental philosophies. It may be defined broadly as the attempt to bring the insights and methods of philosophy to bear on the educational enterprise. Since the philosophical orientation one adopts about the nature of reality, knowledge, and value shapes how one thinks about the nature and purpose of education, philosophy is indispensable to the process of education.

Who can benefit from exploring the philosophy of education? Professional educators, both present and future, teachers, counselors, administrators, and curriculum specialists all need to think carefully about the large philosophical questions that are logically prior to any goals and methods they adopt. Those who are not professional educators—parents, students, legislators, and everyone who recognizes the vital importance of education—will also profit from the philosophy of education.

The example of education simply proves the general need for a guiding conceptual framework in all areas of life and thought. Studying philosophical themes relevant to education offers some people their first opportunity to consider life's great questions and to form their own viewpoints. When we develop our own philosophical outlook, we are then in a position to formulate meaningful educational and career goals. Indeed, from our worldview we draw impetus and motivation for our own study and achievement. The philosophy of education is important because it allows both professionals and nonprofessionals to survey the major philosophies of life and think through a host of significant interconnected issues.

CHRISTIANITY AND EDUCATION

Philosophy of education is an extremely valuable subject for Christians. Contemporary Christians feel an obligation to respond to a multitude of educational issues, from the moral deterioration of our public schools to the creation-evolution controversy in science classes. Many people struggle with the decision of whether to attend or encourage their children to attend a private school, perhaps a Christian school. Some seriously consider the question of home schooling. Other Christians are interested in finding the most effective way to navigate in secular educational settings. These pressing challenges call for more than simplistic answers. We need a whole way of thinking about education—that is, a philosophical outlook that relates religious commitment to educational concerns. Out of this understanding, we can intelligently address whatever educational problems we face.

The main point of contact between educational philosophy and Christianity is their mutual attention to the same basic conceptual questions. These are deep questions about the nature of ultimate reality, the process of gaining knowledge, the demands of morality, and the meaning of life. A complete, systematic set of answers to basic philosophical questions constitutes a worldview, and there is a wide range of competing worldviews, all with their distinctive implications for education. The purpose of this study is to articulate a viable understanding of a Christian worldview, put it in interaction with other worldviews, and show how it provides a more helpful framework for thinking about education.

Speaking accurately of Christianity requires some initial agreement about what Christianity is.[7] Although Christianity is complex and hard to summarize, we may adopt a very basic definition. I find it helpful to characterize Christianity as having two dimensions: a *cognitive* dimension and an *experiential* dimension. The cognitive aspect of Christianity pertains to the beliefs one must embrace, the propositions one must accept as true. The experiential dimension refers to the practical experience of those who are trying to live a Christian life. These two components are intimately connected: to be completely Christian one must be both cognitively and experientially Christian.

An excellent starting place for specifying the cognitive side of Christian faith is what we may call "classical Christianity." Classical *Christianity* is the definition of Christian belief hammered out by councils, synods, and consensual bodies convened during the early life of the church. These large conclaves met on a worldwide basis to establish a precise understanding of Jesus Christ, the Holy Spirit, the Trinity, and other doctrines and, in so doing, to distinguish authentic Christian belief from heresy and error. The seven great councils were Nicea (in the year 325), Constantinople I (381), Ephesus (431) Chalcedon (451), Constantinople II (553), Constantinople III (680–681), and Nicea II (787).[8] Their official declarations commonly bound all Christians, East and West. According to Vincent of Lérins, the councils' legacy is the enduring formulation of "that which has been everywhere and always and by everyone believed" (*quod ubique, quod semper, quod ab omnibus creditum est*).[9] This is historic, ecumenical orthodoxy.

The teachings and doctrines of the many different Christian denominations and traditions have lasting value only insofar as they put us in touch with what is essential and enduring in Christian belief. All valid Christian traditions converge in that

central, consensual core. Coming to us out of the ancient past, the
Apostles' Creed serves as a reminder that the church has always
placed strong emphasis on what each Christian intellectually believes and confidently confesses in the midst of the faithful.[10] This
creedal statement presents necessary Christian belief in outline
form. More elaborate statements of accredited doctrines concerning the Person of Christ, the Trinity, the Atonement, and the like
are found in the consensual documents of the historic councils
and in the writings of the early church fathers.[11]

Each Christian denomination has its own ways of reflecting
its particular journey through time and space, of honoring its
own heroes and commemorating pivotal events. In short, every
faith tradition—Roman Catholic, Eastern Orthodox, Lutheran,
Baptist, Mennonite, and others—has a unique cultural texture.
That is simply a fact of our humanness: we live in a certain
epoch of history, in a certain place, in the midst of a certain
group whose experience is marked by specific events. This gives
concreteness and flavor to our lives. We must not, however,
equate the concrete cultural packaging that mediates to us
Christian faith with the normative content of the faith universal,
timeless and for all. The *Anglican Thirty-Nine Articles* sounds a
moderate tone on this point: "It is not necessary that traditions
and ceremonies be in all places one, or utterly like, for at all
times they have been diverse, and may be changed according to
the diversity of countries, times and [human] manners."[12] There
will always be differences of opinion among Christian traditions on mode of baptism, ordination of women, celibacy of the
priesthood, liturgical style, and other matters. Yet, on the cognitive side of faith, the common, consensual beliefs are primary
while other beliefs and doctrines are secondary.

The other aspect of Christian faith is personal or experiential in nature. Put simply, it is life in Christ. Christianity is not
unique in understanding itself to be founded by a particular
historical personage, since Islam and Buddhism both share that
feature. Yet Mohammed and Siddhartha Gautama, the historical Buddha, exist in an entirely different relationship to the

faiths they inspired than Jesus does to Christianity. Jesus now
and in each historical period is present to the believing faithful.
He is misunderstood, therefore, if considered to be the one
who points the way. He *is* the Way. Being related to him, participating in his life, is the center of Christian faith.

"God was in Christ, reconciling the world unto himself."[13]
Each individual must appropriate the divine gift of God through
Christ. The opening lines of the *Catechism of the Catholic
Church* declare: "God, infinitely perfect and blessed in himself,
in a plan of sheer goodness freely created man to make him
share in his own blessed life. . . . To accomplish this, . . . God
sent his Son as Redeemer and Savior."[14] We were made for God;
we find the meaning of our existence by connection to him.[15]
Experiencing God's life taking root and growing in our lives is
the vital core of Christian life.

Authentic Christian life is not individualistic or idiosyncratic, but is found in the company of the faithful. The church
through the centuries has unwaveringly affirmed that Christ is
present in the midst of his people. Ultimately, life in Christ
occurs within a worshiping community. No theme is clearer in
the New Testament or occurs more often in the earliest documents of orthodoxy: Christianity consists essentially in participating in the cross and resurrection of Jesus Christ.[16] This great
mystery occurs among the people who are called Christ's body.
The *Westminster Confession* states: "All saints that are united to
Jesus Christ their head, by his Spirit and by faith, have fellowship with him in his graces, sufferings, death, resurrection, and
glory, and being united to one another in love, they have communion in each other's gifts and graces. . . ."[17] And, of course,
the Apostles' Creed itself makes "communion of the saints" a
necessary item of belief.

There simply is no Christian tradition without some form
of interpersonal encounter with the living Christ, however diverse that encounter may appear in the many languages, cultures, and eras over more than two millennia. Thomas Oden
suggests an image of light passing through a prism to help us

think about how Christ is related to the rich diversity among Christian groups:

> The varieties of the tradition may be viewed as if Christ were a spectral prism through which God's love is refracted on the changing surfaces of the evoluting world. The lens creates a burst of vibrant colors. It breaks up a single beam of light and reveals all the variety of colors already implicitly within that beam. . . . The colors are strikingly different, just as Christian perceptions of the living Christ have been abundantly diverse. It is as if in certain periods, Christianity has become enamored with soft pastels and aquas, while in another century gaudy iridescent oranges or mellow oyster whites might have captured its imagination. Yet the same unchanging, steadfast love of God in Christ is variably manifested in the entire polychromatic scale. Seen together historically, they manifest the full rainbow of God's presence in the estranged world.[18]

The constant, universal essence of Christian experience is manifested through myriad traditions and settings and times.

Our two-fold conception of Christianity as both cognitive and experiential is illuminating and serves to ground the Christian worldview that emerges in our study. Furthermore, it gives us a positive, properly ecumenical vantage point from which to evaluate alternative philosophies of education and then to develop a sound Christian philosophy of education in response.

DEFINITIONS AND DISTINCTIONS

Before we can make progress in thinking about a distinctively Christian philosophy in general and a Christian philosophy of education in particular, we must clarify the nature of philosophy itself. Philosophy is both a *subject matter* and an *activity*. In other words, it is a field of inquiry with a distinctive content

and a certain method of thinking. These two dimensions will ultimately affect our thinking about education in important ways.

As a *subject matter*, philosophy encompasses the great, ongoing dialogue about life's most important questions. Thus, the
study of philosophy acquaints us with the fundamental intellectual problems that reflective people have always raised and
pondered. The very process of exploring these problems, along
with the principal responses that have been proposed, is instructive and enlightening. The main branches of philosophy
are actually defined by the nature of the questions they address.
For our purposes, we will look at questions concerning the
nature of reality, knowledge, and value.

The branch of philosophy known as *metaphysics* examines
the fundamental questions, "What is the nature of reality?" and
"What exists?" A number of subjects fall within the scope of
metaphysics: the reality of objects, the status of time, causality,
the existence of God, and the nature of a human being.[19] Metaphysics is central to the educational enterprise because education is ultimately designed according to what a society or group
considers reality to be. Different perspectives on the structure
of reality lead to divergent approaches to education. Consider
the distinct educational orientations that emerge when one
compares the view that a person is a rational and spiritual being
to the view that a person is a complex animal.

Epistemology is the branch of philosophy that analyzes
questions related to knowledge. What is truth? What are the
sources of knowledge? How do we know? Concerns of this
sort probe into the nature, kinds, and justification of human
knowledge.[20] Obviously, epistemological issues are critical to
educational theory. Since education deals with knowledge, the
epistemological assumptions held by an educator and educational system will shape pedagogical aims and methodologies.
For example, the assumption that sensory experience is the only
source of knowledge encourages teaching methods that stress
practical, hands-on experience for students and rigorous scientific evidence to support all claims. By contrast, the assump-

tion that insight and intuition provide a legitimate kind of knowledge generates teaching methods that incorporate critical thinking, rational reflection, and exposure to abstract ideas.

The question, "What is valuable?" is central to the branch of philosophy known as *axiology.* Persons are undeniably valuing beings, preferring some things to others. *Ethics* is the area of axiology that studies what "right" and "good" in both conduct and character.[21] *Aesthetics*, another area of axiology, probes the concept of the beautiful. Aesthetics explores the creation and appreciation of beauty in various artistic contexts—music, painting, and so on. There is a very intimate connection between values and education. Education involves the formation of value preferences that extend into the spheres of morality and taste. Consequently, the position taken by an educator or educational community on the matter of values inevitably influences classroom content and procedure, and it can even affect the entire curriculum structure. Great differences exist, for example, between educators who take morality to be absolute and grounded in religion and those who take morality to be relative to individuals and cultures. Educators who embrace the first point of view tend to require that the student learn a particular religious viewpoint as a basis for moral standards. Those holding the latter view typically strive for utter neutrality in discussing ethical issues.

Philosophy as an *activity* or method involves several kinds of intellectual approaches: synthetic, analytic, descriptive, and normative. Philosophers differ about how these approaches are related as well as about their comparative importance. Some identify the proper way of doing philosophy with one specific type of thinking, such as analysis; others propose a combination of types. Without settling these issues here, let us survey the various means of doing philosophy so that we can see how they will relate to our discussion of education.

Those who employ the *synthetic* aspect of philosophical thinking seek a comprehensive interpretation of things. The synthetic approach is an attempt to weave together all of our knowledge and insight about the world into a systematic, unified perspective. Synthetic or synoptic thinking sees life and the universe as a whole rather than as fragmented; a synthetic thinker will attempt to formulate a worldview.[22] A worldview contains interrelated assumptions about the nature of reality, knowledge, and value, as well as their general implications for concepts of society, science, art, and so forth. In philosophy of education, the synthetic approach aims at assembling a total picture of human existence as a context for thinking about the meaning and conduct of education. The synthetic approach to a philosophy of education will help us see how a comprehensive Christian worldview compares—and, indeed, interacts—with competing worldviews.

A philosopher using the *analytic* approach seeks to identify the assumptions and methods upon which common sense and science depend. This method even gives significant attention to the clarification of the meaning of terms and to the rigorous examination of arguments. Without a clear definition of the meaning of such terms as *truth, reality, mind, matter, good,* and *evil,* philosophical dialogue would be ambiguous or vague. Without a precise understanding of the principles of valid argumentation, the case for a given position could be incoherent or misleading. Within the philosophy of education specifically, the analytic approach raises questions about the meaning of such crucial terms as *learning, schooling, training, indoctrination,* and the like. In subsequent chapters, our concern for careful analysis will lead us to scrutinize arguments that support general philosophical positions, as well as the educational theories they support.

Those who use the *descriptive* method in philosophy attempt to represent accurately "what is the case." That is, they describe the facts in a clear and objective fashion. Some of the most significant facts about ourselves as human beings cannot be revealed through scientific procedures. Many of these facts, which are not immediately obvious, must be carefully exposed through philosophical reflection and then characterized as objectively as possible. Robert Beck writes, "Facts must be revealed, the implicit made explicit, and the misinterpreted or uninterpreted brought forward for examination."[23] For example, description in philosophy may produce an account of how conscience operates or of how perception occurs. The descriptive method, then, sets the stage for further theorizing and critique. After all, our explanations and arguments depend wholly on how key facts are represented in the first place. In philosophy of education, for example, we try to describe the structure of human knowledge or the developmental stages of the child. Based on these descriptions, we consider the best methods for teaching certain subjects.

The *normative* method of philosophical inquiry is perhaps closest to the original spirit of philosophy. It is the endeavor to establish standards and ideals for our individual and collective lives. When we apply normative thinking to education, we contemplate and prescribe the ethical and aesthetic values that we think education should foster in students and that should guide the conduct of teachers and administrators. At a very fundamental level, we attempt to project a vision of the kind of person this education should seek to develop and what kind of society we ought to have.

My goal is to equip the reader with a reliable and helpful way of thinking as a Christian about countless educational issues. On some matters, it may turn out that the thoughtful and conscientious Christian can take only one position; on other issues there may be a range of acceptable options. Now, with our working definitions of both Christianity and philosophy, we can launch our exploration of philosophy of education from a Christian perspective.

CHAPTER TWO

Traditional Philosophies
of Education

Our aim is to develop a philosophy of education that is explicitly tied to a Christian
worldview.[1] To achieve this goal we must first
survey other philosophies of education and the worldviews from which they emanate.[2] Here we will examine
three influential traditional philosophies of education:
idealism, naturalism, and Thomistic realism. I label these
positions "traditional" because they seek to fulfill one of
the historical functions of philosophy, which is the articu-
lation of an all-encompassing interpretation of existence.
This enterprise arises from the long-standing belief that
the human mind can reliably know reality and develop a
reasonable interpretation of it.

I will employ a three-part approach in examining
each philosophical perspective. First, I will sketch their
major assumptions about reality (metaphysics), knowledge (epistemology), and value (axiology). Second, I will
explore the educational implications of those assumptions. Metaphysical assumptions have clear implications
for educational aims and curricula. Epistemological assumptions generate logical consequences for styles of
teaching and learning. Axiological assumptions have important ramifications for methods of ethical nurture and
aesthetic cultivation. Third, I will evaluate each perspective in regard to its philosophical adequacy, educational

appropriateness, and theological acceptability. In order to make this discussion more concrete, I will present the ideas of one or two representative thinkers for each philosophy.

IDEALISM: MINDS AND IDEAS

A philosophical idealist believes that reality is composed of minds, ideas, or selves rather than material things. We must distinguish this metaphysical outlook from idealism considered as an attitude toward life, such as the desire to pursue high ideals and lofty goals. William Hocking explains that the term "idea-ism" would be more to the point than "idealism."[3] The central vision of idealism is the primacy of mind over anything we would call material or physical. Physical objects are either unreal or much less real than ideas. While idealism may seem strange at first, it has been held in one form or another by some great thinkers, past and present, East and West, such as Parmenides, G. W. F. Hegel, F. H. Bradley, and S. Radhakrishnan.

George Berkeley held a philosophical position known as "subjective idealism." He asserted that the very existence of objects is donated by mind and that the reality we experience depends on thought. His famous dictum, "to be is to be perceived," affirms that to exist is to be present in consciousness.[4] Berkeley's idealism dispensed with the concept of an objective, material world that exists outside the mind.

A direct implication of idealistic metaphysics is that a human person is essentially a spiritual or rational being. After all, thinking, feeling, and valuing are fundamental to our human nature. Immanuel Kant vigorously argued that personhood has intrinsic worth that is incommensurable with the value of anything else. For Kant, as for other idealists, neither the body nor its physical attributes are relevant to the ultimate value of a human being; it is the soul or mind that truly constitutes our nature. Most idealists, furthermore, recognize some kind of Supreme Being or Supreme Mind behind the universe.

Most idealistic thinkers say that the universe is a rational system or at least that we must think of it in these terms. Kant, for example, argues that the rational structure of objects in our empirical experience is actually contributed by the structure of the mind.[5] His "transcendental idealism" maintains that the human mind is the organizing and unifying factor in all knowledge. The world is rendered intelligible, then, as the mind interprets our sensory awareness of things in space and time through the categories of the understanding, such as quantity and quality. These same rational categories are innate in all rational minds and thus constitute the universal and necessary features of all human knowledge.

Historically, idealism has been concerned with denying skepticism and with assuring us of the possibility of success in the quest for knowledge. It does this by offering an account of how the mind acquires truth or how it comes into contact with God's mind. Most idealists, including Kant, contend that there are universal and necessary truths that are ultimately anchored in consciousness, either human or divine.

An idealist theory of value is perfectly compatible with an idealist understanding of reality and knowledge. For idealists, values are absolute and unchanging. Although many idealists say that the source of these values is the Infinite Person or God, Kant claims that they originate in the structure of rationality itself. Let us consider how the Kantian position shapes thinking in both ethics and aesthetics.

In Kant's view, since moral laws are grounded in the structure of rationality, they constitute an objective, absolute standard. The general form of moral law, which he called the "categorical imperative," demands our unconditional obedience and disregard for egocentric interests.[6] Thus, moral law reflects what is universally right for all humankind.[7] Interestingly, according to Kant, a truly moral action cannot merely conform to the objective requirements of moral law. A moral action must also be done from the proper motive, which he designates "the good will." He conceives of the good will as sheer respect for duty for its own sake. Our subjective intention must be to obey moral law simply because it is the right thing to do. Kant's attention here to the inner component of morality would prevent us from thinking that a person is moral when he merely acts in accord with objective duty but has subjective reasons that are base or unworthy, such as manipulation or self-aggrandizement.

Kant connects morality and religion by arguing that belief in God is required to make full sense of the moral life. Although he argues in his *Critique of Pure Reason* that God's existence cannot be deduced through the arguments of speculative theology, he maintains that rationality must "postulate" God to give meaning to moral life.[8] Moral duties, then, should be viewed as divine commands. Of course, this approach does not so much bring religion into morality as it virtually reduces religion to morality; religion exists to serve the moral life. A Kantian thinker would believe that the historical particulars of a religion, such as Christianity, can be minimized, reinterpreted, or eliminated in order to highlight the universal moral code.[9]

Idealistic thinking in aesthetics involves ideas similar to those present in idealist ethics. For most idealists, an object, whether natural or humanly created, is beautiful according to how well it expresses a transcendent ideal of beauty. In painting, sculpture, music, poetry, and other art forms, idealistic artists generally think of themselves as "idealizing" something, of using a particular instance to embody a larger ideal. Idealistic artists might even minimize blemishes or remove idiosyncratic traits from the object they are creating so that it better expresses the universal ideal. Of course, the ideal is never fully realizable in experience, but the secret to artistic creation and aesthetic taste is the ability to bring a particular under a general norm or rule or to work with the particular object to express the norm more excellently.[10]

The Kantian position on beauty moves in an interesting direction. According to Kant, we do actually make universal aesthetic judgments. But the universal character of such judgments is not based on an objective quality in the object. A person is entitled to pronounce an object beautiful when he realizes that his pleasure in contemplating it is disinterested: that the pleasure is such that it could be experienced by all who contemplate the same object. Thus, Kant erects an objective standard of aesthetic judgment, but anchors it in the shared experience of the human race.

IDEALISM AND EDUCATION

Proponents of philosophical idealism perceive the world as rational and purposeful. Indeed, for many idealists, the universe is deeply personal. In keeping with this vision, the aim of education is to bring about the full intellectual, moral, and spiritual development of the student. To the extent that students emulate the Divine Being or realize the ideals of personhood in meaningful community, they will grow and mature correctly. A particularly Kantian approach would emphasize that students should acquire discipline and self-mastery, hone mental skills, and develop solid moral character. When cultivated, these dispositions serve the proper ends of humankind. Clearly, students need practical competencies to navigate in the everyday world, but the main orientation of idealist education accents those subjects and educational processes that more clearly reflect the ideal, perfect, transcendent realm which truly defines human existence.[11]

According to Kant and most other idealists who think about education, the curriculum should be strongly intellectual. It should enable students to become adept at using ideas and symbols, and it should acquaint them with positive models (exemplars, heroes, and heroines) so they will grow and flourish as persons. A course of study intended to reflect the rational structure of the cosmos and to develop the qualities of personhood in the student would include literature, art, intellectual history, philosophy, religion, and even mathematics. At the college level, such studies are called the humanities. But this sort of humane learning can occur at elementary, middle, and secondary levels as long as instruction strengthens intellectual ability and cultivates sound personhood.[12]

Typical idealists prefer teaching methods that are based on pure cognitive activity rather than on practical application or concrete experience. Lectures and discussions are primary classroom exercises; reading and research in the library are also extremely important. By contrast, field trips, "hands-on" presentations, classroom demonstrations, and the like are not considered important or effective. Interestingly, Kant does say that aesthetic ability requires less verbal instruction and more example and practice. While detractors of idealism say it creates an "ivory tower" situation for teachers and learners, Kant and other idealists insist that the mission of education is to impart mental proficiency so that students will be able to cope with everyday life. Furthermore, idealists defend themselves by saying that emphasis on an ideal realm of truth, goodness, and beauty helps students to live a more complete and enriched life.[13]

The teacher, according to the idealist educational perspective, does more than simply initiate the pupils into abstract or intuitive thinking. He or she is strategically placed in front of young people as a model human being charged with helping them attain fuller selfhood. Kant particularly advocates modeling freedom, autonomy, and pure motives. Teachers and administrators, moreover, have a responsibility to create a healthy social and psychological environment among students so that their personhood is nourished in a climate of rapport and mutual respect.

Idealist value theory leads educators to think in specific ways about shaping moral character and refining aesthetic taste. In moral education, universal ethical principles are communicated to the student—both through didactic instruction and exemplary action—so that they can be applied in concrete situations. Useful pedagogical tools include examples and lessons found in fairy tales, fiction, and biography. Although some idealists believe that the collective wisdom of historical societies (found in their traditions, cultural conventions, and so forth) is the repository of moral principles, Kant was suspicious of this. He feared rivalry and competitiveness between existing peoples and nations and therefore posited an abstract, theoretical construct of a "unity of selves" or moral community that transcends personal and national interests.[14]

Regarding art and aesthetic education, the idealist thinker conceives of art as the idealization of the world. The value of art is measured by how well it captures the universal amid the transient particulars of everyday life. For Kant, neither aesthetic taste nor creative talent can be directly communicated: these are abilities that cannot be taught. Effective aesthetic pedagogy exposes students to great art, explains how it exhibits universal features, and then allows students to practice creating beautiful art for themselves. Artistic sensibility may then emerge in students who are stimulated in both the intellectual and affective areas of learning.

EVALUATING IDEALISM

Many very capable thinkers endorse idealistic philosophy in one form or another. For them, idealism provides an adequate account of the rationality and meaningfulness of the world and of the dignity and worth of the human self. They envisage idealism as providing a basis for moral and religious values by making those values either structural features of the universe or necessary categories of rationality itself. Most idealists think that their position explains the existence of a Personal Being or Supreme Mind better than alternative worldviews.

It is not clear, however, that idealists have established that reality is somehow rooted in the processes of the mind. Idealists who follow Berkeley hold that objects are dependent on consciousness for their very existence. Kantian idealists hold that objects are dependent on mind for their rational structure. Now it is one thing to claim that reality is rationally understandable and a much stronger claim to say, as Berkeley and Kant do in their own ways, that reality is essentially mental. We ordinarily make a distinction between thought about our environment and the external environment itself, between the perceiver and the perceived.[15] Hence, there is a realism already implicit in our ordinary experience that contradicts the idea that consciousness completely accounts either for the existence or the rational structure of things.

This brings us to the divide between all philosophies that are realist and those that are idealist in orientation. Idealism asserts that reality itself is somehow rooted in the processes of the mind. Conversely, realism asserts the general reliability of our senses and our ordinary beliefs about a realm of physical objects that are independent of our minds and yet are inherently knowable. It is hard to imagine what sort of argument could possibly overturn these inveterate realist convictions. By making all reality rely on mind in one way or another, idealism devalues the external dimension of reality in which we find ourselves. Thus idealism drives its epistemology to a metaphysical dead end.

What shall we say about idealist educational thinking? First, it is not surprising that idealistic educational theory endorses abstract and highly intellectual methods, since it emphasizes mind so strongly. Kant believes that education is basically "formal training."[16] Clearly, schools at all levels would do well to emphasize rigorous intellectual work, particularly in an era of declining academic skills. But the Kantian recommendation lacks balance, stressing the intellectual but underplaying the practical and experiential aspects of education that help round out our humanity.

A second criticism of idealistic educational approaches is that they are frequently intended to maintain the status quo. Because philosophical idealists believe in a higher, changeless Reality above the vacillating world, many view the social function of the school as the preservation of the heritage of the past.

The school is not typically regarded as an agent of social change or reconstruction. Kant's own idealism, however, is not preservationist, since he advocates changing current social and political realities according to an ideal of human harmony.

Several criticisms of the idealist stance emerge from a Christian point of view. In spite of the fact that idealism may appear to be compatible with many Christian beliefs, it actually distorts them in peculiar ways. For instance, the idealist Supreme Being only faintly resembles the God of historic Christian faith. A Supreme Mind is a highly intellectualized entity conceived to function within a certain philosophical system, not the God of Abraham, Isaac, and Jacob. Among its other deficiencies, the idealist concept of God excludes relational concepts of grace and redeeming love.

The idealists' nonhistorical, impersonal view of God and their reduction of religion to morality have far-reaching consequences.[17] Kant believes that young children are not capable of understanding many religious ideas because these ideas rest on a knowledge of moral duty and a grasp of the abstractions of theology. Kant recommends, therefore, that religious instruction of the young be limited to teaching them about the value of humanity and conveying only a minimal idea of the Supreme Being. This approach rejects the rich and concrete ways in which children can be introduced to the great truths of Christianity through well-known Bible stories as well as through creative activities.

A final Christian criticism concerns the idealist concept of the material world. In denying that external, physical objects exist or that we can have valid knowledge of their natures, idealism does not comport well with historic Christianity, which attests to the reality and intelligibility of created things. Christian faith sees our mental powers as God-given abilities that are suited to make cognitive contact with an orderly world. What is more, the denigration of the physical in idealist metaphysics cannot make sense of the Incarnation. In the Incarnation, God takes on full humanity, which is intimately identified with the physical reality of the world.

NATURALISM: OBJECTS AND ORDER

Naturalism is the polar opposite of idealism. Its fundamental metaphysical thesis is that nature alone is real, that all reality is physical. Conversely, there are no nonmaterial entities: there is no realm of immaterial spirit or mind, no God or Supreme Being. Every tenet of naturalism follows from the belief that matter is the sole reality and is eternal: the cosmos is a closed, self-existent system; a human being is a complex physical organism; mind is a product of brain processes; human achievement and values are ultimate; death means personal extinction.

Since the late 1600s, beginning with the work of Sir Francis Bacon, naturalistic thought—as opposed to supernaturalistic thought—very gradually became the dominant perspective in Western culture. Its list of representatives includes such diverse thinkers as David Hume, Charles Darwin, Ernest Nagel, and Richard Dawkins. Materialism is a type of naturalism which asserts that all reality derives strictly from the material components of the universe and their operations. The names of Epicurus, Lucretius, Thomas Hobbes, and Karl Marx only begin the long list of materialist thinkers. Although naturalists differ among themselves on matters of emphasis and detail, their common insight is expressed well by the late-twentieth-century astronomer, Carl Sagan: "The cosmos is all that is or ever was or ever will be."[18]

Nagel affirms the "existential and causal primacy of organized matter in the executive order of nature."[19] In other words, every thing is dependent on the existence, configuration, and operation of physical things. Their belief that the physical laws of cause and effect govern everything in the whole universe leads many naturalists to embrace total determinism. A few, however, try to make room for a kind of human freedom that is compatible with determination within the causal system.[20] In any case, those who embrace naturalism understand the workings of the universe to be caused by evolutionary processes, not teleology. That is to say, there is no overarching purpose and meaning to the universe. Indeed, Jacques Monod says that the universe itself is "a game of pure chance."[21]

The concept of humanity does not fare well in the naturalist view of the world. For Nagel, humanity is a relatively temporary phenomenon in our local region of the cosmos. Explaining that the physical and physiological conditions for human existence have not and will not always endure, he states that "human destiny is an episode between two oblivions."[22] Yet Nagel still stresses that our humanness makes us special in the cosmos: "Man undoubtedly possesses characteristics which are shared by everything that exists; but he also manifests traits and capacities that appear to be distinctive of him."[23] Nagel admits, however, that our special human traits—our actions, aspirations, tragic failures, and splendid works of ingenuity—are ultimately dependent on subhuman physical properties. Julian Huxley identifies the uniqueness of humans among the animals as our capability for conceptual thought, use of speech, and possession of a cumulative tradition or culture. He denies, however, that these special traits provide reason to suppose that there is a transcendent power above the complex order of nature.[24]

The epistemological position of naturalism fits its metaphysical stance. The great majority of naturalist thinkers embrace empiricism, which is the view that all knowledge is derived from sense experience. Simply put, what we can see, touch, hear, taste, and smell is the basis for what we can know. Nagel and other naturalists take modern empirical science to be the highest achievement in human thinking about the physical universe, since its methods of observation, experiment, and verification are so sophisticated and successful.

The goal of the empirical method is to discover the regularities of the natural world and codify them into generalizations that represent scientific laws. In principle, through the scientific method, humanity will be able to explain everything in the universe. By recognizing the empirical method as the only legitimate avenue to knowledge, naturalists thereby rule out any other form of knowledge. Religious claims, for example, are discredited. It is not because religious beliefs about transempirical realities have been decisively shown to be false but because there is no empirical evidence to support them, to "prove" that they are true.

Naturalists generally embrace relativism with respect to all values; they deny that values, ethical or aesthetic, reflect ultimate or universal norms. In regard to ethics, naturalists say that, in one way or another, values are based on humanity. Many naturalists maintain that values are created by human beings living together in society. Thus, people in societies formulate ethical rules out of their perceptions of what is necessary to survive and maintain a stable communal environment. Values are instilled in the members of society by the natural process of conditioning. Nagel proposes that ethical norms should be interpreted as "hypotheses" for the intelligent management of the various interests and energies of human beings.[25] These hypotheses are tested in the life experiences of the group and modified as needed. Ethicist Peter Singer explains that the whole project of balancing and maximizing competing interests forms the basis of his naturalist and utilitarian conception of ethics.[26]

Identifying himself as a "humanist," Nagel advocates disciplined reason as the only instrument we have for achieving human goods. Nagel's humanism is secular: it envisions humanity as a product of the physical universe and not as the creation of a supernatural being. There are, of course, other forms of humanism that are supported by the great religious traditions, such as Judaism and Christianity. These forms of religious humanism anchor the importance of humanity in God's overall design rather than declaring our autonomy and self-reliance in a nontheistic universe.

For secular humanism, it is we humans who must take responsibility for our own survival, destiny, and fulfillment. The *Humanist Manifesto II* contains an official public statement of this position:

> We affirm that moral values derive their source from human experience. Ethics is *autonomous* and *situational*, needing

no theological or ideological sanction. Ethics stems from human need and interest. To deny this distorts the whole basis of life. Human life has meaning because we can create and develop our futures. Happiness and the creative realization of human needs and desires, individually and in shared enjoyment, are continuous themes of humanism.[27]

The document goes on to discuss desirable attitudes for human advancement that must accompany the instrumentality of reason—such as caring, compassion, empathy, fairness, and tolerance. But once again we see that if all ethical traits are anchored in human nature and human nature is merely a product of the natural world, then impersonal Nature is the sole ground of all value.

NATURALISM AND EDUCATION

In accord with their metaphysical picture of reality, those who profess a naturalistic philosophy in education hold that the aim of education is to produce people who understand the realities of the material world. Students need to know how to exercise rational control over their environment and to develop their capabilities as natural agents. Such education produces people who lead orderly lives, draw accurate conclusions from observations of nature and human affairs, deal effectively with the environment, and find appropriate expression for their abilities. Science, the chief method for dealing with the physical world, is employed in formulating appropriate instructional procedures to achieve these ends.

This naturalistic orientation promotes a school curriculum focusing on the study of physical objects and the order they exhibit. The basic ideas of the cosmos are most clearly contained in the fields of physics, chemistry, biology, zoology, astronomy, geology, and other natural or "hard" sciences (that is, fields of study in which knowledge is primarily attained through empirical methods and in which mathematics is used as a means of expressing that knowledge). These studies should be at the core of the curriculum. Consequently, the study of mathematics is very important, as it is a precise symbolic language for dealing with quantity and relationship in the material realm.

Philosophical naturalists in education assume an interesting posture toward subjects outside the physical sciences. They agree that subjects such as psychology, sociology, economics, and other social sciences are valuable to the extent that they avoid excessive speculation and concentrate on formulating statistical generalizations about human behavior based on concrete data. Some extreme naturalists minimize the importance of subjects such as literature, philosophy, art, and the like because they do not involve hard facts and quantities; therefore they cannot be considered knowledge per se. Other naturalists accept the humanities as important expressions of our natural human creativity and do make a place for them in the curriculum.

Whereas the naturalist view of reality influences curriculum design, the naturalist view of knowledge affects preferences for teaching and learning. Since the tangible world is the fundamental reality and sense perception is the basic way of knowing it, teachers should emphasize classroom demonstrations, laboratory experiments, field trips, audiovisual aids, object lessons, and other methods of instruction that employ sensory experience. Teaching by direct experience demands that the teacher understand the principles of the natural world so that he or she can properly select the learning situations in which they can be taught. Most naturalists believe that students should learn the scientific method and similar rational problem-solving procedures. Proponents of naturalism in education regard the teacher primarily as an agent for connecting students with the world of facts. Those who promote the humanistic aspect of naturalism say that the teacher assists students in developing their own natural abilities. Unlike the idealist teacher, who is to be a model of appropriate personality and character traits, the naturalist teacher should refrain from imposing her own value judgments on the subject matter. In a sense, teachers are to be neutral channels through which students contact the natural world.

One of the more influential proposals for teaching and learning stems from the work of Harvard professor B. F. Skinner. A professional research psychologist, Skinner adopts certain underlying philosophical assumptions that are naturalistic. He rejects the traditional dualistic concept that psychology is the study of the immaterial mind or self, since such nonphysical entities lack observable, empirical dimensions. Instead, he conceives of psychology as the science of human behavior: the description of which specific external conditions and stimuli elicit certain responses.

Skinner recommends that education be based on the technology of behavior. He applies his findings about the reinforcement of responses in animals to the education of humans.[28] Thus, behaviorism need not postulate "inner states" (motives, intentions, and volitions) in order to assert that desired behaviors can be produced by properly arranging the conditions of reinforcement. The current educational scene displays various signs of behavioristic thinking: computer teaching programs are in vogue, performance objectives are typically incorporated into instructional planning, and competency-based teacher certification is widely practiced.

Obviously, behavioral engineering offers more than a means of developing skills and imparting information. It is a methodology that can shape many kinds of student responses, including ethical responses. Skinner, however, refuses to prescribe what sorts of performances are desirable or what kind of individuals ought to be developed because he thinks these preferences must be established by society's needs and ideals. His behaviorism simply offers effective ways to obtain desired outcomes.

Other naturalists are not neutral about values and are willing to assert a general theory of value for the educational venture. Some say that moral education should present the child with the lessons of the natural world in order to promote right conduct. At the elementary level, for example, showing students the habits of robins caring for their babies in the nest might foster moral sentiments about the love of life. The virtue of patience might be taught by letting children observe that, in many natural processes, time is needed to obtain proper results. Growing plants or observing the gestation periods of animals can convey this lesson. At more advanced levels, students can proceed to abstract judgments about the natural order of things. Studying the complexity of the material world, discovering the economy of its processes, and even analyzing the behavior patterns of individuals and cultures can be touchstones for moral education.

The general goal of naturalist moral education is that students should learn what actions bring about the greatest good for the greatest number of people. This utilitarian perspective makes deciding on ethical matters a purely factual, even statistical, procedure that is open to careful observation and inquiry. In this vein, there is no need to introduce ideas of proper motivation or virtue or unchanging norms. Ultimately, naturalist moral education is simply concerned with results, with practical human behaviors. Educators must inculcate in students tendencies to act in optimum ways. Harry Broudy explains,

> We want our children to develop reliable tendencies to tell the truth, to respect the codes of right and wrong of the community, to be courageous, to be persevering in the face of obstacles, to withstand the temptations of disapproved pleasures, to be able to sacrifice present pleasures in favor of more remote ones, to have a sense of justice and fair play.[29]

Propensities toward these kinds of behaviors are seen as being in harmony with the patterns of nature. There is no need to justify these behavioral objectives by a scale of absolute values; we only need to see that society generally approves them.

In teaching art and aesthetic appreciation, most naturalists stress the primacy of form and balance, as these elements are intrinsic to the natural processes of things. Beauty in art relates to its representation of some aspect of nature. The naturalist who teaches aesthetic appreciation employs hands-on experience or immediate sensory contact with various art media. Hence, naturalists emphasize direct involvement in the arts, in contrast to idealists, who emphasize the abstract, intellectual understanding of art.

For example, the naturalist would wish to have younger students finger-paint in order to gain a basic sense of the dynamics of painting or keep a simple beat with an instrument in order to acquire a feeling for rhythm. Older students might write and produce a drama or play an instrument in order to acquire appreciation for theater or music. By gaining a sense of technique, the importance of physical control, or the ability to combine colors, students begin to develop taste for what constitutes greatness in these arts.

Some naturalists are radical critics of modern education, insisting that it must be completely overhauled. For example, Karl Marx considered the educational systems of modern capitalistic culture as instruments of class domination rather than a means of liberating and enhancing our human abilities.[30] Many studies confirm a strong correlation between economic class and educational opportunity, which in turn translates to a correlation between economic class and career options. All of this would suggest to a Marxist that even free, public education is shaped by the underlying structures of Western industrialized society.

A Marxist would contend that education should combine theoretical and practical activities, being and doing. It should especially recognize the active, dynamic nature of knowing. In this manner, education will no longer contribute to human alienation but instead will develop people who find dignity in their labor. Of course, traditional Marxists believe that the ills of present educational systems cannot be completely cured until the larger society undergoes fundamental economic restructuring—that is, until this capitalistic epoch in history gives way to socialism. The aim is for the working class to gain influence in our educational institutions and use it to help usher in the new era of socialism. However, Marxists believe that the aspiration of outright educational liberalism—specifically, that all necessary social changes can be brought about through nonviolent political action—is naive.[31]

Evaluating Naturalism

Naturalism clearly exhibits a number of positive features. In its more humanistic forms, naturalism emphasizes distinctively human qualities. It correctly endorses the scientific method as an important rational procedure for solving problems. And it faces the hard facts of the universe, including our struggle for survival in it, with courage and determination. Finally, there is admirable confidence among naturalists that creative intelligence can actually improve our world.

Yet naturalism does not adequately explain certain important aspects of the reality we experience: those aspects that seem to have a nonphysical or nonmaterial quality. Admittedly, the naturalist's recognition that the physical world is real and not dependent on our minds is a corrective to the error of idealism, but it then goes to the opposite extreme. The naturalist's assertion that physical stuff is the sum total of reality is as difficult to accept as the idealist's claim that mind is all that exists. Mind and thought are phenomena that are not totally explicable in physical terms. Mind seems to be different in kind from physical things and hence demands a different kind of explanation.[32]

The naturalist position on the centrality of physical cause and effect in the operation of the universe makes determinism virtually unavoidable. A telling objection to determinism is that it denies the reality of free, responsible action. If human choices and actions are ultimately caused by brute, impersonal forces, then they cannot be significantly free. Significant freedom, or libertarian freedom, is classically defined as the power to do otherwise than what one did in fact do. If persons are not free in this sense, it is difficult to envision how they can be held responsible for their actions. Thus, libertarian free will is widely considered a necessary condition for moral life. Clearly, the great danger here is that naturalism would undercut our best understanding of morality.

The problem of determinism can be pressed even further. C. S. Lewis argues that the view that all events are physically caused cannot account for rational thought. He contends that free, rational thought is invalidated if it is produced by physical causes. The classical view is that a belief is rational only if it is held on the basis of evidence and logic; it cannot be coerced in any way. Lewis identifies a damaging irony in the naturalist perspective: if naturalism really is true, then the belief that it is true cannot be rationally held.[33] This is because the naturalist is implicitly stating that his belief is caused rather than free. So, it appears that rationality is also undermined. Other versions of naturalism typically tend to have the same basic defect. Marxist materialism, for example, is troublesome because it posits historical or economic forces as causing all events.

Naturalism is also philosophically impoverished regarding the nature of value. Nagel, for example, denies that anything whatsoever is intrinsically good or evil. Values are simply tentative hypotheses people make to guide them in the exercise of their interests. But why should we think that it is desirable to maximize human interests? Is that intrinsically valuable? Either the value of maximizing human interests is fundamental or it is derived from some value that is. It is unreasonable for naturalists to think that nothing is intrinsically valuable or good and that we can still have ethical norms. One who declares that there are no bedrock values will always unwittingly assume that something is. So, as objective as Nagel tries to be about ethics, his theory is as prone to sentimentality, selectivity, and projection as the idealistic position he rejects.

The philosophy of education arising from naturalism includes some aspects that seem reasonable. For example, it appropriately recognizes that some important learning occurs through direct observation and practical experience. However, its emphasis on empirical inquiry as the sole source of knowledge is disproportionate. Nagel admits that there are other ways of experiencing the universe than by rationally apprehending it, but he insists that the only mode of real knowledge is empirical. This approach ignores the fact that different domains of intellectual investigation have a legitimacy of their own, regardless of whether they meet strict empirical criteria. Metaphysics, theology, ethics, and aesthetics are disciplines that naturalists have either denigrated or dismissed because they do not contain information that can be measured or transmitted empirically. This has contributed to a kind of intellectual imperialism in which all fields of inquiry are forced to conform to the standards of one particular field.

Another problem with some naturalistic theories of instruction is their reliance on conditioning and socialization techniques. These methods have been touted for producing not only academic performance but also ethical behavior. Skinner and other behaviorists have identified significant similarities between humans and other animals in the way our responses can be guided and controlled. It may be that these similarities can be used in one phase of training children, particularly during early years when their powers of reflective thought are minimal and some conditioning is required. The problem is that behavioral engineering can be manipulative and can damage the capacity for self-direction. An exclusively behavioral approach to moral training focuses on publicly observable behavior and may reduce the student's ability to act on the basis of internalized principles and proper motivation.[34] When this behaviorist difficulty is added to naturalism's inability to designate ends for moral life, we have strong reason to doubt that naturalism could provide a healthy moral education.

Naturalism's theological inadequacy stems from its twofold rejection of anything nonempirical. Metaphysically, it holds that nonempirical reality simply does not exist; epistemologically, it asserts that such realities cannot be known. So, it immediately invalidates all Christian claims about God (a nonempirical reality) as well as the ability of the Bible and church tradition to communicate theological truth (information that is not obtained through exclusively empirical means).

Naturalistic philosophy opposes any theological position that affirms the reality of a supernatural deity or any dimension beyond observable, testable reality. For Christianity, God is the eternal, sovereign Creator of the universe. He is transcendent of creation, not part of it. Yet God is also immanent in the world; he is present within the creaturely realm. These are spiritual matters that naturalistic philosophy cannot countenance. Furthermore, the naturalistic concept of humanity as sheerly a product of physical processes drastically conflicts with the orthodox Christian doctrine that persons are created in the "image of God" (*imago Dei*).

Although naturalism concurs with Christianity in affirming the reality of nature, it goes too far and asserts the primacy of nature. For naturalism, the worth of nature is the worth of an unquestionable "given." By contrast, the Christian understanding is that nature has worth as a creature brought into being by a perfectly good God. The insistence by naturalists that physical nature must be known by empirical methods would be largely accepted by most thoughtful Christians. However, they would not agree that empirical investigation is the only avenue of authentic knowledge. A reasonable Christian approach suggests instead that there are many domains of created reality and each domain must be known by intellectual methods appropriate to the kind of reality it is.

THOMISTIC REALISM: BEING AND ESSENCE

St. Thomas Aquinas produced a comprehensive Christian philosophy that combines principles from Aristotle and Christian orthodoxy. It has been of continual interest to philosophers, with followers of Aquinas over the centuries applying his teachings and insights to a large number of subjects, including education.

In the area of metaphysics, Aquinas, following Aristotle, held that only individual things are real. This clearly contradicts all forms of idealism and dualism, which hold that the most real things are universal rather than particular, abstract rather than concrete. For Aquinas, a particular thing is real because it has *existence* or *being*.[35] He sometimes speaks of this as the "act of existing" or the "act of being."

All things that have being are things of some kind or another. More precisely, each thing has a definite nature that makes it the kind of thing it is. Our universe contains trees, rainbows, sea anemones, granite rocks, super novas, persons, and many more kinds of things. The nature of any given thing—its *essence*—is a combination of form and matter. *Form* is that aspect which makes it intelligible to mind; *matter* is that aspect which makes it tangible and concrete. This position avoids both the idealist fixation on pure ideas and the naturalist insistence on the exclusive existence of matter. For Aquinas, the essence of a thing is the basis of "what" a thing is. The complete reality of any particular entity, then, consists in the combination of its *existence* and its *essence*—that is, by the "act of being" uniting with a specific "nature."

Aquinas envisions a grand structure to reality in which everything is arranged hierarchically. The location of an entity in the hierarchy is determined by its proportion of actuality and potentiality. *Actuality* is the portion of being, the measure of reality accorded to something having a particular nature; *potentiality* is the capability to change in certain ways. Change occurs in the temporal world when some potentiality inherent in a thing becomes actual.[36] It is the intrinsic nature of a thing that establishes both what it is and what it can become. An actual acorn, for example, contains the potential to become an oak tree, but it does not contain the potential to become a ostrich.

All along the scale of reality—from inorganic material near the bottom, through progressively more complex plants, to orders of the animal realm, and eventually to humans and angels near the top—there are finite beings. They are characterized by limitation and dependency, which means that there is always some potentiality present. At the very top of the magnificent scale of being is God. Of course, in God there is only form and no matter. God, for Aquinas, is full actuality with no potentiality. God's very essence is pure existence; He cannot *not* exist. He is Being Itself—the great "I Am" in biblical terms.[37] He is the source and fountainhead of all other existence.

The worldview of Thomism is a purposive one: the universe and everything in it is moving toward a destiny. The divinely created natures of things tend toward fulfillment—that is, the actualization of their unique potentials. Humanity is special in this overall scheme. Traits of the physical side of our humanity resemble traits of the higher animals, but our rational and spiritual aspects fit us for a destiny above all other created things. That destiny is the flourishing of our total personhood in relation to God.

The epistemology of Thomism rests on its metaphysics. Since reality is a rationally structured system and the human person is by nature rational, we are capable of knowing reality. As Mortimer Adler puts it, "the human mind naturally tends to learn, to acquire knowledge, just as the earth naturally tends to support vegetation."[38] For the Thomistic tradition, *truth* is the correspondence of thought with the way things are, a view borne out of the confidence that the stable, orderly reality we inhabit is accommodating to the mind's quest.

Aquinas recognized different intellectual powers that may be employed to gain knowledge. Sense experience leads to revisable, scientific knowledge (for example, that there are nine planets in our solar system). Truths that are evident to the senses comprise ordinary, day-to-day knowledge. But there is also intuition, which leads to unchangeable knowledge (for example, the truth that every event has a cause). Truths grasped by intuition or pure rational insight are ultimately a more important type of knowledge that we take as self-evident.

Aquinas also refers to revelation as a source of knowledge. Whereas some knowledge comes through the active functioning of our own intellectual powers, we receive revealed knowledge through God's initiative. We can comprehend by revelation some truths that can also be known by reason (such as the existence of God). However, through revelation we can also learn truths that cannot be acquired by human reason (such as the Trinitarian structure of the Godhead). Aquinas believes that the truths delivered by reason and revelation are compatible.

The Thomistic view that reality is ordered by degrees of potentiality/actuality shapes its perspective on both ethics and aesthetics. Just as human nature seeks truth, it also reaches out for goodness and beauty. This does not mean that every person always acts according to what is good or creates beauty. It does mean that there is a tendency in all human beings toward these values, a potential which strives to become actual. Furthermore, in the hierarchical order of things, there is a priority of some kinds of goodness and beauty over others. The role of the rational agent, then, is to understand the hierarchical pattern of things good and beautiful and to align his or her activities with them.

In the area of ethics, goodness flows from the proper activity of reason. It is the rational creature's role to grasp the proper end toward which we should aim our actions. The field of ethics articulates the ways we must seek our end in terms of universal principles. Although the intellect's grasp of the good is fundamental, moral action also involves the will. Reason or intellect originates an order to "do this." Yet, as Etienne Gilson says, the "moving force of the order belongs to the will."[39] In the Thomistic conception of ethics, the will is still subservient to the intellect. Consequently, moral error stems from either ignorance on the part of the intellect or weakness on the part of the will. Two major goals of moral development, therefore, are training the intellect to recognize what is right and strengthening the will to do it.

The intellect knows what is good by understanding the objective values inherent in reality. Commenting on the Thomistic ethical system, William McGucken identifies three areas of moral obligation, which are, in ascending order, duties to one-self, to fellow human beings, and to God.[40] He further indicates that there are more specific duties within these broad divisions. It is important to understand that moral values in this system are not dependent on human preferences but are rooted in the nature of reality.

According to Aquinas, the will can be habituated to con-form to the good. By consistently striving and acting upon what we know to be good, we develop habits. These habits in us are inclinations or dispositions to act and react appropriately in certain circumstances. Cultivating moral dispositions supports what Aquinas calls "virtues." Although Aquinas recognizes an important level of morality that can be taught, discussed, and embraced in the form of rules or principles, he sees moral life as being concerned at a deeper level with the development of virtues, such as justice and temperance.[41]

Although most people do not readily associate art with reason, Aquinas and his intellectual descendants make reason central to aesthetics. Jacques Maritain represents this position:

> Creativity, or the power of engendering, does not belong only to material organisms, it is a mark and privilege of life in spiritual things also. . . . The intellect in us strives to en-gender. It is anxious to produce, not only the inner word, the concept, which remains inside us, but a work at once mate-rial and spiritual like ourselves, and into which something of our soul overflows. Through a natural super-abundance the intellect tends to express and utter outward, it tends to sing, to manifest itself in a work.[42]

The role of reason in art is an expression of the natural ten-dency in human beings to create beauty.

Maritain explains that aesthetic creativity is manifested in two areas: the fine arts and the practical arts. Those who create in the realm of the fine arts (music, painting, sculpture, and so on) create beauty for its own sake, purified of all extraneous elements. Those who create in the sphere of practical arts (weaving, pottery, and so on) aim to produce useful objects that are also pleasing or beautiful to the intellect. According to Thomists such as Maritain, since the practical arts have function in addition to the pure representation of beauty, they are inferior to the fine arts.

In both areas of art, the creative intellect makes aesthetic judgments employing the concept of excellence. Maritain writes, "beauty delights the intellect . . . because it essentially means a certain excellence in the proportion of things to the intellect."[43] Among the specific criteria for judging excellence are integrity, proportion, and clarity.

THOMISTIC REALISM AND EDUCATION

A Thomist sees the world as a rationally ordered system that is laden with value. A chief purpose of humanity is to know the nature and structure of things in that complex system. Fascinating educational proposals can be generated from this view. The ecclesiastical wing of Thomism (represented by such thinkers as Jacques Maritain and John Henry Newman) recommends subjects that deal with theistic themes and Christian doctrines. Historically, this kind of emphasis formed the foundation of Catholic education. Although they do not give high priority to the religious dimension, the lay Thomists (represented by Robert Hutchins and Mortimer Adler) endorse subjects that exhibit the absolute truths of the cosmos and that treat the enduring themes of human nature.[44] Their approach supplies broad justification for the inclusion of logic, mathematics, languages, philosophy, and the like in a school curriculum.

A Thomist theory of knowledge provides many fruitful directions for teaching and learning. Maritain says that the ultimate goal of education is to develop our essential nature as human beings.[45] Since he considers the intellect to be the core of human nature, he argues that education is primarily the nurturing of our mental powers. Teaching abstract ideas, imparting important facts, and reinforcing good mental habits are some of the methods that can be employed toward this end.

All pedagogical methods must aim at increasing the power of the student's mind. The goal is to teach all subjects so that the learner becomes able to grasp general principles and logical connections and thereby comes to understand the structure of reality. Maritain believes that the formal discipline of education is as important as its content. A well-trained mind has the ability to handle life's situations, including the need for continued learning. All discipline, however, must occur in a context of love, creativity, and proper freedom.

Maritain's moral theory focuses on both the intellect and the will in moral education.[46] It is of utmost importance, he argues, for reason to be able to form accurate moral evaluations. This ability includes not simply grasping universal moral laws but also applying them to concrete situations. At one level, we are talking about the intellectual procedures that must be learned; at another, the development of the will to follow the judgments of reason. Maritain advocates determining and employing the best methods for training the will in younger people (showing approval and disapproval, rewarding and punishing, and the like). The methods aim at moving the young person toward responsible adulthood, to a state in which his or her actions flow from the inner wellspring of moral reason. To be sure, Maritain embraces the historic Christian doctrine of the Fall, which asserts that both the intellect and the will are in a weakened condition. He argues, however, that enough of our natural endowment as rational and moral beings remains intact such that it can be educated, strengthened, and assisted in its cooperation with divine grace.

Training the intellect is also primary in aesthetic education. Although many people associate art with the expression of feeling, Maritain holds that reason is intimately involved in both the appreciation and creation of beauty. Hence, the intellects of students must be prepared for aesthetically meaningful activity; they must be brought to a point of clarity concerning what constitutes excellence and beauty.

After students have mastered the basic content and techniques relevant to the aesthetic endeavor, the teacher can then cultivate and refine their intuitive perceptions and creative drives. Their intuitive capability probes into the essence of the work of art, and their creative capacity displays their own inner nature. Maritain supports the contemplative side of aesthetic pursuit: persons by nature enjoy and appreciate what is beautiful. He likewise endorses the productive side: persons have an innate drive to create, to bring about things of beauty, to produce works of art.

EVALUATING THOMISTIC REALISM

Thomism navigates between the two extremes of idealism and naturalism. Whereas naturalism recognizes only matter as the basis of reality and idealism recognizes only mind, Thomism affirms the dual but inseparable aspects of reality. Its emphasis on the reality, structure, and cognitive accessibility of the creaturely world reveals the influence of the Aristotelian system. Its affirmation of the immeasurable value of creation and affirmation of its theistic dimensions derive from Aquinas's explicitly Christian view.

One objection to Thomism is that its purposive or teleological universe has no room for genuine freedom. Some critics think that significant human choice is impossible if everything operates automatically toward an end. However, Aquinas argues that human nature includes free choice, which he defines as the power of the will to enact the practical directives of the intellect. This means that human beings can make changes in circumstances and make things happen that would not otherwise occur. Free will also includes the ability to go against the moral order of creation.

Thomistic epistemology is more adequate than that of either idealism or naturalism, as it recognizes both empirical experience and the cognition of abstract truths rather than making one or the other the exclusive form of knowledge. Aquinas states that most truths we know originate in sensory experience but are finally understood conceptually. For example, we do not first have the general idea of dog and then later discover that there are dogs. We first come into contact with particular material things through the senses and later move to knowledge of general and abstract ideas about them. This is the natural order of human knowledge.

Another strength of Thomistic philosophy is its insistence that there are universal values that are anchored in the stable, enduring natures of things. Recognizing a relationship between the conceptual and the empirical, between absolute and relative, allows us to see how abstract and universal principles can be applied to variable, concrete life situations. All of this makes better sense of the actual human moral situation than most other views.

As a philosophy of education, Thomism has had a large following.[47] Early in the twentieth century, it was crucial to the cultural revival in Roman Catholicism. In its lay expression, Thomism has appealed to many in other Christian traditions and even to some secular thinkers. This fact is testimony to the power and richness of its ideas. Amid signs that Thomism is again experiencing a resurgence, I believe that the time is right for seriously considering its ideas in educational philosophy today.[48]

Maritain, as a chief representative, offers a description of what happens to a human being in the process of education that is magnificent and compelling. He believes that the idealist's "imitation of the Absolute Mind" is hopelessly romantic and that the naturalist's "conformity to nature" is utterly dehumanizing. He argues instead that education develops the natural powers of the mind, which are those aspects of our being that make us distinctively human. Therefore, he places a high premium on the cultivation of the intellect and on intelligent self-direction as keys to human dignity. This natural law approach contrasts drastically with naturalist approaches that focus on producing desired behaviors as though humans were merely higher animals living in groups.

Some critics argue that Thomist educators are committed to the "calisthenics theory of learning" and the "spinach theory of education." The calisthenics image suggests that the student learns by the arduous drill of his intellectual faculties and that a dominating teacher plays the role of the drill sergeant. The spinach image suggests that if intellect and character are shaped through the toughening of the powers of self-discipline, then whatever is unpleasant to do in school can be used to develop them. Winston Churchill once remarked, "It doesn't much matter what you teach a boy, so long as he doesn't enjoy it." At the extreme, this view leads one to think that the most distasteful subjects must be the most beneficial and therefore must be given highest priority.

Some educators, Thomists and others, have held unacceptable views about the disciplinary aspects of education. However, it is a distortion to stereotype Thomists on this point. Educational good comes only through intellectual hard work. Clearly, a much higher degree of academic rigor is needed at a time in American history when students' academic skills are declining at an alarming rate. Along with healthy discipline, Thomists such as Maritain want education to encourage the creative and free expressions of children because the sheer delight in learning motivates them to actualize their human potentials. Maritain even points out that the student is actually the primary agent in educational transactions, while the teacher is the secondary agent.[49]

How should we think of the philosophy of Aquinas in relation to Christianity? Critics say that the Thomistic metaphysical position is theologically flawed. They contend that Greek thought forms, adopted from Aristotle, distort rather than clarify biblical ideas. They admit, however, that Aquinas's general picture of the world, which affirms the existence of

God and a hierarchically-ordered creation, is a plausible Christian theory of reality. Their concern is that the categories Aquinas employs to explain the nature of reality make God static, impersonal, and unchanging rather than dynamic, personal, and responsive.[50] Rejoinders to this criticism expose inaccurate caricatures of how Aquinas employs the concepts of substance, being, change, and so forth.

The epistemology of Thomism benefits by being based on metaphysics; that is, it starts with being. Thus, from the outset, knowledge is indeed possible and not undercut by skeptical and critical doubts. Furthermore, the importance of human rationality and its ability to seek truth form the basis of a feasible Christian view of human knowing. Some critics fear, however, that this emphasis on rationality leads to an overly intellectual approach to faith. Thomists respond that the activity of gaining accurate knowledge of natural truths and connecting them to truths about the existence and nature of God is a kind of prelude to faith. Faith is exercised in light of all that we know and believe to be true. Consequently, what we believe intellectually is extremely important.

Thomistic moral theory also reflects some basic Christian understandings. It stresses the objective character of values, the need for the rational perception of moral principles, and the priority of developing virtues as the very core of moral life. Opponents of Thomism accuse it of giving priority to being over doing, theory over practice. Defenders answer that genuine moral living involves more than simply knowing abstractly what is good and right; it requires acting in accordance with this moral knowledge and, ultimately, becoming a certain kind of person.

CHAPTER THREE

Contemporary Philosophies of Education

Although traditional philosophical perspectives seek to provide a total worldview, what I call "contemporary" perspectives do not offer a comprehensive vision. The shift away from grand, synoptic thinking began in the seventeenth century, the onset of the modern period. René Descartes struggled with doubt about our most basic beliefs; David Hume recommended skepticism; Immanuel Kant asserted that we could not know reality in itself.[1] It is not surprising that those who proffered philosophical views in such an intellectual climate would reduce their scope and avoid attempting to decipher the nature of things.

Here I present four contemporary philosophies that have clearly influenced education: experimentalism, existentialism, philosophical analysis, and postmodernism. Although each one denies that a synoptic vision of the world is possible, none can avoid being shaped by tacit assumptions about the nature of reality, knowledge, and value. Our task is to draw out the implicit components of each worldview and then evaluate their impact on education.

EXPERIMENTALISM: EXPERIENCE AND SOCIETY

Experimentalism, which is sometimes called pragmatism or instrumentalism, developed in the early twentieth century. This philosophical view exerted strong influence on twentieth-century American education and still appeals to many educational thinkers in one form or another. Experimentalism rejects any concept of a transcendent, ultimate, fixed reality (such as the idealist's realm of ideas and supreme mind, the Aristotelian's pure form, and the Thomist's absolute being). According to experimentalism, all traditional, otherworldly views rest on unfounded metaphysical presumption. Experience—common human experience—is the only basis for philosophy. Since experience is constantly changing, experimentalists think about how we can adapt to as well as control changes in our environment. This approach has far-reaching implications for education, whether conceived narrowly as curriculum reform and teacher training or broadly as the basis for the adjustment process of the individual in the social and physical environment.

John Dewey, arguably the most influential experimentalist on education, maintains that the realm of "experience" does not pertain exclusively to sensory experience: it encompasses all that human beings do and think and feel, from passive reflection to active doing. He held that this world of human experience is adequate for the fulfillment of human purposes and the satisfaction of human understanding. Whatever lies beyond the world of ordinary experience is unknowable and thus cannot be a legitimate subject for philosophical reflection.

Emphasis on the world of ordinary experience contrasts markedly with the traditional realistic position. Thomistic realism, as we saw, asserts that there is an objective reality to which our beliefs must conform and that our intellectual processes are well-suited for this purpose. Dewey, however, settles for experience as the very reality we seek, thereby trying to steer clear of any dualism between the objective world and subjective belief.

It is not merely the traditional subject-object dualism that disappears. John Childs explains that in experience all dichotomies melt away:

> The divisions between the natural and the supernatural, the real and the ideal, reality and appearance, subject and object, mind, body, thought and activity, all seem to many to be obviously natural dualisms. . . . [The] experimentalist . . . asserts unqualifiedly that experience is all that we have. . . . Hence, if human experience cannot give us an adequate account of realities, then man has no possibility of gaining such an account.[2]

When experimentalists insist on experience as the ultimate ground of human discourse, they mean that it is the only sure measure of whether our ideas are true.

Dewey conceives of human experience as the collective experience of human beings, not as the private, inner feelings of isolated individuals. Limited private experience can be corrected by the shared experience of those living in society. That is, whatever claims one makes about "reality" may be inspected by all in the community and tested in the realm of shared experience. According to Dewey, the "reality of experience" is in continual flux and flow. Experience—and therefore reality—is in constant process.

In contrast to "intellectually-oriented" epistemologies, Dewey offers an "experientially-oriented" one. Since reality is characterized by experiential change, knowledge is temporary, tentative, and provisional. Knowledge is not an item for passive contemplation but an instrument for solving problems and actively managing the ever-changing world. The test of a given hypothesis or claim is whether it really "works" when put into practice. To the degree that it has practical effectiveness, it can be said to be "true." Public consensus about what works in certain human situations or what best solves empirical problems is the sole criterion of truth.

Experience, as Dewey says, has a "transactional" character, which means that human beings are in a great dialectic with their world. Through raw experience, people develop certain ideas and hunches about the way things are. They act upon these ideas and then undergo their consequences. Depending on how things turn out, they may revise their initial hypotheses. Dewey refers to the "complete act of thought," which proceeds from a perceived difficulty in the flow of events, through subsequent diagnosis and inventory of possible solutions, to testing for consequences of proposed solutions.[3] Dewey's "controlled transaction" is simply the layperson's version of the scientific method.

Experimentalism applies scientific methodology to ethical and aesthetic questions as well, rejecting the notion that we must search for moral and aesthetic absolutes in some transcendent realm. We must instead explore the questions of value in the very place where people in fact develop and apply their values: within the boundaries of experience.

According to Dewey, ethical values do not have an objective or fixed status. Values are not verities to be discovered; instead they are practical proposals that are constructed by human beings. Risky as it might be, human beings have to create values and make normative claims without transcendental help. They have to make revisable, conditional recommendations about what is good or right. Ethical proposals express a longing to rearrange experience, or at least specific features of experience, in a more desirable way. Dewey states, "we create new ideals and values in the face of the perplexities of a new world."[4]

The ethical question "What ought I to do?" becomes for Dewey an invitation to designate certain ends or purposes as desirable and then to try them out. In light of the results of our experiment with certain values, we will retain, revise, or reject them. Again, the dictum "what works is good" means not merely what works for the individual but what works for the community. Actions that seem to bring "good" to the individual, such as lying and stealing, have negative effects in larger society. Hence, they are not really good. The ultimate test of values, then, is their application to the environment, both social and physical. The experimental method is our guide to determining the suitability of any ethical strategy.

Dewey's aesthetic views also revolve around the concept of experience. He denies the more traditional position that a work of art is a special type of entity or object that produces a specific effect in us. Coupled with this denial is his rejection of objective standards that one may use to evaluate the quality of a piece of art or the appropriateness of one's response to it. Rather, the work of art is a catalyst for changing the experience of those who take it seriously. The dynamic, experiential consequences of a work of art provide the measure of its aesthetic worth. Experimentalists say that many traditional philosophies look for objective norms beyond the world of human beings; conversely, they present themselves as locating the criterion of artistic value in how people feel or respond.

The task of the artist is to acquire new insights, experiences, feelings, and intuitions—and to stimulate those same reactions in us. Dewey writes that "[e]very art communicates because it expresses. It enables us to share vividly and deeply in meaning to which we had been dumb. . . . Communication is the process of creating participation, of making common what had been isolated and singular."[5] The democratic tone of experimentalist aesthetics allows common citizens to proclaim something to be a true work of art if they find new meanings to life in its presence, experience new dimensions of feeling, and, perhaps as a result, relate better to other people.

EXPERIMENTALISM AND EDUCATION

For experimentalists, ultimate reality is social experience: the ever-changing collective feelings, hopes, problems, and pains of the community. It is a realm in the dynamic process of becoming—or what William James called "the universe with the lid off." Therefore, the school curriculum, which should be designed to reflect the nature of reality, must be a series of well-planned experiences in which the process-oriented quality of our world is represented. The purpose of formal schooling is not to impart static knowledge, which is usually broken into so many departments, because such a curriculum would give students an entirely fallacious impression of their world. The point of schooling is instead to enable students to solve problems that arise within their experience.

Dewey prefers "procedural" subjects to "substantive" ones. Studies that portray social life and problems are considered more important than those that examine nonhuman phenomena. Procedural-type courses of study help students learn how to approach and solve the problems of life instead of encouraging a "spectator mentality." Courses with socially-oriented content enable students to understand the flux and flow of human experience and how to manage it intelligently.

The subject called social studies is a prime candidate for inclusion in an experimentalist curriculum. In general, experimentalists prefer courses that explore current problems and issues over those that cover established material. For example, the study of modern family structures or problems in American democracy might be encouraged in middle schools and high schools. Seminars on environmental concerns, race relations, nuclear weapons, and changing sexual attitudes would be important in the college setting. Traditional courses in history and physics would be included because they are useful for understanding and managing our present world. As Morris and Pai say, "the entire curriculum will be inverted from subject matter intended to be applied later to life situations to the life situations themselves that provoke the kinds of learning in or between subject matter areas that intelligent living calls for."[6]

Rather than simply "telling" the student that a certain situation or problem is interesting or important, Dewey suggests that the teacher try to arouse the student's sense of curiosity in order to motivate her study. In this "learner-centered" approach, the teacher should discover and use the interests of the student. The underlying conviction here is that learning is likely to be richer and last longer if it grows out of the pupil's own needs and questions.

In addition to being problem-oriented and learner-centered, Dewey's theory of learning is also activity-based. The problems identified by the learner's interest must be actively confronted. The learner must get involved with whatever topic or problem she selects, grasping its peculiar characteristics as well as the general skills of problem solving. In short, one learns by doing. Traditionally, the logical method of pedagogy would present a systematic, organized body of material that is "predigested." However, the psychological method links the subject to the learner's life situation and then lets her work through it until she intellectually "digests" it and gains clearer understanding. Dewey advises teachers to resist the "strong temptation to assume that presenting subject matter in its perfected form provides a royal road to learning."[7]

Consider the contrast between two different ways of teaching geography. A traditional approach to teaching geography might begin with the explanation that the earth is a planet in our solar system and then proceed to an explanation of the seasons and climates around the globe. The instructor could discuss the land and water masses, the northern and southern hemispheres, and the physical characteristics of the various continents. Later, the class might focus on the United States, its regions and its climate, its flora and fauna, and eventually the students' home state or town. A psychological approach would reverse the conventional sequence of study, beginning with the learners' own location and moving outward to larger geographical entities as their interest naturally expands. This method anchors learning in immediate experience.

Dewey's conception of value education, character building, and the cultivation of aesthetic taste reflect the high priority that experimentalists place on society. Dewey does not look to abstract ideals to determine values but instead consults communally

accepted precepts and norms. The values that society endorses
are best taught through experience. Children—indeed all
people—learn what they live. Real life, with all of its problems
and pressures, its interests and satisfactions, is a better catalyst
for learning than purely didactic instruction.

In ethical and aesthetic education, then, the experimentalist
educator must aid the group in identifying problem situations,
allowing it to experiment with solutions and their consequences, and let the disposition of the majority hold sway. The
emphasis on group values should operate in situations ranging
from the school playground, where young children learn that it
is better to take turns on the swings than to allow bullies to
wrest seats from weaker pupils, to graduate programs, where
students realize that cooperative research is more productive
than their splintered, competitive efforts.

According to Dewey, science helps us determine areas of
social agreement. We can find unity through empirical means
about what is right and wrong, good and bad. Morris and Pai
write,

> It is this possibility of a kind of nonmetaphysical, non-
> theistic, wholly secular brotherhood that some people feel
> is most nearly realized in the free, universal, secular public
> school in America. It is the "melting pot" idea expanded to
> include not only language and custom and style of dress but
> basic beliefs and life values.[8]

Moreover, if students find that their most workable morality
differs from that of the larger society, the teacher may recommend that they shoulder some responsibility in changing the
prevailing social pattern. Hence, the school has a greater duty
than merely inculcating existing social practices; it must engage
in intelligent criticism of the public standard.

In teaching aesthetic values and cultivating taste, the socialization approach is again the key. Rather than fostering
deeply private intuitions or radically divergent artistic senti-

ments among students, the experimentalist tries to expose them
to what society considers appropriate. The experimentalist
teacher will endeavor to get pupils involved in the whole aesthetic venture, to make some aesthetic judgments, to try
various media in the attempt to create art, and so forth. The
ultimate purpose of aesthetic education is not merely to have
the student grow up to appreciate the classic works of art but
also to help the student, through aesthetic enjoyment and production, to find more meaning in life.

EVALUATING EXPERIMENTALISM

With its emphasis on technology and satisfactory consequences, experimentalism particularly expresses the mood of
contemporary American life. If we accept the attitude that life
can be improved, then we are more likely to work toward and
achieve a better world. Furthermore, the pragmatic emphasis
on democracy, human freedom, and certain forward-looking
social movements must be applauded.

Nonetheless, the experimentalist claim that the nature of
reality is beyond human grasp is problematic. Every philosophical position at least tacitly embraces a general idea of what
reality is like. Dewey's talk about the "world-as-experienced"
simply replaces more traditional candidates for ultimate reality
with a newer candidate. His "naturalization" of experience actually suggests an underlying metaphysical position that is basically naturalistic. The problem is that experimentalists simply
refuse to pay sufficient critical attention to the genuine metaphysical issues underlying their own position.

In the experimentalist position, truth is always relative to
some individual or group. In other words, whatever ideas
enable us to maneuver effectively in the world are "true."
However, we cannot expect the things that were true for people
in medieval times still to be true for us today. Our changing
experience causes us to alter the ideas we need for dealing with

life. As William James declares, "True ideas are those that we can assimilate, validate, corroborate and verify. False ideas are those that we can not."[9] The notion that there are truths that exist independently of what people think is emphatically rejected by experimentalists.

One of the easiest ways to criticize an experimentalist theory of knowledge is simply to subject it to its own relativism: that is, one may say that experimentalism itself may be true for some people but not for others. A more weighty criticism engages "workability" as a test of truth: it has not been shown to apply to certain significant areas of truth. The truths of logic and mathematics, for example, seem to be independent of what people think and thus elude experimentalist efforts to make all knowledge relative.

Stroll and Popkin present a standard criticism of pragmatic philosophy:

> Some have contended that "working" is too vague a concept, and, as a result, that it is difficult, if not impossible, to determine whether an idea or a belief has "worked." If ideas and beliefs are to be evaluated in terms of whether their consequences "work" out satisfactorily in experience, how does one determine the possible consequences in order to test ideas and beliefs?[10]

Potential consequences branch off in many directions and are virtually infinite in number. They also reach indefinitely into the future, making a thorough test of them very difficult.

In ethical theory, experimentalist standards of morality become relativized and popularized: what is right for one person or one society can be wrong for another, depending upon their different experiences. However, we must point out that this position has not been convincingly established. Although ethical codes and perspectives may differ among various people and groups, it does not follow that there are no universal moral principles. Changing situations may, of course, necessitate variation in how people apply certain moral principles, but that does not prove that the principles themselves display wide variations in group opinion and experience.

The experimentalist attempt to make beauty and aesthetic taste relative encounters difficulties as well. We can certainly agree there is a need for art (beautiful objects and aesthetically pleasing experiences) to be available to a wide public, but we can reasonably disagree that the public sets the standard for what is beautiful. Dewey argues that beauty is what people do in fact enjoy, that what *is* admired *ought* to be admired. It is useless, he thinks, to maintain that a work of art has a certain intrinsic excellence that is admirable regardless of whether or not it is enjoyed in common society. But we can reply that this position fails to distinguish between enjoyable beauty (a subjective matter) and admirable beauty (an objective matter). Dewey provides no adequate reason to think that the latter collapses into the former. This flaw in experimentalist aesthetics parallels the flaw in its ethical theory: its recurring failure to distinguish between relative and absolute factors in the realm of value.[11]

All of the educational implications of experimentalism have been quite controversial. One thesis—that student experience is the focus of education—deserves close scrutiny at this stage of our study. Clearly, there is a degree of truth in this thesis. Who would deny that stirring the interest, arousing the curiosity, and inviting the participation of the student is desirable? However, there is serious danger in giving students the impression that their desires are the center of the educational enterprise, that they are almost autonomous agents in the education process. This does nothing to temper the natural tendency of youth to become too egocentric and preoccupied with their own immediate needs and desires. Without proper guidance, they may fail to come to understand and appreciate a larger perspective on human life and history.[12] Unfortunately, decades of experimentalist education, which has been dominant in the public school movement, have given us several generations of students who match this description.

Another intriguing difficulty in experimentalist educational thinking is its conviction that the school is to be both the mirror of society (a prime agent in the socialization process) and a constructive critic of society (a catalyst for needed change). Dewey emphasizes the role of the social group in setting standards and expectations for individual behavior; but he also advocates that teachers help students become aware of social actions that have negative results and urge them to work for constructive change as they assume their roles in society.[13] Two problems surface at this point. First, Dewey identifies no discernible agreement on values and goals in our diverse society, thereby relinquishing any prospect for a consensus on social problems. Second, he offers no clear means of preventing teachers from importing hidden agendas for moral and social progress into the classroom.

The underlying naturalism of the experimentalist perspective unavoidably contradicts a Christian worldview. Christianity asserts that the cosmos is created by a supreme spiritual being, governed by certain unchanging moral principles, and made to be a kind of prelude to eternity. Experimentalist philosophy, by contrast, denies the existence of God, views all moral principles as relative and changeable tools, and rejects any concept of life after death. Experimentalists also dismiss the ideas that humankind is sinful and in need of redemption and that miraculous divine intervention in the world is possible.

One thing Christian thinkers can say about experimentalist theory is that the various natural mechanisms for adaptation and control which it recognizes are actually important aspects of our lives as creaturely beings under God. Experimentalists have unwittingly affirmed certain ways we are made to function as experiential beings. A Christian worldview concurs, for example, that human cooperation is paramount in learning and other enterprises. The democratic ideal, along with its vision for legitimate pluralism and mutual respect among people, can be deduced from enlightened Christian thinking. That we are creatures who devise means to desired ends is simply a fact about the way God made us; it does not require a purely naturalistic explanation. Of course, these and other theoretical weaknesses in experimentalism have not diminished its practical appeal. Here again the Christian thinker can respond that its rather successful practical methods (for example, direct experience, problem solving, and the like) emerge out of the structures of divinely created human reality.

EXISTENTIALISM: INDIVIDUAL AND CHOICE

The hallmark of existentialism is its radical personalizing of the enduring questions of philosophy. The major intellectual issues that have been debated through the centuries cannot, according to existentialists, be considered purely objective and theoretical. These issues have deep, subjective significance in that they bear on the individual's quest for meaning in life. The intellectual ancestry of existentialism is usually traced to Søren Kierkegaard and Friedrich Nietzsche in the nineteenth century. However, the subsequent theoretical work, which solidified existentialism into a leading philosophical perspective, was done by European writers in the twentieth century.

The metaphysics of existentialism does not endorse a fixed and absolute reality, such as the idealist's Mind or the naturalist's Nature. Existentialists tend to deny that there is any rationality or order in the universe and to reject any intellectual system that insists there is. If existentialist thinkers say anything at all about reality, they generally assert the primacy of the existing individual, focusing on the solitary human being rather than on shared, social experience.

According to the French philosopher Jean Paul Sartre, human nature is basically undefined. In traditional metaphysical and theological systems, there is a universal or essence that defines every individual thing that exists. The essence of a thing reveals to us the kind of thing it is, its general characteristics and its purpose: "Essence precedes existence," it is said. For existentialism, however, there are no universals or pure essences by which we can understand the meaning of things, much less the meaning of human life. Sartre explains that the traditional understanding of reality must be reversed, declaring that "existence precedes essence." In other words, we first become aware *that* we are, that we exist: we did not ask to be born and yet wake up one day to find out that we are here. From this starting point, we commence the long process of trying to fashion *what* we are, our essence: *we* create the meaning of our own lives. Sartre writes, "Man is nothing but what he makes of himself."[14]

The chief attribute of the individual is the necessity of making choices, the inescapable burden of choosing who I am and what I will be. Even religious believers who search for answers in the will and plan of God or metaphysicians who explore the transcendental principles of existence must choose to accept or reject what is offered. Even experimentalists, who claim that questions about the ultimate meaning of life need not be addressed, are thereby still making a choice. Thus the concept of choice is detectable in most philosophical systems, but it is preeminent in existentialist thought.

On the issue of God's existence, the existentialist movement is divided into theistic and atheistic wings. The theistic or religious wing looks to Kierkegaard as its fountainhead. Actually, we could find prototype existentialists as far back as Blaise Pascal and, in a certain sense, Socrates. The list of religious existentialists includes Gabriel Marcel, Karl Barth, Paul Tillich, Martin Buber, and Jacques Ellul. The atheistic wing of existentialism draws much of its original inspiration from Friedrich Nietzsche and includes Jean Paul Sartre, Albert Camus, and others.

Traditional Christian theology and metaphysics affirm God's existence and perfection; they also affirm the human ability to know him. Theistic existentialism, by contrast, starts at the very same place as its sibling, atheistic existentialism: the aloneness and riskiness of the human condition. Theistic existentialists insist that we cannot know in any objective sense

whether God really exists; they deny that there are any convincing rational arguments for the reality of a divine being. Even if
there were impressive arguments for God's existence, they
would be beside the point, since we would still be faced with the
choice of whether or not to direct our lives toward God. For
these existentialists, we must exercise pure faith in God and live
as if he exists. This "as if" posture for faith reminds us of our
responsibility without specifying what our choices should be.
Thus, existential faith is always perilous and never easy.

Atheistic existentialists take a stark and cold view of the
world in which we find ourselves. They do not believe in a transcendent deity and absolute moral principles. This means that
we humans have no hope of discovering a pre-existent meaning
to human life. Sartre explains:

> The [atheistic] existentialist . . . thinks it very distressing
> that God does not exist, because all possibility of finding
> values in a heaven of ideas disappears along with Him. . . .
> Existentialism isn't so atheistic that it wears itself out
> showing that God doesn't exist. Rather, it declares that even
> if God did exist, that would change nothing. . . . Not that
> we believe that God exists, but we think that the problem of
> His existence is not the issue.[15]

The issue for atheistic existentialists is the responsibility of personal choice—a point with which even their religious counterparts agree.

According to Sartre, human civilization, supported by traditional philosophy, has emphasized the objective knowledge
of things: facts, quantity, and data. The attempt to objectify all
knowledge finds strong expression in the scientific method,
which began in the natural sciences but has been extended to
the social and behavioral sciences. This trend reveals the growing assumption that all aspects of humanity can be investigated
and known in the same way that atoms, machines, and laboratory animals can be known. Sartre, however, argues that we

cannot attain self-knowledge or interpersonal knowledge in the same way we know impersonal objects.

Commenting on existentialist epistemology, George Kneller says, "the validity of knowledge is determined by its value to the individual."[16] The concept of truth takes a somewhat different shape in the thought of existentialists. According to the classical conception of truth, propositions are true when they correspond to the way things really are. Sartre, on the other hand, expands the concept of truth, suggesting that the true is the real or the genuine. Hence, a person is a "true" person when he or she has cast off sham and superficiality and has embarked on an earnest search for meaning and personal integrity.

Existentialists have been preoccupied with the theory of value broadly conceived. Sartre's writings on ethics and aesthetics are representative in underscoring the importance of the individual and the necessity of choice. Of course, the individual must make his ethical decisions without any moral absolutes or any way of knowing them. According to Sartre, if there were absolutes, and if we could know them with certainty, surely we would lose our essential freedom as human beings. H. J. Blackham writes, "My freedom is the unique foundation of values."[17] Theistic existentialists also stress the inevitability of decision, although they envision a different fundamental choice about life than that of the atheistic existentialists.

Existentialists see each ethical choice as an element in the larger orientation of one's life. Implicit in every single decision is an axiological assumption about the meaning and worth of human existence. Over the years of our lives, in countless daily choices, we actually construct our own picture of humankind, a definition of what it means to be a person. Since we cannot avoid choosing our values and shaping the meaning of our lives by our cumulative choices, existentialists say we should face the whole business squarely and earnestly. Theistic existentialists are willing to build a life on the human longing for an Ultimate Being, although they say they know it can have no objective verification.

Atheistic existentialists think that recognizing our aloneness in the universe and accepting the necessity of making moral decisions is to be human in the noblest and most heroic sense.

In the aesthetic realm, existentialists hold that each individual must decide what is pleasing, delightful, and beautiful rather than consult common public beliefs or transcendent principles for the standard of aesthetic taste. Traditional aesthetics constructs the meaning of art either from an objective world of things or from a set of universal ideas. The value of a portrait, according to this approach, would be determined perhaps by how well it represents the actual person in question or by how well it exemplifies an accepted standard of excellence. Existentialists flatly deny that art must be judged by its relationship to some object outside of it, whether the object is in the empirical world or in the ideal realm.

In the mid-twentieth century, existentialism influenced the development of various nonrepresentational theories of art. Under existentialist influence, artists in the fields of music, painting, and film deliberately ignored prevailing norms of composition in order to make an "existential statement" about the human condition.[18] Their underlying theme was that art must personally "engage" both the artist and the recipient of art.

EXISTENTIALISM AND EDUCATION

Because existentialists recognize no fixed and unchanging reality, their theories of education are decidedly unconventional. Numerous existentialist writings have influenced educational philosophy.

Sartre and other existentialists would have the curriculum include a heavy offering of courses that emphasize the elusive, inner recesses of personhood. Courses in the sciences, which deal with objective facts and quantifiable data, are of secondary importance to those courses that encourage the growth of selfhood in the student. The exact subjects of study and the materials for teaching them would be selected according to how well they elicit the student's "awareness of freedom and responsibility." Some thinkers who reflect existential themes but are less individualistic, such as Martin Buber, say that the awareness of freedom is the basis for fulfilling interpersonal relationships.[19]

Sartre suggests that the arts give opportunity for self-expression. The social sciences also provide occasions for the student to react to important issues and problems; great literature allows the student to "feel his way" into the situation of another character and vicariously work through the relevant choices. While these subjects are especially helpful, any subject is acceptable as long as it provides the right conditions for individual reflection and decision. Van Cleve Morris says that the existentialist curriculum aims at intensifying personal involvement.[20]

Courses in the existentialist curriculum are not viewed as static, packaged bodies of information. Genuine education is a dynamic process in which the student is brought to face his or her own existence. This means that all courses, as well as the total learning environment, must be constructed so that there are opportunities for attaining self-knowledge, which leads to inward growth, ethical development, and individual decision-making.

The subjective takes precedence over the objective, since even seemingly secure truths about the objective world must be validated by the "I" which is responsible for all believing and knowing. One must appropriate knowledge for oneself. Existentialists claim that prevailing educational structures fail to recognize this because they rest on the modern dichotomies of objective and subjective, thought and emotion, fact and value. This is why Sartre insists that the educational process needs serious revision, a revision that fosters personal wholeness.[21]

According to Kneller, the teaching approach that best elicits the type of learning the existentialists want is the "Socratic method."[22] The Socratic method involves asking hard questions that may threaten the status quo and make the learner uncomfortable. Always wary that learners might retreat to the comfortable ideas of an established orthodoxy or group consensus, the existentialist educator will devise ways to stir students into an awareness of their own selfhood and to move them toward enlightened self-knowledge.

For Sartre, moral and aesthetic education must be based upon individual involvement. Character formation is aided by helping each student discover that he or she is the sole judge of what is valuable. Students must realize that the teachings of absolutist theological and metaphysical systems are not binding upon them and that they alone must shoulder the responsibility of choosing their values and thereby shaping their own lives. Sartre holds that we should not demand that anyone be perfectly compliant with any social system, set of beliefs, or code of conduct. The child's moral development is a deeply private matter.

The refinement of aesthetic sensibilities, according to existentialists, is a twofold process. First, it involves freeing children from traditional forms of artistic production and criticism as well as from social pressure to feel and respond in prescribed ways. Second, it involves helping children to create art as their own statement about life and to respond to art on the basis of their own existential situations. Conformity to tradition and popularity with peers cannot be used as criteria for appraising an existentialist work of art. Sartre particularly emphasizes the role of the free imagination in art.[23] In order to help generate imaginative energy, many existentialist educators use a nondirective approach, attempting to construct an environment that is open and sensitive to individual feelings.[24]

EVALUATING EXISTENTIALISM

Emphasis on the primacy of the individual is both the boon and the bane of existentialism. On the one hand, existentialism beckons us to awaken to our responsibility as individual human beings. On the other hand, its understanding of human selfhood is troublesome.

Sartre's contention that the cosmos is devoid of meaning and thus that one must shape one's own destiny is philosophically perilous. He says that the individual must ultimately decide what is real and what is true. But the claim that it is the individual who certifies reality and truth quickly escalates to the more radical thesis that individual choice actually produces reality and truth. When intellect is subordinated to will, the downward slide into pure individualism and arbitrariness is difficult to avoid.

Excessive individualism also afflicts Sartre's ethics and aesthetics. Although there may be a need for appropriate self-expression, Sartre goes too far in his assertion that the individual's wants and needs are paramount. This opposes centuries of human history that tell us that proper personal development requires learning how to enter into reciprocal relations within a social context. Particularly in ethics, Sartre's position fails to explain the objective status most people assign to moral judgments. Most people not only tend to attribute objectivity and universality to basic ethical principles but also cannot fathom how the concepts of duty and obligation, good and evil, make sense if they are founded wholly on individual willing. It is difficult for many to accept the case that Sartre and others make that the very act of choosing creates the value of what is chosen.

The implications of existentialist thought for educational philosophy are of mixed worth. Sartre's emphasis on the necessity of the individual appropriation of truth is clearly fundamental, an excellent axiom for the educational enterprise. Yet his desire for a minimum of structure, as well as the encouragement of extreme forms of self-expression, can have negative educational results. To a significant degree, selfhood is discovered through relationships with what is not the self—in both the otherness of people and that of an impersonal, external environment. Most existentialist prescriptions for self-development do not place sufficient stress on self-control, self-editing, self-denial, and self-giving in relation to others.

Focus on the individual, out of proportion to the common heritage of humanity, can undermine a student's interest in understanding and participating in our shared civilization and culture. In the end, it can foster the illusion that the individual is the center of the universe, which is a very damaging orientation for living. What begins with the promise of total freedom and complete responsibility can end in profound unhappiness and estrangement. Of course, there is no question that the existentialist theme of the inward, personal struggle for meaning captures an important aspect of the human situation. Historic Christianity affirms that persons are made in the image of God and that being so created makes us long for moral and spiritual fulfillment. We should not be surprised, therefore, that sensitive, reflective people recognize that it is a struggle to be authentically human.

Much in Christian faith resonates with the theistic existentialist's plea for total, unconditional commitment to God. However, the existential characterization of religious faith is problematic. Typically, existentialists declare that reason is ineffectual in making religious commitments; instead a passionate act of choice must decide such matters. Radical willing is the basis of faith. Although the recognition that there are limitations to reason is good in certain regards, a view that reason is impotent and ineffective in matters of faith excludes a vital human quality from one of the most important areas of life.

It is difficult to see how the typical existential description of faith as a subjective, volitional response can be saved from self-projection and wish fulfillment. Surely, it is the eternal nature of God that determines whether any particular subjective response is appropriate. However, in searching for the properly personal or intuitive dimension of religious life, some theistic existentialists denigrate the factual, historical, and doctrinal elements of a faith tradition. Instead of taking these elements as objective truths to be embraced, they look for the "personal truth" or "existential meaning" behind historical narratives or theological formulations. Thus, existentialists abandon the traditional assumption that theological beliefs are objective.

On theological grounds, the Christian view of a fallen but needy humanity actually provides an explanation of why the world appears meaningless and absurd to the atheistic existentialist. It gives us an idea why he would think that to make life meaningful one must engage in a strenuous quest. If one looks to science or formal philosophy alone for the ultimate answer to human existence, without realizing that the very world that science and philosophy investigate is a creation of a holy and loving God, disappointment is inevitable. When the world itself is elevated to the status of final answer, despair and desolation of the human spirit occur. A Christian perspective departs from atheistic existentialism in affirming that the world—understood as the creation of a supremely intelligent and powerful creator— is orderly and purposeful.

PHILOSOPHICAL ANALYSIS: LOGIC AND LINGUISTICS

Analytic philosophy rejects the aims of systematic philosophy by refusing to advance statements about reality, knowledge, value, God, and the meaning of life. Analysis is concerned instead with clarification of the concepts and language we employ in making these kinds of statements. Since the method of analysis purports to be a neutral procedure for elucidation, philosophers with quite divergent philosophical positions can use it. We will see, however, that those using analysis inevitably adopt philosophical assumptions that affect their intellectual work.

In spite of disagreements among those in various schools of analysis, their rallying point is the conviction that philosophy must clarify the ways we use language and thereby clarify our concepts. They insist that the classical problems of philosophy—the mind-body problem, the problem of free will and determinism, and the like—either arise from or are aggravated by misleading forms of discourse. Clarifying relevant ways of speaking actually promises to solve, or perhaps dissolve, the problems. Beginning early in the twentieth century, analysis flourished and eventually became the dominant philosophical method in the United States and Great Britain.

The analytic movement can be divided roughly into two broad schools of thought: ideal language analysis and ordinary language analysis. Many analysts look to Ludwig Wittgenstein's *Tractatus Logico-Philosophicus* as setting forth the ideal language project:

> Philosophy is aimed at the logical clarification of thoughts.
> Philosophy is not a body of doctrine but an activity.
> A philosophical work consists essentially of elucidations.
> Philosophy does not result in "philosophical propositions," but rather in the clarification of propositions.
> Without philosophy, thoughts are, as it were, cloudy and indistinct: its task is to make them clear and to give them sharp boundaries.[25]

These lines, written at the outset of Wittgentstein's career, were interpreted as criticizing the ambiguity of ordinary language.

The quest for an ideal language eventually spawned the influential movement known as logical positivism, whose followers conceived of analysis in a very specific way. With historical roots in the empiricism of John Locke and David Hume, positivism connected the meaning of all language to empirical verification. The meaning of a statement is identified with the empirical experiences one must have in order to verify it. Since positivists were particularly interested in devising an inclusive logical system for all of the special sciences, they declared that statements which are not verifiable by empirical, scientific criteria are meaningless.[26] This view throws into question all propositions of metaphysics, theology, and ethics: assertions about reality, God, and moral duty become highly problematic. Vigorous debates ensued, with some philosophers denying that nonempirical language could be cognitively meaningful and others proposing ways in which it could have some other kind of meaning. After its heyday in the 1920s and 1930s, logical positivism was supplanted by the ordinary language approach.

Interestingly, ordinary language analysis was also inspired by Wittgenstein. His later writings, especially the *Philosophical Investigations*, stimulated much activity among ordinary language philosophers. These philosophers—Peter Strawson, John Austin, John Wisdom, and others—assert that common language is adequate for human purposes; we simply need to understand better its various functions and structure. Ordinary language philosophers try to elucidate and clarify the concepts and beliefs that language embodies rather than attempting to impose alien criteria (from the area of science, for example) on all other areas of language use. They are open to the different ways in which various types of language gain meaning without conforming to strict positivist standards: religious language, romantic language, poetic language, and the like. Nevertheless, ordinary language analysts still believe that philosophical problems are rooted in linguistic confusion.[27]

Philosophical Analysis and Education

The relation of analytic philosophy to education is quite different from that of other philosophies to the educational endeavor. Up to this point, we have considered each philosophical position through its concepts of reality, knowledge, and value and have examined its educational implications. According to analyst R. S. Peters, the historical function of philosophical systems is "the formulation of high-level directives which would guide educational practice and shape the organization of schools."[28] But this is not the role of analysis.

Analytic philosophers do not see their task as that of asserting philosophical premises and then drawing educational prescriptions from them, for the initial premises would have to come from substantive philosophical commitments. Analysts argue that the task of philosophy is instead the clarification of the ways we think and speak about educational matters. Peters writes that the job of the analytic philosopher is to place our basic ideas "under the analytic guillotine,"[29] meaning that analysis should dissect our educational concepts and terms, with the goal of elucidating their meaning and use.

The aim of clarity requires neutrality. Arnold Levison writes,

> Analytic philosophy can help analyze and clarify language, provide models of theory, state criteria for meaning and verification, and in general, help unsnarl the logical and linguistic tangles in pedagogical knowledge.[30]

Analytic philosophers refrain from prescribing educational goals or norms, and they make no proposals about such issues as curriculum structure and pedagogy.

Those who employ the analytic approach look at statements generated by other philosophies and subject them to scrutiny. For example, the experimentalist dictum "Teachers should provide real life experiences for their students" would interest analytic philosophers. This rule is intended to discourage a disproportionate amount of formal, and supposedly artificial, academic exercises. But the analytic philosopher could ask what is meant by the term "real life." Investigation would determine that the term "real life" is a descriptive term that refers to all of the activities of human beings. Grammar is an activity of human beings. Therefore, why should conjugating verbs by rote be ruled out of the original prescription— something that the experimentalist wants to do?[31] Other important terms that need analysis include "good life," "learning," "liberal education," "culture," "curriculum," and so on.

William Frankena goes further than the typical analytic philosopher with an interest in educational language and claims that philosophy should also map the overall logic of educational philosophy as an entire region of discourse. This "conceptual mapping" would allow us to navigate successfully within a subject. Frankena believes that analysis helps us understand various normative philosophies of education and equips us with clear, useful concepts for building our own philosophy of education.[32]

FIGURE 2

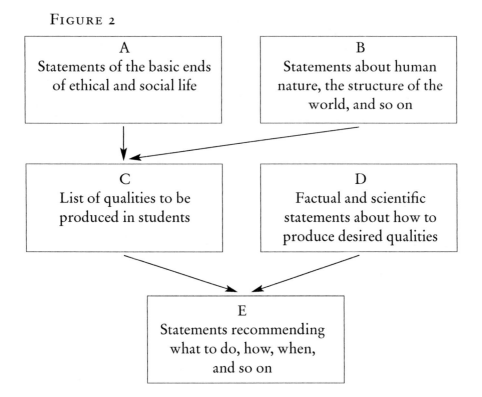

"Education," Frankena maintains, "is the process by which society makes of its members what it is desirable that they should become, . . . either in general or in so far as this may be carried on by what are called 'schools.'"[33] Hence, the main task of a normative philosophy of education is to list and define a set of dispositions to be fostered in students by parents and teachers. This set of statements is logically connected to other important types of statements, some more general and some more specific. Frankena proposes a model (figure 2) of how all of these statements fit together in a philosophy of education.[34]

If providing a list of desirable traits to instill in students is central to normative philosophy of education, then that list would both constitute a conclusion from more general assumptions and serve as a premise for articulating more specific directions for education. On the one hand, a complete theoretical philosophy of education provides justification that the specified dispositions (C) are indeed desirable. The rationale will come from our most basic normative judgments about life (A) and from our overall worldview and general knowledge (B). On the other hand, the list of qualities (C), together with certain factual information about how such qualities are produced (D), serves as grounds for making more detailed recommendations about how and when to produce them (E). This list of concrete recommendations pertains to curriculum, pedagogy, and so on.

Obviously, a total normative philosophy of education has a more theoretical side (the ABC pattern) and a more practical side (the CDE pattern). Frankena explains that a philosophy of education may use some premises from box B to draw conclusions in box D; it may also use premises from boxes A and B to draw conclusions in box E.[35] He also recognizes that the character of a philosophy of education depends heavily on the nature of the statements it includes in B and D. Whether it is scientific or unscientific, naturalistic or supernaturalistic, secular or religious, idealistic or pragmatic, positivistic or metaphysical, depends entirely on what propositions it employs in B and D in order to reach conclusions in C and E. Frankena clearly stresses the importance of the propositions affirmed in A, since no normative conclusions can be drawn in C and E without them. Whether a position is hedonistic or not, utilitarian or not, depends completely on the initial premises asserted in A.[36]

Frankena says that his method of analysis can be applied to the thought of various philosophers on education (for example, Plato, Rousseau, Whitehead, Dewey, Maritain). He briefly discusses Aristotle to illustrate the power of his model. He shows that a portion of Aristotle's work on education exhibits the ABC pattern. Aristotle's statement that the good life is a happy one consisting of intrinsically excellent activities (such as contemplation) belongs to box A. Furthermore, Aristotle's claim that if we are to achieve the good life we must cultivate certain dispositions (for example, moderation, practical wisdom, and a knowledge of mathematics, physics, and philosophy) belongs to box B. His conclusion that we ought to cultivate such dispositions belongs to box C. This conclusion, conjoined with certain other philosophical beliefs in box B and empirical observations in box D, generates definite recommendations about the most effective methods for cultivating desired dispositions (for example, habit formation) in box E.[37]

EVALUATING PHILOSOPHICAL ANALYSIS

Analytic procedures can improve educational philosophy by clarifying key terms and concepts, pointing out implications of philosophical statements, and examining the structure of educational theories. Philosophers who practice analysis differ in the degree to which they employ analytic procedures. For Peters, philosophy of education is exclusively analytic, and the educational philosopher can make no substantive theoretical proposals. Frankena, on the other hand, believes that philosophy of education should include both analytic and normative aspects. Analysis hones our logic and makes our thinking more precise, whereas the normative approach projects a comprehensive vision of education.[38]

Although analytic philosophers typically portray themselves as having metaphysically and morally neutral positions, they have to make certain tacit assumptions. Historically, many analytic philosophers have held assumptions compatible with naturalistic metaphysics and empiricist epistemology, and hence they are vulnerable to the same criticisms as those positions. Peters is a case in point, since he restricts the premises allowable in box B of our model to empirical or scientific ones.

Narrow empirical assumptions combined with analytic methods cause trouble when applied to the linguistic and conceptual structures of Christianity. Such an approach places the cognitive integrity of many theological matters in question: God, atonement, morality, the nature of humanity, and the like. We can readily see that, when Christian themes are applied to educational concerns, the problem is compounded. Talk of a transcendent purpose to life and the inherent worth of students as persons could not be seriously considered by analytic philosophers if their work is too empirical.

Although there are no logical positivists any longer, some analytic philosophers still approach things as empiricists and thus have difficulty making sense of Christian claims. There is, however, a growing number of analytic philosophers who are actually theists.[39] Most of them practice analysis without embracing empiricist assumptions and are doing very interesting things in their investigation of religious language. They have, for example, provided rigorous analysis of the use of masculine terms applied to God;[40] William Alston has even argued, contrary to prevailing opinion, that we can speak literally of God.[41]

We can see that there is no necessary link between a certain philosophical position and analytic methods per se. Analysis as a technique or means of doing philosophy should not be rejected out of hand since it asserts that rigorously clarifying and investigating the linguistic and conceptual features of our basic beliefs is essential. Clarity and precision become a prerequisite to productive philosophical discussion and evaluation, even discussion of a Christian worldview and philosophy of education. The caveat here is to be aware of presuppositions that may distort the results of analysis.[42]

POSTMODERNISM: CRITICISM AND DECONSTRUCTION

The intellectual movement known as "postmodernism" has attracted considerable attention. Although the early use of the term "postmodern" can be traced to the fields of architecture and sociology, virtually every academic discipline has felt its influence in recent decades. Many aspects of popular culture also exhibit postmodern characteristics.[43]

The ideas of Modernity are identified with the period called the Enlightenment (mid-1600s to 1800) and the important assumptions that undergirded its intellectual activity—such as the ability of empirical, scientific reason to establish all important truths, confidence in the orderly and rational operation of the universe, and the idea of progress.[44] Postmodernism criticizes and attempts to forge beyond modernism. It involves a series of related challenges to what we might call the "modern mind-set." A list of important postmodern voices includes Ferdinand de Saussure, Claude Levi-Strauss, Jean-François Lyotard, Martin Heidegger, and Søren Kierkegaard. Friedrich Nietzsche should be recognized as perhaps the first truly postmodern voice.[45]

Postmodernism is not merely the general view that we are entering a time when certain aspects of modern thought are waning. It is, rather, a philosophical stance which, in its extreme expression, asserts very radical views about reality, knowledge, language, meaning, value, and a host of other important topics. These views provide the theoretical underpinnings of postmodernism. Let us look closely at the philosophy of postmodernism, paying particular attention to the thought of Jacques Derrida and Michel Foucault.

In the area of metaphysics, postmodernism attempts to expose and discard the notion of an independent, external, stable reality. It denounces as myth the traditional belief that there is a fixed reality that is not created by mind and to which the mind must conform in the acquisition of knowledge. This conventional wisdom is meant to assure us that what we call knowledge is a more or less accurate description of "the way things are." Postmodernism explodes that assumption by showing how what we take to be reality is created by our language. What we actually have, postmodernists insist, are "linguistic descriptions" masquerading as reality. If we can speak of any "reality" at all, it is language itself, which is quite variable and fluid.

The epistemology of postmodernism emphatically denies that we can make secure cognitive contact with the world at all.

Whatever independent reality there may be, we cannot know it. Everything we suppose about what is "out there" is actually filtered and distorted by cultural assumptions, frameworks of ideas, and categories residing in the mind itself. The key influence on our perceptions of the world is language, which serves as the medium and filter through which all assumptions and categories enter the mind. Because we actually cannot know an objective reality, language has no fixed reference point, no anchor.[46]

Abandoning objective reality as the ground of language, postmodernists argue that our language is simply part of a larger narrative, a more encompassing linguistic context. That is what human beings have done through the centuries in the creation and preservation of culture. They have told stories, developed theories, constructed narratives. We create the myths through which we interpret the world, and there have been many: the classical Greek myth of the contemplative lifestyle, the Judeo-Christian myth of eternal salvation, the capitalist myth of economic productivity, and so on. However, if we cannot measure our narratives against an objective order of things and thereby determine which are accurate, adequate, or true, we are forced to acknowledge the relativity of all narratives. For postmodernists, even the fables and stories of peoples untouched by science and rationalism are on equal footing with any cognitive structures produced by modern inquiry. Any proposed universal rational standard is itself simply an artifact of some particular narrative or other. There is, as postmodernists say, no master story or "meta-narrative" that allows us to select among competing narratives.

If no theory or interpretation of reality is better than any other, how is it that some theories and interpretations have succeeded historically while others have failed? Postmodernist thinkers answer by attributing this success to political forces. They hold that there are no truer or better interpretations, only stronger interpretations—that is, interpretations that are more persuasive at a particular time for a particular audience. What is persuasive in a given narrative is really what is rhetorically

powerful for one social group at the expense of another. Our
current list of culturally and intellectually accepted theories is
thus a political instrument that elevates one social group into
power (aristocratic, white, European males) while suppressing
other social groups (lower socioeconomic classes, women, non-
Europeans).

The postmodernist thinker wants to expose how this social
power mechanism works by "deconstructing" the prevailing
language system. Derrida's method of deconstruction is intended to reveal the gap between word and object, language and
reality, and to show that what we think is reality is actually created by language itself. Prevailing linguistic myths that the
postmodernists work to unmask include the myth of truth as
the correspondence of thought to reality, the myth of universal
cross-cultural objectivity and rationality, the myth of neutral,
value-free scientific investigation, and the myth of a fundamental moral nature in human beings.

What is deconstructed, according to Derrida, are traditional, Western, value-laden dichotomies or "binaries":
presence/absence, nature/culture, male/female, central/mar-
ginal, true/false, correct/incorrect. In each case, the first item in
the pair is preferred and ranks above the second. These hierarchical binaries provide the foundation for our Western intellectual tradition, and we use them to distinguish true from false,
correct from incorrect, real from illusory. We consider them to
be beyond dispute, foundational. Without such binaries, there
can be no foundation.

For Derrida, "presence" (and its binary opposite, "absence") is the root idea in Western culture. It engenders the view
that knowledge begins in perception, by just *seeing* the object
"right there in front of us." With this knowledge, we then proceed to compare "representations" (i.e., interpretations) of the
object to the object that is actually "present" to us. For example,
one person may say that a given object is yellow, another person
may say that it is green. We can look at the object ourselves and
see that it is yellow, which makes the first person right and the

second wrong. Without presence, there can be no representation, and without representation there can be no stability of meaning. When this process is deconstructed, there are no longer common, non-subjective grounds for determining the final, complete, definitive truth about anything.

According to postmodernists, value-laden binaries limit and confine thought and language to a supposed presence—that is, everything is tied to objective truths to which they must conform. The rejection of presence frees thought and language to "play," as Derrida explains, with the "reading" or interpretation of the "text." By play, he means that we may interpret an object or event freely without being restricted by considerations of correctness or truth. The idea of the text can be understood so broadly as to encompass even nonverbal texts or nonwritten realities, such as human actions. For Derrida, all the world is a text. This is tantamount to the endorsement of epistemic relativism: there is no objective truth.

The axiological position of postmodernism matches its relativistic epistemology. Postmodernists maintain that ethical knowledge, like all other knowledge, is a linguistic construct. There are no unchanging, bedrock values; there are only linguistic constructions of value accepted by certain people and groups and cultures. What comes to be accepted as good is what those wielding the power want it to be. The deconstructionist Foucault also recommends that the greatest good is an individual's freedom to maximize her own pleasure; indeed, he argues that "society constitutes a conspiracy to stifle the individual's longing for self-expression."[47] Regarding civil law as an instrument of repression, Foucault even recommends decriminalization in the name of true freedom.[48] Ultimately, Foucault embraces anarchy, which is the undeniable political and social consequence of his ethical thought.

Postmodern philosophers are very interested in aesthetics, particularly in literary theory. Although advances in philosophy and physical science led the way to cultural change during the Enlightenment, literary theory leads the way in a postmodern era. Stanley Fish's "reader response theory" is a prime example. Denying the classical view that a literary text has a structure of meaning that is stable and self-sufficient, Fish substitutes the structure of the reader's experience for the formal structures of the text. Consequently, interpretation of a text is accomplished not by discovering the author's meanings but by developing one's own meaning in interaction with one's own expectations, projections, judgments, and assumptions.[49]

POSTMODERNISM AND EDUCATION

Perhaps no part of modern society has been more influenced by postmodern thought than education. Since postmodernism rejects objective knowledge of the world, it also rejects the classical concept of education. Traditionally, education has been charged with the transmission of historical knowledge, the great ideas of the past, and a sense of the inherent dignity of being human to young students. It also has equipped students with the skills of objective thinking, evaluation of facts, and logical extrapolation of conclusions from data—all with the purpose of sending them into the world with the ability to tell truth from error and the means to understand the patterns of thought that circulate in society.

Metaphysically speaking, postmodernist thinkers recognize no fixed, orderly reality which educators can impart to students. The curriculum does not mirror the structure of an orderly, external reality but reflects the "version" of truth held by those who have power. All traditional curricula, as well as all of the academic disciplines, which purport to represent domains of reality, are actually means of consolidating power and maintaining social control. For the teacher to teach them without questioning their very foundations is to teach error, to participate, even if unwittingly, in the perpetuation of repressive thought systems. The postmodernist curriculum, by contrast, shows students how their consciousness has been distorted by repressive systems; it submits all such systems to radical critique.

The epistemological perspective of postmodernism includes certain revolutionary approaches for the teacher-student relationship. If knowledge is essentially subjective, then teachers should not portray themselves as "authorities" or "unbiased transmitters" of information. Lecture, memorization, recitation, and the like are oppressive pedagogical techniques that attempt to inculcate prescribed patterns. Postmodern educators would lead students into the construction of their own knowledge and guide them in deciding what they think is true. Various techniques can be used to achieve this goal: examinations of the hidden assumptions behind accepted truths and norms, independent investigations of some problem, opportunities for creativity, and socialization exercises.

With the abandonment of objective knowledge, *content* is no longer the main focus of learning. Instead, *relationships* become primary. Christine Sleeter writes,

> Critical [or postmodern] pedagogy emphasizes the collective analysis of oppression, and feminist pedagogy focuses more on personal feelings and experiences, but both place the student at the center of teaching and learning. Neither imposes the teachers' view of reality on the students.[50]

The teacher should not impose his or her own views in such areas as history, art, religion, or anything else. The goal of education is to help students achieve greater self-awareness, more liberated creativity, heightened sensitivity. Students must be affirmed for their efforts and not be judged according to artificial, power-based standards of correctness.

Most academic fields show clear signs of postmodern influence. Many historians, for example, are moving from a modernist view of historical scholarship, which assumes that the meaning of events is found in their historical context, to a postmodern approach, which denies any fixity or objective truth about the past while affirming that the reality of the past is whatever the historian chooses to make of it.[51] Even the trend away from carefully citing references in footnotes exemplifies this attitude.[52]

Although it does not appear that postmodernism is having much effect on physical science itself, postmodernist thinkers are rewriting the history and philosophy of science. These thinkers assert that "scientific truth" is simply the language we use to get what we want. Lyotard writes: "There is no other proof that the rules [of scientific inquiry] are good than the consensus extended to them by the experts."[53]

Moral education as envisioned by postmodernists amounts to encouraging and empowering students to follow a lifestyle of personal anarchy. This makes sense to them because if values are rooted in power, then expression of one's personal power would indeed be primary in moral life. Living out one's own "narrative" is of fundamental importance. Since all narratives may influence others, any one narrative promoted by some to the status of meta-narrative for all is oppressive. Therefore, postmodernists urge that we teach students to reject all of the stories that society tries to force on them—stories about what is good and bad, about ideals for moral living, and about the ways to happiness.

Postmodernists exhort educators to awaken students to the fact that morality is really just a linguistic construct and thus also a social construct. Indeed, as Foucault claims, the very human self to which common ideas of morality are addressed is itself a kind of linguistic construct.[54] Modernity, as reflected in the works Descartes, Locke, and others, taught us to speak of the self as an entity, a substance, a thing of one sort or another in which moral values were anchored. Conversely, the post-modern educator is adamant that there are no innate moral values. Richard Rorty explains the postmodern position regarding the self:

> There is nothing deep down inside us except what we have put there ourselves, no criterion that we have not created in the course of creating a practice, no standard of rationality that is not an appeal to such a criterion, no rigorous argumentation that is not obedience to our own conventions.[55]

Students must be taught how to critique and throw off conventional moral demands and create their own rules. In effect, they create themselves. In this regard, Nietzsche could be considered a proto-postmodernist, prefiguring the call to throw off the conventions of society and to create who we are by our own choices—to tell our own stories, as it were.

As we would expect, the postmodern attack on the very idea of meaning profoundly influences aesthetic education. Every art form—literature, painting, sculpture, music, drama, photography, and the rest—must be carefully critiqued to show that there really is no transcendental order to be captured, no objective world to be creatively interpreted through the artist's particular medium. Students must come to see that all talk about art—its structure, content, and significance—is nothing more than a language game. For too long, the language game has been dominated by modernists who advance a largely structuralist and objectivist agenda: art could be "great"; art could be "meaningful." Once this agenda is exposed, students will become free artistically and not bound by bogus rules.

In literary theory, postmodernists reject the traditionalist notion, represented by E. D. Hirsh,[56] that a literary work "means" what the author intended it to mean. Understandably, the traditionalist student is taught to work at uncovering the author's original intention. This work involves studying the author's history, cultural background, education, personal influences, use of language and symbols, and the like. The postmodern student, however, is taught the method of deconstruction: how to uncover contradictions in literary or philosophical texts and reveal the veiled power hierarchies involved. Deconstructing a text destroys any fixed meaning and allows the student reader to interpret it freely in a manner that seems compelling or attractive to him.[57] There are no external standards (or even internal standards) of personal or cultural consistency and coherence to restrict his interpretation. Postmodernist recommendations about teaching other modes of art advance these same themes, including the denial of objective standards, the assertion of constructivist views of artistic meaning, and the encouragement of highly personal and idiosyncratic aesthetic judgments.

EVALUATING POSTMODERNISM

The effects of postmodern thought are almost ubiquitous in Western society today—in academic areas, ranging from literary theory to theology, and in the culture at large, from pop music to forms of religious worship. Many people are disturbed by postmodernist thought because it severs our ties with the stable boundary markers of true/false, right/wrong, good/bad, correct/incorrect. Others are attracted to it because it automatically legitimizes any individual's or any group's "reading" or interpretation of a text or event, no matter how deviant it may be from the opinion of experts or from established knowledge in a given field.

Of course, postmodernism's rejection of objective reality is not a denial that anything really exists or a refusal to admit that there is an external world that we inhabit. Instead it is the denial that we have cognitive access to what is there, a denial arising from the deeply rooted conviction that reality is forever hidden from us. For postmodernists, as for modernists, the discussion of reality quickly turns into an analysis of knowledge. Whereas modernists were overly optimistic about the capacity of human reason to know certain objective truths, postmodernists can recommend only skepticism.

To claim that knowledge is nothing but a linguistic construct is equivalent to claiming that there is no such thing as truth or "the way things are." We may then pose the following question: Is the postmodern description of knowledge as linguistically constructed the way things really are? The postmodernist needs to answer in the affirmative but can do so only on pain of inconsistency. We could even turn the issue another way and ask, if all linguistic utterances are power plays, then is the language expressing the postmodernist position itself a power play? To be consistent, the postmodern thinker must say that the postmodern position is yet another power play aimed at gaining the upper hand and marginalizing those with other points of view. Postmodernism cannot avoid being self-refuting if it follows its own tenets.[58]

Interestingly, the extreme epistemological position of postmodernism can actually help us develop a more realistic and modest understanding of objectivity and truth. To be objective does not mean that one has no biases or assumptions; it means one responsibly identifies them and keeps them from distorting the results of intellectual investigation. Likewise, our search for truth does not enjoy an unconditional guarantee. Rather, our search is progressive, fallible, and partial. Plato's dialectical method for the pursuit of truth is helpful: our current view of the truth must be subjected to intense examination and debate, perhaps leading us to modify it and to subject it to further scrutiny. Thus, we can admit that knowledge is contingent— and that it even has social and historical dimensions—without having to conclude that it is purely arbitrary.

In addition to these serious philosophical difficulties, postmodern ideas yield unacceptable consequences for education. By undercutting the objectivity of all rules and standards, postmodernism reduces grammar, mathematics, logic, science, and other basic disciplines to mere matters of opinion. Students are thus cut off from a vital dialogue with the reality they inhabit and in which they must navigate. The documented decline of basic skills in America, which has occurred within an increasingly postmodern climate, portends frustration and failure for students. The postmodern posture also breeds a lack of humility in students concerning the accumulated knowledge of the various disciplines and flouts the collective wisdom of the human race. A learned arrogance about the important of their own ideas and opinions diminishes their capacity to understand and cope with the world.

The problem runs much deeper than the deterioration in basic skills; it involves debunking our most cherished human values and ideals. By promoting an educational process intended to show students how systems of reason reinforce patterns of dominance and submission and by working to expose how these systems "normalize" people into the ideals of social order, postmodern education creates suspicion about all patterns of ideas, all organized systems of inquiry, all consciously planned communities. According to this model of education, the postmodern educated person, the one who really knows what is going on, must renounce fidelity, loyalty, faith, courage, and dedication to a cause, since these once-admirable qualities are merely fictions that enable a dominant social group to maintain power. The epitome of the postmodern person is one who stands completely alone, outside any organized human endeavor. For the student, this stance means acting autonomously and authentically and deciding for himself how to interpret the world. This is supposedly "liberation" from preconception and distortion. The tragedy, however, is that the enduring, intangible values that give meaning to life and worth to the world have become completely invisible to the postmodern student. C. S. Lewis warns that this outcome is, in effect, the abolition of our very humanity, for the claim to "see through" all things is the same as not being able to "see" at all.[59]

We can follow the deficiencies of postmodernism into theological territory. It is obvious to postmodernists that genuine knowledge of God is impossible because all supposed knowledge is embedded in language, all language is embedded in culture, and all cultures differ. The meta-narrative of God must be rejected along with all other meta-narratives. Postmodern relativism maintains that all little narratives, or petite narratives, are on equal footing, with no one narrative being truer or more valid than another. The Christian narrative, then, cannot claim to be the definitive truth about God and his ways; it can only claim to have truth within its own linguistic framework. Some religious believers, intimidated by the stringent demands of modernist rationality, welcome the postmodern era as though it provides a fresh opportunity for stating their faith position. They seem happy merely to say that their faith is "true for them," but this is a serious mistake.

When bona fide cognitive knowledge of God is eliminated, voluntary trust and faith in God are simultaneously undercut. Real faith is exercised only within the ambit of things that one believes to be true about God, the human condition, and the means of salvation. With the cognitive side of Christian commitment gone, it is difficult to imagine what sort of grounding the volitional side of faith might have. Any "faith" exercised under a postmodern description of our epistemic condition would have to be purely arbitrary.[60] Yet this voluntaristic and arbitrary type of faith is not what consensual, orthodox Christianity has proclaimed for more than two millennia. Wholehearted trust in the God of Christianity has always been considered reasonable based on the cognitive information we have about him (in the Bible, the classic creeds, accredited church tradition, and so forth).

None of this means that in order to be rational in believing in God Christians are obliged to follow some universally prescribed intellectual procedure which unequivocally demonstrates the truth of Christianity. But neither must we feel forced to conclude from the fact that persons and cultures differ about the truth that we cannot make warranted claims about the truth or that we cannot justifiably adopt Christianity as a metanarrative. Admitting that our apprehension of the truth, including Christian truth, is in some sense finite and mediated is not equivalent to saying that we have no grasp of truth whatsoever. As long as we are duly humble in our assertions, willing to scrutinize the grounds of our beliefs, and ready to engage in dialogue with those who differ from us, we have the proper mental posture to support ourselves in making reasonable claims concerning truth.

In fact, Christian theology affords some rich theological glimpses into the human epistemic condition. God created persons with the capacity for forming beliefs and gaining knowledge. We are rational beings, knowers. We are also social, linguistic, and historically conditioned beings; so, the beliefs we hold and the knowledge we attain are mediated to us in important ways. While we all have different vantage points on reality,

sometimes resulting in challenges in communication and persuasion, all humans share the same basic epistemic abilities (perception, memory, logical reasoning, and the like) and inhabit a
common environment in which those abilities operate. In a
world order conceived this way, there just is no compelling
reason to think that our different narratives are radically incommensurable.

It is because God made the heavens and the earth and all
that is within them, and gave humans the cognitive powers they
have, that even atheistic postmodernists can nonetheless find
within the universe and human beings grounds for some sort of
significant life. Further Christian reflection on the human cognitive condition might focus on the theme of Christ as the eternal word (logos) and on how this supports confidence in the
general validity of the quest for knowledge.

The postmodern position on philosophical anthropology
provides occasion for further theological critique. Foucault
argues that human beings "make" themselves—that is, they
create their own nature through the languages they construct
about themselves, particularly through the language systems of
the contemporary human sciences. He readily grasps the unset-
tling implications of the claim that there is no enduring self:

> To all those who still wish to think about man, his reign, or
> his liberation, to all those who still ask themselves questions
> about what man is in his essence, to all those who wish to
> take him as their starting point in their attempts to reach the
> truth . . . to all these warped and twisted forms of reflection
> we can answer only with a laugh—which means, to a cer-
> tain extent, a silent one.[61]

The cynical tone here seems warranted when anything resembling an enduring human nature is abandoned.

In marked contrast, the Judeo-Christian scriptures address
the question, What is humanity? and give reason for confidence
and hope. Indeed, they inspire humble thanksgiving for our
place and privilege in the created order:

When I look at your heavens, the work of your fingers,
the moon and the stars that you have established;
    what are human beings that you are mindful of them,
mortals that you care for them?
    Yet you have made them a little lower than God, and
crowned them with glory and honor.
    You have given them dominion over the works of your
hands; you have put all things under their feet,
    all sheep and oxen, and also the beasts of the field,
    the birds of the air, and the fish of the sea, whatever
passes along the paths of the seas.
    O LORD, our Sovereign, how majestic is your name in
all the earth![62]

Quite frankly, postmodernists simply have no categories for
apprehending the profound truth that humanity has inherent
worth because we are created by a sovereign and loving deity.

CHAPTER FOUR

——— ·◆· ———

Toward a Christian
Perspective on Education

W hat we need is a systematic and well-rounded
Christian understanding of reality, knowledge, and value that can direct our thinking
about curriculum structure, methods of teaching and
learning, and instruction in morals and values. In the
previous chapters, I have examined the relationship of
Christianity and education indirectly by commenting on
other philosophies; now I will address the relationship
directly.

Not all Christians see the relationship between faith
and learning as a positive one. Seventeen centuries ago,
the church father Tertullian asked, "What, indeed, has
Athens to do with Jerusalem? What concord is there
between the Academy and the Church?"[1] His concern
here was the relationship between reason and the pursuit
of worldly knowledge, on the one hand, and faith and the
revelation of God, on the other. His own answer is im-
plied rhetorically in the question itself, for he held not
only that Christian revelation is self-sufficient but also
that there is tension or conflict between the spiritual mission of the church and the intellectual role of the academy.
Those who agreed with Tertullian comprised a minority
in the history of Christian thought, but this opinion provides an instructive contrast to our present view.

The majority of Christian thinkers has always envisioned a positive, intimate relationship between the life of the mind and the life of faith and has particularly affirmed the importance of education.[2] The Christian vision of education unfolding here is in this vein. It is grounded in many enduring insights from the Thomistic tradition, which I will supplement with philosophical and theological insights from other traditions as well.

CHRISTIANITY AND METAPHYSICS

Metaphysics is fundamental to any worldview, and creational metaphysics is fundamental to a Christian worldview. Christian orthodoxy recognizes two broad dimensions of reality: God, the Creator, and the world, his creation. Beyond these two realities there is nothing else. When we recite the Apostle's Creed ("I believe in God the Father Almighty, Maker of heaven and earth . . ."), we affirm this truth.

Historic Christian thought holds that the infinite and sovereign God, who alone is eternal and self-sufficient, freely chose to create everything that is out of absolutely nothing. The classical doctrine of "creation out of nothing" (*creatio ex nihilo*) entails that everything depends on God, while he depends on nothing else. He alone endowed creatures with their own natures and structures and powers. Out of these basic creational concepts, we can construct an explanation of the world and the meaning of the human endeavor.

Daniel O'Connor and Francis Oakley write that the ancient Christian doctrine of creation is completely radical. Not only is it the central motif in a Christian worldview, but it also projects a conception of reality that is utterly distinct from that of competing religions and philosophies:

The idea of creation brings in its wake a whole chain of implications. Not that they were all perceived at once. Centuries were required before some of them—for example, those affecting conceptions of personality or the nature of the political life—were clearly understood.[3]

From this focal point, we can engage in distinctively Christian thinking about a wide range of issues.

It is not so much the idea of a beginning that makes the doctrine of creation unique. The real distinctiveness of the biblical doctrine is its stress on the fact that all beings are totally dependent on a transcendent, personal source. Yet this principle must be carefully interpreted to maintain the philosophical uniqueness and superiority of Judeo-Christian monotheism. For instance, the biblical account of creation, in effect, denies that the actual creation is divine or part of the divine. This contrasts sharply with other religious cosmologies such as Hindu pantheism, which teaches that the world is permeated by the divine essence, and Neo-Platonism, which maintains that the world is an emanation of God's own being. Neither does the doctrine of creation allow us to think of the world as caught in a struggle between supremely Good and supremely Evil forces, as Cosmic Dualism maintains, or as manipulated by unseen spiritual personalities, as ancient polytheism asserts.

The contrast is just as striking between biblical monotheism and naturalistic cosmologies. Whether in the ancient materialism of Lucretius or the modern naturalism of Ernest Nagel and Stephen Hawking, the consistent message is that the physical universe is eternal and persists throughout countless permutations.[4] The Christian view, however, insists that the universe and everything it contains are creaturely realities, brought into being by a sovereign and loving God, dependent completely on his will for their source and sustenance.

The metaphysically unique and rich insights of the doctrine of creation yield many important implications. One implication is the notion of a meaningful history understood as the arena in which human beings act. Their plans and activities are not determined by an arbitrary deity, by the endless and repetitive cycles of nature, or by the stuff out of which they are made.

God interacts with human choices in the arena of history, but he protects the significance of those choices. After all, he made us by fiat and endowed us with powers of reason, emotion, and will that reflect in a finite way his own infinite powers. He intends for us to work out the meaning of our lives, to shape our individual and collective destinies.

Another implication of the doctrine of creation is that humans bear moral responsibility. Unlike many rival views, Christian theism does not hold that humans are part of some divine or primordial substance; neither does it insist that they are exploited or controlled by unseen spiritual forces. Thus, it is possible for human choices to be genuinely free. Since the world is created and sustained by a transcendent deity, we are obliged to conform to the moral structures he has established. When we choose not to do so, the evil we commit is our own. Blame cannot be shifted. The Old Testament picture of a God of covenantal relations rests on the abiding perception that God is moral and that our transactions with him and with our fellows must be based on moral grounds.

Some ramifications of the doctrine of creation bear more directly on the philosophy of education. Its affirmations that the world we inhabit is real, rational, and good are rich and suggestive; such insights correct all claims that the reality we inhabit is illusory, unintelligible, or evil. The first implication is that the world, the one we see and touch, is truly real, having an ontological status of its own that is donated by God. Its reality cannot be minimized or relegated to second-class status by otherworldly definitions of spirituality, as the errors of Gnosticism and Docetism do. These errors are well known in the history of the church but still tend to recur in new guise century after century.

Second, it follows from our understanding of creation that nature is intelligible. In other words, the things of this world are knowable by minds, accessible to our cognitive activities. Since nature is a creature of a supremely creative mind, it is open to rational investigation by finite minds. Indeed, the Creator's intent was that humans "have dominion" over all other things in creation.[5] At the very least, having dominion implies rational supervision and control of a knowable environment.

The idea of creation also implies that the whole created world is good, since it comes without flaw from the creative activity of a perfect being. In spite of the fact that sin has alienated the creation from its Creator, the world's basic value remains intact. Since the created world is immensely valuable, all responsible interaction with it falls under divine mandate. This is the creational justification for our efforts to understand and manage our environment.

The concept of creation also lays the foundation for a biblical anthropology. The starting place for a proper view of humanity is that point of similarity we have with all of nature: our status as creatures. Human beings are finite, imperfect, and perishable—characteristics we share with the nonhuman creation. Like all created beings, persons depend upon a source higher than nature for their existence. Yet somehow our frail, creaturely nature bears the "image of God" (*imago Dei*), which distinguishes us as special and superior to the rest of the nonhuman creation. Although different Christian traditions have their own theories of exactly what constitutes the image of God in persons, all of them affirm that this makes us unique in the order of creation.

In this context, personhood must be defined in that rich and full sense that involves the many powers of reason, the vistas of emotion and feeling, and the ability to choose. A person, in a way, is a miniature creator, capable of understanding and doing things within a limited sphere of existence that parallel what the omnipotent deity can accomplish in an unlimited way. A more extensive analysis of personhood in the image of God would include the concept of singular center of consciousness that has a special privacy or interiority to itself. Further, it would include the ideas that a personal being seeks fulfillment in relationship, that there is a need for "the other" that may well mirror the social nature of the Triune God. Still further expansion of a biblical anthropology would encompass a Christological point of reference because the key to reality, and the key to human reality in particular, is Jesus Christ.[6]

CHRISTIANITY AND EPISTEMOLOGY

The fact that God has made persons as creatures who form beliefs and seek knowledge ushers us right to the threshold of epistemology. To be sure, God's knowledge is total, perfect, and impeccable, while ours is partial, defective, and fallible. Nevertheless, by virtue of bearing the image of God, we are able to think, judge, and know in ways that reflect his rational abilities. A theistic worldview does not guarantee that our efforts to attain knowledge will always be free from error, but it does assure us that knowledge is possible when earnestly pursued.

Since a Christian perspective affirms that reality is variegated and multifaceted, it follows that it recognizes that knowledge will be complex. There simply is no single way to discover all the different truths there are. Each domain of truth must be approached on its own terms: for example, we must discover scientific truths through observation and experiment, historical truths through records and artifacts, logical and mathematical truths by abstract reasoning. Any theory of knowledge that denies or distorts the different kinds of truth occurring in a theistic universe must be rejected as too narrow. Total empiricism, for instance, which holds that knowledge comes exclusively through the senses, must be rejected because it denies the possibility of theological and moral knowledge. Many forms of rationalism and idealism, by contrast, hold that knowledge is innate and thus denigrate the empirical. There is simply no reason to adopt any of these extremes.

God has endowed human beings in many different ways so that they may make the best of their opportunities to seek truth. Some truths are acquired through our basic noetic powers, such as memory, perception, and rational intuition, all of which produce beliefs in us under the appropriate circumstances.[7] Other beliefs about what is true result from constructing arguments. We also have the ability to form hypotheses that can be confirmed or disconfirmed by rigorous test. Although our various mental capabilities for finding truth are finite and fallible, they must be seen as gracious endowments for navigating in God's world. Christians have no special shortcuts for acquiring truth; they possess the same basic intellectual powers and opportunities as other humans. The important advantage for Christians lies in their perspective and motivation.

Some Christian thinkers ponder whether our moral and spiritual condition affects the search for truth. They argue that a disciplined will, balanced emotions, and even virtuous character may be relevant. After all, if I have diligently trained my will to maintain a strong mental focus and accurate judgment, would that not be an advantage in my quest for truth? If a person's affections are such that he actually loves truth and wisdom and earnestly wants to align his life accordingly, does he not thereby gain strong motivation in the human knowledge venture? If one possesses dispositions to be just, benevolent, and courageous, does he not see the world differently and therefore see some truths better? Conversely, might it be that sin could cloud our eyes to the truth? We often comment, for example, that the extremely self-centered person has difficulty coming to know certain truths about himself and that the overly ambitious individual has a tendency to distort reality. All of these matters are worthy of further discussion from a Christian point of view.

Though it offers no guarantees to those who seek specific truths, the Christian perspective still supports the search in interesting and important ways. It gives truth an appropriate residence, since it provides an understanding of how knowledge is genuinely possible within a real, rational, created order. It explains our innate desire for truth, and it explains how our intellectual quest is situated within a cosmos that is amenable to our knowledge-gathering efforts. Since there is such a thing as truth, one of the deepest longings of our being can be satisfied. In a way, Christians should simply feel more at home in the universe they are exploring than anyone else.

Arthur Holmes declares that all truth is God's truth wherever it may be found.[8] God created the whole universe and everything it contains. Thus, the truth about anything is ultimately related to God. Aquinas teaches, "All things are called true because of their orientation toward the truth of God's mind."[9] Knowledge of any truth, then, indirectly bears witness to God. A Christian worldview affirms that the unity and integrity of God mean that there is a unity and integration to all truth—truths within disciplines, truths across disciplines. The God-centeredness of truth—whether all who seek truth recognize it or not—makes knowledge of truth intensely personal, not detached and indifferent.

Several marvelous passages in the New Testament further amplify this point by proclaiming that the center of all truth is ultimately God himself as revealed through Jesus Christ. Jesus Christ is said to be "the word of God," "the one in whom are hid all of the treasures of wisdom and knowledge," "the one through whom all things were created and hold together," and "he in whom we live and move and have our being."[10] This Christological concept signifies that the very heart of reality is personal, rational, and knowable and that all other knowledge takes on proper perspective through relationship to Christ. Pope John Paul II writes, "God has placed in the human heart a desire to know the truth—in a word, to know himself—so that, by knowing and loving God, men and women may also come to the fullness of truth about themselves."[11]

In addition to providing the deeper meaning of the search for truth, a Christian perspective can actually provide fruitful leads, insights, and hunches in the quest for certain truths. Christian ideas about human nature, for example, should point in key directions for a Christian doing research or theory construction in psychology, sociology, or cultural anthropology. Likewise, the Christian idea of humanity as made in the image of God should guide how the Christian philosopher and ethicist think of morality. A Christian understanding of moral life would clearly affect what Christian teachers emphasize when they discuss ethical behavior in grade school. A Christian working in biology, for example, should be supported by the conviction that all biological structures and processes are part of a creaturely order to be explored. Moreover, when a Christian thinks in large terms about the entire range of human knowledge, her worldview should assist her in detecting relationships and discovering interconnections across different domains of truth.

CHRISTIANITY AND AXIOLOGY

A Christian theory of value fits consistently with Christian theories of reality and knowledge. We know that the Maker of reality is perfectly good and supremely creative. Therefore, all of his creation is charged with great value and worth; created personhood has special dignity and significance. It is not difficult to sketch how the main contours of ethics and aesthetics are shaped by this Christian frame of reference.

In the area of ethics, a Christian view compares favorably with other prominent theories. Christian theism opposes, for example, all positions that take fundamental moral principles to be either subjective or relative.[12] A Christian and theistic position holds that moral principles are objectively meaningful and absolute because they reflect constant moral realities inherent to creation. Persons and cultures sometimes differ in their formulations of fundamental moral norms, or they apply them in different ways in varying situations. But the fact that we do actually communicate on moral issues—disagreeing, persuading one another, and reaching decisions—indicates that there is a reliable cognitive content to moral judgments. Virtually all societies agree on the most basic values (justice, benevolence, and so forth), which undermines the claims of some that all moral

judgments are relative and demonstrates that there is a common
moral perception among people.[13]

A striking difference between Christian theism and many
other ethical views is that it is committed to a concept of intrinsic goodness. Most other views deny that any actions or kinds
of actions can be inherently good or evil; thus, they lack an objective grounding for ethics.[14] Creational metaphysics, however,
with its premium on personhood, provides important insight
into a sound basis for values.[15] The concept of persons being
made in the image of God puts ethics on solid ontological
ground.[16] Because humans are the kind of creatures they are—
rational, moral, social beings—definite moral considerations
are due them. Our created human nature means that we must
act and be treated in certain ways. Certain actions and not
others move us toward the fulfillment of our created nature.
Likewise, if persons must be treated in certain ways, then we
are all ethically obligated to treat each other accordingly. Keith
Yandell explains that the structure of personhood accords it
"inherent value" which cannot be outweighed by the moral
consideration of anything that is nonpersonal.[17] Thus, we have
a firm anchor for moral law and our duty to obey it.

A Christian approach also addresses the inner or subjective
side of moral life.[18] Once again, the pivotal concept is the nature
of created personhood. This rich, holistic understanding sees a
finite person as endowed with powers and capabilities that
reflect the nature of the Supreme Person: thought, volition,
agency, and emotion. These powers are part of our own
creaturely existence and can be cultivated, strengthened, and
shaped. Some non-Christian philosophers, most notably, Aristotle, even recognize the fact that we have innate mechanisms
for forming habits in light of our perception of moral law. Traditional moral theory gives the name "virtue" to properly
formed habits or dispositions. We can see that the moral community through the ages has prized a number of important
virtues: honesty, loyalty, benevolence, courage, and the like.
The possession of such virtues in aggregate constitutes good

"character." Thus, *being* a good person is necessarily related to *doing* the right things.[19]

Indeed, performing morally right actions and building morally good character is the fulfillment of a vital aspect of divinely created human nature. Aquinas indicates that the person who acts morally obeys the "natural law," which is "nothing else than the rational creature's participation in the eternal law."[20] C. S. Lewis draws a comparison with the Tao of Chinese religion to speak of the moral law.[21] To live in accord with the Tao, the universal moral law, is to be in conformity with the way things are meant to be. One thereby has an inner harmony and sense of well-being.

The Sermon on the Mount reinforces the idea that moral life is an avenue of fulfillment in God's order. In this sermon, Jesus enumerates a number of inward attitudes and dispositions which one needs to possess in order to be blessed. Interestingly, the Greek word *makarioi,* which occurs throughout this passage, typically translates as "blessed." It may also be translated "fulfilled," "profoundly happy," or "deeply contented."[22] Blessed are the meek, blessed are the merciful, blessed are the peaceable. That is, deeply fulfilled, intensely satisfied, profoundly happy are they whose lives display these virtues. This quality of life is nothing less than the life of God taking root and growing in us.

To be sure, sin infects the human condition, and any Christian moral philosophy must take this fact into account. Christian traditions differ, of course, over the precise impact of sin on human nature. Although a complete analysis of sin lies beyond the scope of this book, let us recall that consensual orthodoxy through the centuries has never held that sin prevents us from taking moral development seriously.

It is only when we properly identify the key elements of the creational order that we can begin to understand the context and significance of the redemptional order. The Christian doctrines regarding sin and the fall, justification and atonement that pertain to God's redemptional program logically entail that only a certain *kind* of being can have moral transactions with its fellows, experience a fall, be addressed by God, know God's presence, and so forth. The doctrine of creation signifies that we human beings are precisely this kind of creature. Claude Tresmontant explains that the human fall into sin does not change the ontological facts: "What is altered is not human nature itself, but the relations, properly supernatural, between God and man. . . . Nothing has been taken away from the nature originally created; nothing has been added."[23]

Scripture proclaims that the universe is filled with the glory of God and thus provides the impetus for a theory of aesthetic or nonmoral values. From this central declaration, we rightly conclude that the whole world is charged with value: "The heavens are telling the glory of God; and the firmament proclaims his handiwork."[24] God makes available to his creatures a host of goods and values that are not exclusively related to moral duty and virtue: friendship, knowledge, pleasure, and so forth. Christianity understands all such goods to be gracious gifts of God, manifestations of his love in creation.

Beauty is one of these important creational goods. Although thoughtful Christians may differ on the controversial issue of beauty, we can develop some general insights in harmony with the preceding metaphysical and epistemological themes. For example, we can distinguish between the objective and subjective aspects of beauty. Objectively, beauty can genuinely be "in" things, objects can really be "beautiful." Just as reality is not illusory and truth is not completely subjective, beauty is not merely a private preference. Beauty in an object is a kind of excellence or perfection; it is an important aspect of our divinely created world. Of course, the elements of beauty—such as unity, proportion, clarity, and the like—are subject to discussion and even to contextual study within any specific artistic field.[25] The ability to perceive beauty as an arrangement of such elements must be taught and cultivated in persons. Although there can still be disagreement about the exact standards of beauty or about what specimens (whether natural or humanly made) are in fact beautiful, judgments about what is beautiful can have an objective reference.

The counterpart of objective beauty in objects is the subjective response of persons. Certain things please individuals in various ways. We often talk about objects as being beautiful not so much because they have an intrinsically excellent nature but because we have certain emotional reactions to them. When we claim that things we enjoy are beautiful, we are essentially expressing our taste. Both ways to appreciate beauty are legitimate, subjective enjoyment and objective appraisal. Subjective beauty within the sphere of taste has a very affective aspect, whereas objective beauty involves certain cognitive functions, such as evaluation according to accepted standards. God has created persons with drives leading them to seek beauty and its appropriate pleasures. The beauty and pleasure we find are actually hints of God in the created order, glimpses of his perfection and grace.

A CHRISTIAN JUSTIFICATION OF EDUCATION

Neither the Bible nor a general Christian view of life contains an explicit, systematic philosophy of education. So, our task is to draw out a number of important implications and insights for the educational process from these basic sources.

Of course, the natural starting place for justifying education from a Christian perspective is the innate human drive for understanding. This divinely created tendency finds sophisticated social expression in formal education, which represents an organized, sustained effort to transmit the knowledge and achievements of human civilization. Education is not only an outgrowth of a natural disposition; it is also mandated in God's command for Adam to take dominion over the created order. Hence, we may say that schooling is, in principle, a divinely ordained human institution.

Interestingly, some theologies of education justify schooling by tying it to other institutions. They typically say that the school derives its biblical sanction from one of three more basic institutions, which they take to be more directly ordained by God: the family, the church, and the state. Education is thus viewed as an outgrowth of the family's fundamental right to educate, or as a projection of the Church's mission on earth, or as founded on the right of civil society to insure a competent citizenry. The convergence of these three means of justifying education add legitimacy to deliberate, organized education.

Historically, many educational enterprises did grow out of these other three institutions, which still remain committed to various kinds of education and training.[26] The rise of the home schooling movement in America in recent decades clearly attests to the feeling of responsibility many families have to educate their young. There are also impressive examples of organized religion taking a strong role in education. Within the Protestant tradition, the *Heidelberg Catechism* and the *Westminster Shorter Catechism* are evidence of its sense of obligation to teach even the very young so that they might know the truth of God and thus better glorify him.[27] Under the auspices of the Roman Catholic Church, education at all levels has had a long and distinguished history.[28] Insofar as the existence of the civil state is biblically justified, its efforts in public education gain some degree of justification as well.

Debates arise when the presumed rights of any of these institutions seem to conflict. There are many notable examples in which interests of the state seem inconsistent with the rights of family or church.[29] Whether the disputes are about sex education, the demise of academic standards, or some other pressing issue, we need sane theoretical guidance to help us analyze matters and determine which rights are more fundamental. From a Christian point of view, it would be difficult to elevate any rights, such as those alleged for the state, above those of family. Moreover, from a Christian vantage point, it would be difficult to envision as proper a family approach to education that did not recognize the need to guide its children toward Christ and the church. A humane and enlightened democracy would take these deeply rooted rights of family and church into account. All of this clearly embroils us in complicated issues that informed Christians must pursue in greater depth.

The Christian justification of education, in effect, collapses the sacred-secular distinction. Both the general creational mandate for education and the redemptional theme of glorifying Christ with our minds show that there is no bifurcation of spiritual knowledge and worldly knowledge. God is one; he is a unity. All truth stems from him and is known by him; thus, there is no basis for insisting that only "religious knowledge" has spiritual significance.[30] Neither are there grounds for saying that a religious vocation is of greater value than any other. When pursued for the glory of God, the most mundane tasks, such as business ownership, full-time homemaking, political involvement, and disciplined study, have eternal worth.

CHRISTIANITY AND THE CURRICULUM

Christian theism strongly justifies a high view of education, and that perspective further shapes the contours of an educational philosophy. In a well-formed philosophy of education, Christian commitments about the nature of reality will virtually determine curriculum structure: the subjects and sequence of studies should reflect the various areas of reality to be explored by students. And the priority placed on the different areas as well as on the methods of exploration is determined by another metaphysical consideration: the very nature of humanity. Christian theism proclaims that each person is valuable and should develop his or her God-given potentials to the fullest.

In a holistic Christian concept of human nature, persons are complex and yet integrated beings with rational, emotional, moral, aesthetic, physical, and practical aspects. Christian thinking clarifies what it means to develop each aspect of our humanity and how that development can best be accomplished. Limiting our discussion here to the rational and practical dimensions of personhood, what can we say about the kinds of curricula that enhance them?

For one thing, every human being should be intellectually nurtured on unchanging truths, great ideas, and universal values. The lofty educational themes that support and nourish our eternal aspect pertain to humanity itself, our moral quest, our place in the universe, the meaning of suffering, and the like. Although people and cultures down through the centuries have held many differing beliefs on such subjects, studying those beliefs provides the opportunity for each person and each generation to think through the fundamental issues of life. Those who try to understand the reasons why people disagree will come to appreciate the portion of truth contained in each view, discern any underlying agreement, and gain deeper insight into what it is to be human. If we take our essential humanity seriously from a Christian point of view, we will have excellent grounds for providing this kind of education at all age levels and in any creative way possible. No child, youth, or adult should be deprived of the opportunity to be exposed to this kind of broad, humanizing education. In short, everyone deserves a liberal education.

A Christian approach to education gives a legitimate place to the practical part of our personhood as well. What I call the practical aspect of life may involve any human activity from manual labor to sophisticated technical invention and may be understood along two related lines of thought. According to one line, the practical dimension of our humanity attends to all the needs of creaturely survival, maintenance, and advancement. We are not pure spirits, unembodied intelligences that can spend our existence in detached contemplation. Rather, humans must have food, shelter, and physical security. We act upon our environment in order to attain these things.

Another line of thought maintains that the practical dimension of our humanity mirrors the fact that God himself is an agent. He is a doer and a maker: he envisions plans, carries out his intentions, and works for creative change. It is no surprise that the practical abilities of persons can function at levels far beyond sheer survival needs. This active, productive aspect projects our inner thoughts and motives out to the wider world, allowing us to dream lofty dreams, devise positive plans, and constructively alter our environment. The history of civilization and culture is an expression of this marvelous power of human agency. It is yet more evidence that we bear the image of the maker of all things.

But we must realize that a life of purely practical involvement—as well as any form of education that places disproportionate emphasis on practical skills—cannot provide a larger understanding of life and the world. That is why the intellectual aspect of our humanity must guide the practical. That is why nourishing students on the major themes and great ideas of humankind helps them transcend the spatio-temporal boundaries of practical life. Such education enables them to think not simply in terms of their immediate surroundings or needs but also in terms of the global situation in which humanity finds itself. It sensitizes them to moral obligations, religious aspirations, and recurring problems of the race. It brings a wider perspective to practical decisions and actions. When speaking of what this kind of education had done for him, Aristotle remarked that it had allowed him to do freely what most persons do as slaves. In other words, broad understanding and mental freedom are necessary to provide depth and direction to one's practical action.

At the very least, an actual curriculum featuring the enduring themes about God, humanity, and the world would include such subjects as literature, history, philosophy, the natural sciences, the social and human sciences, and mathematics. The continuing discussion of what precisely constitutes humane learning is vigorous and fascinating. The importance of thinking carefully about what type of curricula will provide it cannot be stressed too much.

The content and form of a curriculum aimed at practical training, on the other hand, vary with the skills in demand in a constantly changing job market. Intense educational debates rage over whether technical and professional preparation should be distinct from liberal learning or whether the two forms of education should somehow be combined. In constructing a curriculum that best meets the needs of the whole person, educators must be clear about the kind of realities they seek to prepare students for and the kinds of skills they want to develop.

It is obvious that metaphysics profoundly affects the curriculum at all levels of schooling, from elementary through college. Since Christian theism holds that reality has a definite structure, education has the role of imparting knowledge of that structure and developing in students the skills they will need for continued contemplation of and commerce with it.

Teachers in such a curriculum must, of course, adjust their methods to the developmental state of the learner. Earlier stages of schooling must provide the basic skills, techniques, and categories for acquiring later, more sophisticated forms of knowledge. Jerome Bruner suggests that a sound curriculum would be designed in a "spiral." As students progress from one instructional level to another, "a curriculum . . . should revisit basic ideas repeatedly, building upon them until the student has grasped the full formal apparatus that goes with them."[31] Because of the preparatory function of early schooling, early curricula should also include methods that provide positive emotional support, initial socialization, the beginnings of character development, and physical hygiene and coordination.

Some fascinating studies reveal that significant learning requires that students develop "cognitive frameworks" or schema which will enable them to organize and assign meaning to individual pieces of information. Thus, it is not accurate to conceive of learning simply as the progressive accumulation of data or facts. George Miller, for example, has shown that discrete, disconnected data cannot be reliably held in short-term memory and will soon be lost unless they are connected to a more enduring, stable mental structure.[32] We all need a coherent cognitive framework for accurate intellectual processing and long-term understanding. Experiments provide convincing empirical evidence that a structure of background information is required, whether we are talking about purely verbal learning, such as reading, or learning through any other aspect of experience.[33] This evidence about the nature of the learning process justifies creating courses within the curriculum that place sufficient emphasis on the acquisition of general principles, themes, and concepts as contexts for the interpretation and retention of more specific information.

In any complete learning episode, the learner is not just passively receiving meaning but is actively selecting the appropriate framework for making sense of incoming information. E. D. Hirsch, Jr., proposes that general cultural literacy actually functions as a background framework, that it provides an essential intellectual context for countless learning activities.[34] Without the background, students are not able to interpret the meaning and importance of their learning experience, whether it is texts they read, educational videos they watch, or classroom discussions in which they participate. It is no surprise that among traditional cultures there is a strong precedent for teaching basic cultural literacy in the early years, perhaps by as early as thirteen years of age.[35]

Christians who think about education should take seriously the need of students to be initiated into our shared cultural heritage. The future depends on how well our children will be able to understand and engage the complex reality they face. Without an adequate degree of cultural literacy, which is a kind of intellectual net, too much information slips past them. We can readily see, too, that their ability to grasp the rich vocabulary, nuances, symbols, and images through which Christian belief is expressed also depends on this cultural literacy. Without the proper background, they will miss too much.

Talk of our shared cultural heritage inevitably raises the question of the content and role of the liberal arts. Liberal arts is, in a very deep sense, the keeper of the great tradition—the great works of literature, art, philosophy, and science as well as the ongoing discussion of the great ideas and issues they contain. Robert Paul Wolff recognizes the value of one who is educated in the great tradition: "I confess that I *like* a cultivated man or woman, on whom allusion is not lost, in whose discourse there echo earlier voices, one capable of that special sort of irony which comes from the awareness that one's most precious thoughts have been anticipated."[36]

Education helps develop various human capacities through childhood and adolescence, and these capacities must become ever more mature. Ultimately, it is not the world of the child but the real world—of serious decision, human conflict, work and leisure, success and failure, triumph and tragedy—for which the process of education must prepare the student. It would be a crime against young students if we allowed education to foster, even for a moment, the delusion that the world is just for them, or that reality coincides with their relatively immature ways of thinking about it. In a culture that virtually worships youth, this insight will become increasingly important.

Christianity, Teaching, and Learning

Our thinking about modes of teaching and learning is influenced by our epistemological commitments. For a Christian theist, teaching and learning must be built on the confidence that we can know reality, that truth about the world is accessible to us. Articulating his Thomistic position, Josef Pieper eloquently writes,

> [A]ll existing things . . . are positioned within the knowing soul's field of reference; and this field of reference, the "world" of man the knower, is nothing less extensive or significant than the total universe of all that is. Being able to know means to exist in relation to, and be immersed in, all that is. The mind, and the mind alone, is *capax universi* [capable of grasping the universe].[37]

This is no shortcut to truth. We need to study diligently to refine and modify our findings and to engage in critical dialogue on the truths we think we have found. It is not easy: the principle of commitment to truth must find its expression in rigorous intellectual activity.[38]

Commitment to truth opposes the underlying skepticism of our age, a skepticism that is increasingly infecting all levels of schooling and is particularly evident at the high school and college levels. In many of our educational institutions, the human ability to know truth is undercut in numerous ways. Students eventually get the message that we cannot know truth and that we definitely cannot know the truth about life's most important questions. This kind of message promotes the attitude that education must be reduced to acquiring practical information and specialized techniques in order to control our environment, prosper financially, and satisfy our personal desires. Predictably, technical and pragmatic courses of study flourish in this kind of setting. Those studies that touch upon life's large issues—such as the foundation of morality, the nature and meaning of humanity, and the existence of God—may be perceived as quaint fantasies or word games that people play to advance their own agendas.

In such an intellectual environment, where there is no way of determining the answers to basic human questions, the whole academic enterprise becomes degraded. Skepticism inevitably begets relativism and radical freedom, two pervasive characteristics of our current educational milieu. Relativism treats all of life's major options as if they were of equal value, as if there really is no firm truth about anything: there are no standards, no absolutes, no reasonable guidance about how to live a decent human life. In a relativistic educational environment, students are given no reliable and helpful way of thinking about such matters as ethical norms, social obligations, religious options, family structures, and sexual behavior.

The corollary to relativism is radical freedom. As a response to relativism and skepticism, radical freedom denies that there should be any ultimate constraints on what a person believes or does. Since there is no compass for truth, and since it is socially unacceptable to make critical judgments in the name of truth in the current educational climate, students learn to expect that they have the right to believe anything they want. It has become fashionable to encourage them to inhabit "their own truth." Unfortunately, this distorts our legitimate intellectual duty to pursue truth, hold rational beliefs about it, and be open to discussion and debate that is aimed at conforming our beliefs more closely to it. In the sphere of action, the new freedom has also wreaked havoc, generating and supporting the view that no choice or behavior is inherently wrong. The traditional ideal was that, even with our admitted limitations, we could discern principles for ordering our behavior, that we could tell in general what conduct is really right and really wrong.

There is an important distinction between two types of educational settings: those that promote relativism and those that expose students to a wide variety of ideas and opinions. Sometimes the outside observer mistakes the latter for the former. If all truth is God's truth wherever it may be found, then a variety of important voices in the great, ongoing intellectual discussion must be heard. Students must be assisted in grappling with diverse positions and in making their own evaluations, and this process should take place in ways that are sensitive to their different developmental stages. At the level of higher education, of course, some of the major voices in the great discussion clash and can cause extreme dissonance. Nietzsche's advocacy of the will to power conflicts with the teachings of St. Francis on humble spirituality; the writers of *The Federalist Papers* promote a concept of governance utterly different from that which one finds in Machiavelli's *The Prince*. Yet Christian theism endorses the stimulating and wonderful encounter with the complex realm of ideas when truth is the goal.

An educational enterprise grounded in the human ability to know truth will acquaint itself with the best research on how knowledge is transmitted and acquired. The Christian commitment to truth and the importance it places on the power of the mind should enable us to evaluate critically all proposals for teaching and learning. For example, let us consider the fashionable proposal that educators abandon abstract, didactic instruction methods and instead employ more experiential teaching styles. The rationale for this is that today's students, from preschool through college, are allegedly "concrete" learners: they learn through what they experience. Underlying this shift in pedagogical emphasis is the assumption, endorsed by Dewey and others, that students will naturally draw out general principles from concrete experience.[39] Ironically, serious deterioration in academic performance among our youth is now well documented and has become a serious national concern. Obviously, there are many variables associated with poor educational results, but one factor is the abandonment of teaching traditional content and skills in favor of experience-centered instruction.

Some very promising studies show that students need both specific information and general ideas. These are not mutually exclusive dimensions of learning. In today's educational circles, the experiential, the personal, and the idiosyncratic are promoted as a panacea. A better balance would be struck if we helped liberate students from patterns of thinking that are too experience-oriented and assisted them in gaining the skills of abstract reasoning and interpretation. It is a cruel paradox that many claim that our age knows more and has more information than previous ages but that it regularly produces minds that are weak, underdeveloped, and lacking in historical perspective.

Given the worldview of Christian theism, which affirms that universal truths are knowable and that permanent values exist, what recommendations for teaching might we offer? Mortimer Adler suggests that we adjust modes of teaching and learning to strengthen the basic ways in which the mind can be improved. He identifies three: the acquisition of organized knowledge; the development of intellectual skills; and the enlargement of the understanding, insight, and appreciation.[40] The ideal is that these three types of educational processes will interact in all courses and at all levels of schooling. Naturally, the precise emphasis each type of process receives depends on the developmental stage of the student and the nature of the subject matter.

At the level of organized knowledge—such as language, literature, mathematics, history, social studies, and the natural sciences—it is reasonable to teach using didactic methods, repetition, memorization, standard textbooks exercises, and the like. Much of this will be rote learning. The teaching can be as attractive and creative as possible, but there still is a body of knowledge that students must simply commit to memory. It is work, but we are not being kind to students in allowing them to avoid it. By transmitting knowledge in this fashion, we are building the support for higher forms of learning. This necessary support begins with material appropriate for the lower grades and then builds in quantity and sophistication as the students progress.

The very backbone of education is the development of basic skills: reading, writing, speaking, listening, observing, measuring, calculating, and estimating. Since this type of knowledge is "knowledge how to do," it can most effectively be developed by regular performance, practice, and drill. To help students gain these skills, the teacher must act in much the same way as an athletic coach, guiding students in the doing of certain things, correcting faulty performances, and eventually helping them achieve proficiency.

The enlargement of students' humanistic understanding and appreciation rests on basic knowledge and fundamental skills; but it also transcends them. The goal of this higher level of education is to seed important ideas in the minds of students, improve their critical judgment, tutor their moral sentiments, stimulate the enjoyment and admiration of beauty, enhance the imagination, and increase their tolerance for difference. It is this level of intellectual activity at which all other levels aim. We can consult the information we possess and employ the skills we have acquired when we contemplate and discuss the large ideas that have shaped our civilization. The pedagogical approach that is most appropriate for reaching this consummate phase of education is, as it should be, the Socratic method. The interrogative or discussion format improves both analytic and synthetic powers, and it awakens the creative and inquisitive capacities of students. Of course, other similar methods, such as the writing of critical papers, are also very helpful. It is at this level where the seeds previously sown in skills for gathering information and mastering technique can bear the fruit of insight, appreciation, discernment, and wisdom.

Mortimer Adler himself has long been known for promoting the teaching of the great books as an excellent way of exposing students to the great ideas which have defined our intellectual culture for over 2,500 years. Adler's *Syntopicon*, containing almost 3,000 topics revolving around 102 great ideas in human civilization, remains the centerpiece of the Encyclopedia Britannica's *Great Books of the Western World*.[41] The ideas of beauty, chance, eternity, evolution, family, God, justice, liberty, love, suffering, tyranny, virtue, war and peace are only a small sample of the topics which fuel the great, ongoing conversation in Western civilization. Of course, there will always be controversies about which ideas are "great" and about how to draw the line between books that deserve to be called "great" and those that do not. From a theistic and realistic perspective, however, we must note that the great ideas are valued because they help us think deeply about human life and the universe. Enlightened thinking about such matters, in turn, expands our understanding of the profound significance of the Christian view of life. Therefore, Christians concerned about the health of our general culture and about the ability of contemporary people to grasp Christian truth must not take lightly the place of the great books in the curriculum.

CHRISTIANITY AND VALUE EDUCATION

The value commitments of Christian theism shape our thinking about ethical and aesthetic education. For the Christian, various

objects and actions in God's universe have value, both in the
moral realm and in other areas. Our recognition of this axiological dimension of existence is foundational to a Christian frame
of reference.

The grounding for moral education is the fact that God is
holy and that he created humans as moral beings capable of
reflecting that holiness. We are moral agents, able to know and
do what is right. Thus, the task of moral education is to assist
youth in realizing this aspect of their human nature. A moral
agent, at the very least, is a person who makes moral judgments
and performs morally significant actions. Thus, moral education must address both the cognitive and the behavioral domains. Education in the cognitive domain involves teaching the
young to recognize moral standards as well as to make moral
evaluations in relation to them. Education in the behavioral
realm addresses the need to act in ways that reflect our standards, that is, to put ethical knowledge into practice.

Hence, the most effective process of moral education will
be concerned with determining the proper sources of moral
knowledge and the best means for conveying it to children and
youth. Broadly and ecumenically understood, Christian faith
recognizes several important sources of moral knowledge: the
common moral experience of the human race, the precepts and
principles of the Old and New Testaments, and the insights of
the community of faith through the ages. The first source is
available to all persons insofar as they are rational and moral
creatures; it is part of God's general revelation.[42] This level of
understanding is even reflected in the great religious traditions
of the world. Scripture is God's special revelation that clarifies
and intensifies the nature of our moral obligations and shows
that the whole moral enterprise is rooted in a morally perfect
Creator. Church tradition offers the accumulated moral
wisdom of God's people based upon their reflection on Scripture and human experience. Properly interpreted, the legitimate
sources of moral knowledge converge, providing a trustworthy
framework of understanding within which we can form our
own moral judgments and direct our actions. Ultimately, we

have moral responsibilities to deity, to ourselves, to our fellow human beings, and even to nonhuman nature.

In spite of our access to genuine sources of moral knowledge, something is unmistakably wrong in the human endeavor. We human beings fail to live up to what we know is highest and best, often violating our clear duties and sometimes committing horrible atrocities. All of this underscores the theological fact that we are fallen, that sin infects the human condition. Although Christian traditions have differing interpretations of the impact of sin on the human moral enterprise and of the nature of moral living itself, none of them take moral education to be hopeless. On the contrary, the endeavor to live morally and to provide moral education for our young has always been regarded as one of the primary responsibilities within Christian orthodoxy.

In order to fulfill the responsibility of initiating and nurturing the young in moral life, we must employ the most effective educational means. The Judeo-Christian Scriptures speak of moral education, but most passages address its larger goals rather than offer guidance concerning actual methods. Thus, we must study and reflect on the most effective approaches that both empirical research and common sense can recommend to us. To the extent that we can gain specific information about the natural mechanisms for helping to engender moral life in students, we thereby learn more about the structure of our created humanity. These mechanisms range from the cognitive ability to learn general rules and the propensity to form habits to the capacity for cultivating emotional responses that reinforce our convictions. We should not forget the function of interpersonal relationships in moral education. Our earliest social relationships originate in family life, where basic morality is learned. Over time, meaningful moral life comes to be supported by friendship as well as through connection to a positive, larger community.

We cannot ignore the need for divine grace in moral living. Although we study the natural means of developing moral capabilities, we must also remember that grace uplifts and completes nature. Whatever else the human venture is meant to be, it is certainly meant to be a kind of cooperation between creature and Creator. One aspect of the moral endeavor involves conforming ourselves to the moral structures of God's universe, but another aspect involves being receptive to God's gracious aid and empowerment for living. A holistic Christian approach to morality asserts that God upholds and energizes our efforts that are rendered to him.

Christian theism also supplies fertile ideas for thinking about aesthetic value and aesthetic education. Works of art reflect the incredibly wonderful capacity God has given us for the creative expression of beauty. Art is a kind of mirror of the human condition and thus provides significant avenues for understanding how different individuals and cultures have interpreted God, humanity, and the world. Furthermore, we must not forget the capacity of art to inspire, enlighten, and edify those who are exposed to it. In order for students to reap these benefits from art, aesthetic education must include the explanation and discussion of both the form and the meaning of fine works of art.

Since many people do not instinctively understand the complexities of art, they must be led into experiencing great works in a way appropriate to their nature as art. The viewer must be educated to "see" in a new way. For the educator, this means that students need to be initiated into the enduring issues about how to determine what is beautiful and excellent in art forms, about how art may convey a message to or elicit a response from those in its presence, and about a host of other related conceptual matters. Students will need to know something about how techniques and tastes have changed historically within the various arts in response to shifts in intellectual or aesthetic outlook. All this can be done at levels of sophistication that are appropriate to the developmental level of aesthetic learners.

While discussion of art is important to aesthetic education, participation in art is vital. Art invites participation. Great music needs to be played, great drama needs to be performed, and great painting needs to be viewed at length. One key aspect of aesthetic learning is the attempt to create art oneself. Students at every grade level need the opportunity to create works of art of their very own, thus opening them to a dimension of experience that gives great pleasure and expands the human spirit.

The ultimate goals of aesthetic education are to enable students to become more self-aware and discriminating in what they enjoy and to improve their judgment about what is aesthetically admirable. The hope is that a meaningful aesthetic education will enhance and enrich their lives as they are exposed to the kind of self-transcendence and self-abandonment that comes through art. It may be that those who have had glimpses of beauty will be able to improve a world in which there is increasing tension and pressure.

CHAPTER FIVE

Issues in Educational Theory

C ontroversies abound in educational circles in America. As some problems are resolved, new ones arise. The explosive problem of racial desegregation, for example, is receding into our past, but now we face the problem of racial disharmony in our schools. While religious fundamentalists still challenge the teaching of evolution, many thoughtful Christians are increasingly addressing larger issues stemming from the pervasive secular humanism in our educational systems. The list of issues is seemingly endless: declining proficiencies in basic skills, political correctness, tax credits for private tuition, sex and gender education, drug abuse among younger and younger children, violence and killings in our schools, and so on.

A major strength of the Christian philosophy of education we have been developing is that it provides a framework for thinking critically about all of the relevant issues. Although the issues cannot be neatly categorized, it is helpful to divide the controversial topics into those that address the level of theory and those that involve practical application. Theoretical issues involve general ideas about education and their logical implications; practical issues pertain more directly to the actual conduct of teachers and their activities in the classroom. Let us here select a handful of theoretical issues for close examination: the relationship between liberal learning and general education, the relationship between liberal education and professional training, the integration of faith and learning, ethics and values education, and the nature of pedagogy. My aim throughout is not only to help us reflect on these specific controversies but also to provide a model for how we can bring Christian thinking to bear on many other educational difficulties.

LIBERAL LEARNING AND GENERAL EDUCATION

In discussions about curricula, "liberal learning" is often mistakenly equated with "general education." Yet these two terms are not strictly synonymous. The relationship of a general education to liberal learning is actually that of means to end. Liberal learning—as distinct from vocational training—is the goal, the end, the desired result. The ideal of a liberally educated person is one who has achieved a significant degree of mental freedom, understands moral and civic responsibility, is tolerant and humane, and has a deep sense of the historic aspirations and struggles of the human race. This liberally educated person has been initiated into the important realms of human knowledge and the ongoing discourse that takes place within human culture.

General education, typically conceived as a broad selection of courses rather than as a specialized or technical program, has long been a favored means of reaching the goal of liberal learning. A person who is familiar with broad, fundamental areas of knowledge and is competent in essential skills is well on the way to becoming liberally educated. General education courses are usually arranged in a basic "core curriculum" that students are required to take. From the earliest elementary grades through high school, the core curriculum typically features content and proficiencies that are considered benchmarks for each developmental level. Discussions of the content of the core curriculum at the college level are more wide-ranging and contentious. The underlying conviction is that there is fundamental knowledge that students should be required to learn.

A key to understanding liberal education is to grasp its relationship to general education. Although, there is an interesting connection between general education and liberal education, the former is neither a necessary nor a sufficient condition for the latter. A general education is not necessary for one to become liberally educated because a free and critical mind *could* be developed by the study of just a few key disciplines. Indeed, in ancient Athens, the original liberal arts curriculum was relatively small. There were only seven subjects: the trivium, which consisted of grammar, logic, and rhetoric (that is, the public use of language), and the quadrivium, which included arithmetic, geometry, astronomy, and music. It is clear that people can develop the ability to think critically through study in a certain few disciplines and thereby gain discerning habits of thought and judgment that will stand them in good stead in life.

Moreover, a general education does not guarantee liberal learning, since an uncritical and slavish mind could easily be produced through the study of many and varied subjects. A student might dutifully memorize a multitude of facts in numerous academic fields, believe everything in each textbook and the words of each teacher in turn, and end up a small-minded and role-bound person. Yet presumably this student would have satisfactorily completed the apparent requirements for a liberal arts degree. So, it is obvious that we cannot equate general and liberal education.

There are, however, many reasons to believe that general learning, if properly conducted, can be a good basis for a liberal education. But we must consult our philosophical foundations to identify the primary factors that allow a general education to be authentically liberating. Let us contrast two distinct rationales that support general studies as the heart of the curriculum; they envision very different outcomes for the educational experience. I will name these differing philosophical views after two famous teachers of the ancient world, Plato and Protagoras.

In the *Republic,* Plato proposes that we examine all knowledge claims to determine whether they have objective truth. Following his teacher Socrates, Plato taught that "dialectic," the process of closely questioning ideas through dialogue, was the best process for finding what is really true. Plato believed that human thought and decision are free only insofar as they conform to the truth about reality. Intellectual and moral freedom were the goals of the general education that was offered at his Academy, one of the great learning institutions of the ancient world. In essence, Plato enlisted general education in the service of seeking and knowing the truth. We want broad exposure to ideas and information so that we may challenge, verify, critique, and responsibly arrive at what we think is true. The search is not easy, and we may sometimes have to change our beliefs. But the search itself is a noble one, appropriate to every person's education. Let us call this approach the Platonic concept of general education.

The other concept of general education I shall name after Protagoras, the ancient Sophist. The Protagorean rationale for a general education is that students need wide exposure to different ideas and opinions in order to navigate in society and to persuade others to accept their own views. It is not important to this "rhetorical" theory of general education that a person try to conform his thinking to what is really correct or true. The Sophists taught that there may or may not be objective truth and that there may or may not be a reliable process for seeking it. Objective truth was simply not the point. Hence, the Protagorean model of education is skeptical concerning truth and the means of determining it. Rather, information and ideas are the means of achieving one's own ends. Freedom pertains not to the rational control of impulse and the direction of one's life according to truth and duty but to the ability to succeed in human commerce.

There is a striking difference between these two concepts of general education. The dialectical approach holds that there are certain ideas and truths to which every student should be exposed, whereas the rhetorical approach holds that it does not matter what students study as long as it relates to their current society and helps them prosper. A proper general education based on the dialectical model will give students a broad foundation in knowledge that is essential to our full humanity as well as skills that are necessary for lifelong learning. This requires that students be exposed to a range of subjects which, from one angle or another, touch on the nature of the physical universe, the complexities of our social existence, the meaning of life, and the source of our common duty. Students must also develop their competencies in grammar, communication, calculation, and the like.

Interestingly, the Platonic or dialectical model dominated education for many centuries. Most Hellenic and Roman schools followed it by establishing the trivium and quadrivium as the basis of education. In medieval Europe, monastic schools and their counterparts, the cathedral schools (open to the lay public), included the study of Holy Scripture and theology in the curriculum. The curriculum was shaped around *studium generale* ("general studies"), which was the ancient liberal arts course of studies now dedicated to the greater glory of God. In effect, each *studium generale* functioned as a Christian liberal arts college, and these became the building blocks of the first universities in the twelfth and thirteenth centuries. Thus, the heritage of the liberal arts survived in a Christian form later to become the foundation of education in Western European civilization.

The Christian college model, emerging over the centuries in Europe and Great Britain, was eventually transplanted in American soil. After the Puritans founded Harvard College in 1636, it and other Protestant schools would provide the only higher education available to most Americans for many years. Harvard and other Ivy League colleges eventually imported a German university model in which technical research and graduate programs tend to dominate. Some universities in that vein have been able to retain a solid commitment to undergraduate liberal arts, though others have not. The essential Christian liberal arts model more clearly persists in smaller undergraduate colleges. We see it in Catholic institutions such as St. John's College (Maryland), Thomas Aquinas College (California), and College of the Holy Cross (Massachusetts). The Christian liberal arts lives on as well as in Protestant institutions such as Calvin College (Michigan) and Wheaton College (Illinois), and in Asbury College (Kentucky) and Houghton College (New York), which are both Methodistic in theological outlook.

In modern times, the content of liberal arts education has been understood to include subjects which every educated person should know: world history and civilization, scientific interpretations of the universe, theories of the social sciences, great literature, and philosophy begin the list of subjects. Such subjects provide a broad education, but the intent is not to be broad simply for the sake of being expansive. Instead the intent is to convey important knowledge to students and increase their understanding of vital issues pertaining to our shared human condition. The pursuit of this aim obviously results in *a certain kind* of breadth, a breadth of learning organized around the lofty themes of fundamental humane knowledge.

In the last decades of the twentieth century, educators grew more interested in the Protagorean or rhetorical theory of general education. In the name of exposing students to as many different viewpoints as possible, the classic core of the liberal arts has too often been ravaged or abandoned. There have even been accusations that it is dogmatic to insist that some kinds of knowledge are more worthwhile or humanizing than other kinds. According to this view, the Platonic approach promotes the intellectual tyranny of some subjects over others.

In one way or another, countless American colleges and universities have come to ally themselves with this new perspective. Over the past few decades, we have witnessed the rise of "liberal arts" curricula that incorporate subjects on transcendental meditation as well as psychology, computer programming languages in the place of human foreign language, and gay history as an alternative to world civilization. Although these examples are a bit extreme, they nonetheless expose the bankruptcy of the rhetorical approach to provide an adequate principle of selection for courses in universal humane learning. Thus, we may legitimately doubt the ability of the Protagorean or rhetorical approach to produce a properly liberated intelligence.

One cause of curricular deficiencies in schools and colleges is the lack of coherent understanding of what liberal learning really is. When any general selection of courses is blindly equated with "liberal education," the proper means-to-end relationship of generality and breadth to the liberation of the mind is lost. The idea that some subjects are more important to our humanity than others, and thus should be required of all seeking a liberal arts degree, is completely abandoned. Of course, there are good reasons for a university to offer courses in Eastern religions or feminist studies, for example. Certainly, a liberally educated person must be willing to learn from a variety of perspectives and compare them to traditional Western views. However, the point must be that all studies should be evaluated and included because they advance the project of genuine liberal learning.

Administrators and faculty who design general education curricula that require "a little of each subject" or that let students "pick a course from each area" risk forfeiting the high, Platonic concept of liberal learning. Unfortunately, they have lost sight of the precise kind of general education that a truly liberal education demands. The alternative Protagorean concept often gains influence and sometimes dominates where there is no guiding philosophical consensus about what courses constitute an authentic liberal education. Curriculum decisions become purely political, with departments simply demanding "their share of the core" or curriculum committees restructuring the core to represent fashionable notions of "relevance" or "efficiency" or "political correctness."

While many schools are losing their philosophical moorings, it is heartening to note that many historically liberal arts colleges are retaining theirs. In the face of mounting pressures to make the curriculum "more practical" or "more relevant" or even to redefine it in radical ways, a wise approach is to hold steady. Nothing could be more practical or more relevant for students facing an ever-changing job market than acquiring a knowledge of the enduring values and meanings inherent in our common humanity, appreciation for diverse ideas and cultures, the capacity for abstract thought, and long range vision. In addition simply to being equipped to earn a living, each student must also become capable of building a life and pursing a fuller existence as a human person.[1] Current demographic trends suggest that the failure of much secular educational thinking to provide an anchor in essential learning is driving more people to seek private education—and particularly private Christian education—at all levels. If these trends continue, the strong liberal arts institutions, often stereotyped as conservative, will become the true pioneers.

Since we cannot prescribe a single curriculum format, each institution will have to work out exactly what it considers to be the course of study that is most faithful to the great heritage of liberal education. Educators must simply remember that they need not strive for a core curriculum that is overly general but only one broad enough to cover the important ideas and lasting values of humankind and to transmit the skills of continued learning. This is the way to construct a liberal education that is general in that it encompasses a number of subjects but also quite specialized in the sense that it focuses on the major insights and discoveries of human civilization. In the long run, this approach to liberal education will far surpass other approaches.

INTEGRATING FAITH AND LEARNING

Christians who are concerned about education have long discussed the question of how faith and learning are related, and the discussion is often couched in the language of "integration."

During the early part of the twentieth century, the Catholic educational community considered this topic.[2] In the second half of the century, it was common among Protestant liberal arts colleges to use the term "integration" to describe their missions.[3] Many college teachers and administrators still instinctively feel that they should somehow be engaged in the task of integrating faith and learning. But what exactly does integration mean?

The tradition of liberal education, with roots in both Hellenistic and Judeo-Christian thought, affirms that the world is real, good, and intelligible. The very fact that the world is intelligible implies that knowledge about it is genuinely possible. Moreover, all knowledge about the world is a consistent and unified whole because God, the Creator, is one. A hallmark of authentic liberal education is that it deals with the relationships and connections between truths in various fields of knowledge. It rests on the belief that all aspects of human life and the world are integrally related. Christian liberal arts institutions typically propose not only that the various areas of knowledge are interconnected in their program of studies but also that all areas of knowledge can be integrated with the Christian faith. Many types of Christian schools encourage and pursue this kind of integration, and the topic of integration is vigorously discussed in the literature of Christian higher education.[4]

Christian theism provides some very general ideas for thinking about the integration of knowledge. First, it tells us that areas of knowledge are integrated with one another in that they all make best sense when they are firmly founded on the assumption that reality is orderly, rational, and moral. Of course, the exact nature of that order, rationality, and moral structure and the precise way in which all areas of knowledge fit into it remain open for discussion, but confidence in this assumption provides direction and balance to our study of every subject. Second, domains of knowledge are integrated when each one in its own distinct way sheds light on the nature of the world and the meaning of life. In other words, different domains of knowledge converge and enrich our understanding of the deepest, most enduring human concerns. Third, knowledge is integrated when we see that information and insights in one sphere of human endeavor have an impact on other spheres. To recognize, for example, that mathematics is directly related to music theory, that our moral standards actually have value in economic theorizing, and that the biochemistry of brain states impinges on psychology is to see human knowledge as whole rather than as fragmented.

What about the integration of faith and knowledge? We can again draw from the resources of the Christian perspective to offer some proposals.[5] First, faith is integrated with knowledge when we can show that the metaphysical, epistemological, and axiological assumptions which make the best sense of established knowledge are those inherent in the Christian worldview. Second, faith is integrated with knowledge when we receive the conclusions and insights of the various branches of inquiry as God's provision for our learning more about him and his universe. Third, appropriate integration occurs when the ethical and social convictions of the Christian life are employed to evaluate the process and use of human knowledge. Fourth, knowledge is integrated with faith when our best information and insights are allowed to tutor and refine our understanding of Christianity, the Bible, or some aspect of religious life. Fifth, faith and knowledge are integrated when learning is sought as something that can be used to strengthen practical discipleship or service to God. It would be interesting to explore other possible ways of thinking about what it means for faith and learning to be integrated. Arthur Holmes suggests, for example, that a kind of integration takes place when the motivation for study and learning is distinctively Christian and when the community within which learning takes place is founded on Christian principles.[6]

Integration has potential pitfalls. One concerns the integration of knowledge in one field with that of another field; another concerns the integration of faith and knowledge. We are caught in the first kind of pitfall when, in attempting to relate one area of knowledge to another, we fail to protect the integrity of each area. In an effort to provide efficient integration, some institutions offer "interdisciplinary courses" or "integrative studies." In many cases, when such courses are introduced into the core curriculum in the name of liberal learning, they tend to replace more sustained, rigorous study in the essential but distinct disciplines involved. Beginning students in these courses are typically required to learn very little of the basic information and methods of the various fields before they are asked to think about integrating them. Too often the result is a superficial attempt at integration that leads the students into thinking that they understand the subject better than they really do. As one critic put it, such courses frequently degenerate into "sharing among the mutually uninformed." Robert Paul Wolff asserts that the lesson to be gained from educational experience with these courses is that integration is not a starting point but an achievement. It is only after students have learned something well and have immersed themselves in some discipline or mastered some methodology that they can sensitively and intelligently relate it to other branches of knowledge.[7]

Some educational thinkers propose that we should not thrust relatively inexperienced college students into high-sounding integrative courses but rather should attempt to get them to engage in deliberate integrative thinking later in their college careers.[8] Their argument is that integrative efforts would be more effective after students have studied some of the solid disciplines of liberal learning, developed the appropriate skills of thinking and evaluating, and had the opportunity to gain a greater degree of maturity. In other words, the later years of college would be a better time for attempts at interdisciplinary integration. These attempts could include seminars on topics and problems, interdisciplinary studies, and so forth. We must be careful to uphold the standards of the disciplines involved and not to allow easy models of integration to captivate us.

A second pitfall awaits those who do not think carefully about the integration of faith and knowledge. It is important to protect both the character of the Christian faith as well as the soundness of the knowledge with which it is integrated. This is not an easy matter. E. Harris Harbison raises the issue in the form of a dual question: "Can a liberal education be a Christian education—and (vice versa) can a Christian education be a liberal education?"[9] After all, authentic liberal education rests upon the openness to truth and commitment to rational persuasion. The Christian faith involves a commitment to a certain set of beliefs and way of life. It might appear, on one hand, that a liberal education is straitjacketed by the Christian worldview, that its essential mission must be abandoned in order to have intellectual contact with Christianity. On the other hand, it might seem that unswerving commitment to Christianity is jeopardized by a truly liberal education, which is committed to rigorous study and critique, open to new truth, and dedicated to settling issues only on the best rational grounds. There are actually two possible ways of going wrong here—one from the side of education and one from the side of faith—which we must now examine.

Clearly, not all allegedly liberal education can be Christian because not all concepts of liberal learning can make a fruitful connection with faith. As long as a liberal learning is equated with purely general education and embraces the assumption that all viewpoints are equally valid, the definitive character of Christianity is impossible to recognize. As long as education's only creed is humanism, and its main goal is the students' self-advancement, then the Christian view will not be able to illuminate its course of studies. Hence, this model of liberal education, which is the rhetorical one described earlier, cannot enter into a worthwhile intellectual relationship with the Christian faith.

However, the dialectical model of education can be employed to forge a more profound relationship with faith. The dialectical approach to liberal learning assumes that truth genuinely exists, that persons have intrinsic dignity, and that moral duty provides practical guidance—all affirmations of Christian theism. In essence, then, liberal education—which seeks real truth, ponders the significance of the human enterprise, and explores the wonders of nature—is learning in search of a worldview. Certainly, not all efforts in the realm of liberal learning have been set within an explicitly Christian frame of reference, but the Christian worldview, which holds that there is a personal and moral deity whose creation we study, ultimately puts in proper perspective everything that liberal education wants. Apart from the Christian faith, even the classical dialectical form of liberal education can only sense and long for this superior meaning. Ironically, liberal education, with its ideal of complete understanding, may forever fall short of its own goal unless it is enlightened by Christianity.

Approaching the matter from the other side, we can also recognize that not all Christian education can be properly liberal or liberating. Only a few decades ago, some Christian schools claimed to teach distinctively "Christian" subjects, presumably, such things as "Christian sociology" and "Christian biology." These kinds of courses purport to convey the correct Christian view of every subject and issue. Endeavors of this sort, however, misunderstand the more appropriate and effective forms of integration of faith and learning. They tend to be instruction-in-the-faith, aimed primarily at perpetuating a fairly rigid view of faith or the beliefs of a particular sect. By their very nature, they compromise the intellectual integrity of various academic fields in the name of a religious point of view. In both subtle and overt ways, such programs drive in but do not draw out; they demand conformity but do not invite free response. They transmit information, but they fail to cultivate critical thinking. In short, there is instruction but not education—and there is certainly not liberal education in the highest sense of the term.

An educational institution need not give prepackaged answers to every issue, curtail the presentation of diverse points of view, avoid the debate of controversial topics, oversimplify and distort the positions of opponents, or restrict the pursuit of conscientious scholarship in order to be Christian. Particularly at the college and university level, a Christian institution should be the most aggressive of all institutions in seeking open encounter with opposing views, stimulating creativity, and searching for understanding. Where better to expose error than in an open climate devoted to seeking the truth? Where better to evoke creative activity than in a place that appreciates the source of all creation? Where better to seek a wider understanding of the Christian faith than in a setting that seeks wisdom in all areas of life and thought? When this world-class understanding of Christianity interacts with the best form of learning available, neither the faith nor the educational process lose integrity. Indeed, a version of the Christian faith that is neither dogmatic nor paranoid and that maintains a proper understanding of Christian liberty can be both the ground and the fulfillment of liberal learning.

An essential attitude that we cultivate in seeking a Christian education that is truly liberal, or liberating, is humility. We need humility in our quest for knowledge and in our search for answers at the interface of knowledge and faith. Knowledge has traditionally been understood as the mind's conformity to a reality that it did not create. This conformity is actually a kind of humility before reality itself—a reality that Christians believe God created. In many fields of knowledge, answers are not always readily available, and the intellectual hard work that people perform to discover answers then becomes an expression of humility. Therefore, we balance the affirmation of what we do know with the admission of what we as yet do not know. In the intersection of faith and learning, we must also not pretend that Christian sources provide more ready or more detailed solutions to complex problems than they actually do. We must be willing to work through questions and ambiguities and be ready to revise our understanding along the way. This kind of intellectual integrity is really an outgrowth of Christian piety, not subversive to it. We must be confident that genuine knowledge, honestly gained through discipline and diligence, will shed light on religious faith and even correct misunderstandings of it. This kind of humble attitude creates an atmosphere in which a Christian education can be a truly liberal one.

LIBERAL EDUCATION AND PROFESSIONAL TRAINING

Christian theism endorses both the intrinsic value and the utility value of knowledge. On one hand, knowledge is important because it helps us understand reality, including the reality of our God-given humanity. On the other hand, knowledge is useful: it facilitates our practical interaction with God's creation. These two orientations toward knowledge are embodied in two different educational visions: liberal education and career training. Both orientations find some justification within a Christian framework. An examination of the relationship between these two models can be quite revealing, especially regarding the structure of education at the high school and college levels. Is one kind of education just as good as the other? Should they be two separate and distinct tracks? Or can liberal education and career training be incorporated into a single, coherent system of education?

Such questions can first be approached by asking what type of person, or what type of mentality, each form of education tends to produce. Career training, by its very nature, aims to equip a person with the skills needed for competent functioning in the job market. Many students who are attracted to a professional or technical course of study are tempted to minimize their exposure to the liberal arts simply to complete their career training. While recognizing the legitimacy of work and productivity in society—and hence the possible justification of a well-conceived place for professional, preprofessional, and technical programs within a liberal arts context—a Christian perspective affirms that life is more than employment and that people are more than the job they perform.[10] A purely vocational or professional approach to education does little toward acquainting the student with the enduring issues, profound ideas, and great achievements of human civilization. It is not designed to stir the student to develop his or her own unique human potentials. Neither is it intended to awaken one's consciousness to social duty or to religious service. One is reminded of the British scientist who defined a technician as one who understands everything about his job except its place in the universe.

Jacques Maritain says that purely vocational training constitutes a "servile education." The ancient Latin term *artes serviles* literally means "useful arts." Maritain sharply contrasts this kind of education with a bona fide "liberal education" (*artes liberales*). Interestingly, the Latin root here is *libere*, which means "to make free" or "to liberate." Thus, a liberal education is somehow meant to free us. But how, precisely? Historically, this meaning applied to the free men of a state who were capable of self-governance. For centuries, the label continued to be used to signify that a liberal education "liberates." It does so by freeing the mind from ignorance and prejudice, uplifting it with high ideas and ennobling possibilities, and strengthening its capacity to reason and evaluate. Although racial slavery no longer exists in modern America, the danger of another kind of slavery remains: slavery to self-interest, self-indulgence, impulse, and emotion. There is nothing inherent in a vocational or technical education that counteracts the slavery of mental and emotional immaturity, which threatens a society increasingly preoccupied with comfort, pleasure, and acquisition. A practical education serves our ends—whether those ends are base or noble.

It is not necessary to denigrate the need for gainful employment or the need to receive training for it in order to recognize the wisdom of locating such training within a context of liberal learning. The goal of liberal education has always been to enable students to become thinkers and leaders and not simply to prepare them to be the functionaries of society. From an educational viewpoint alone, the benefits of liberal learning are of a different order of magnitude than those of vocational preparation. From a Christian viewpoint, it is important that Christians in the modern world are people who can think, who are sensitive to the enduring questions of life, who can formulate plans and instill vision, and who can intelligently persuade others of the adequacy of Christ for the human condition. This is a strong argument for a Christian liberal arts education as a matrix within which some technical or professional training can be conducted. Liberal education is deeply concerned with the same issues that Christianity addresses: the meaning of life, the nature of values, the shape of human history, and the contours of the world order. It acquaints Christian students with the ongoing cultural dialogue about these things so that they may one day intelligently and responsibly enter that discussion.

Although the concept of liberal education is often discussed in relation to higher education, it does not apply exclusively to the college level. Mortimer Adler and others point out that liberal education is appropriate for all levels of schooling and for all ages.[11] Adler decries the "abominable discrimination" which lies at the heart of our system of public education, saying that it offers two divergent tracks to students, the vocational track (technical) or the liberal track (the sciences and the humanities). Students, particularly at the high school stage, are often placed into one of these tracks, often by formal evaluation and counselor encouragement, sometimes by their own choosing. Adler's proposal for a liberal education for all public or state school students, which he wrote on behalf of the Paideia Group, boldly recommends teaching all children the indispensable skills of learning and exposing all of them to those concepts and experiences which can awaken their full humanity. Although some children may be more capable of absorbing liberal learning than others, Adler still advocates providing quality liberal education to all children.

Because the process of self-definition is especially acute during the years of late adolescence and young adulthood, exposure to liberal learning during these stages is very significant. Whether they attend a large university or a small college, students should seek a dimension of liberal learning in their formal education. Although a number of sizeable universities claim to offer a liberal education, most seem to have drifted away from authentic, potent liberal arts programs. This places a heavier burden on young students somehow to select courses and read books that provide important elements of liberal learning as well as to seek out those rare professors who teach in ways that liberate young minds.

EDUCATION IN ETHICS AND VALUES

In the face of the perceived moral decline of our nation, no topic is more important than the teaching of ethical values. To be sure, educators, parents, and religious organizations will continue debating how we determine the content of morality and how we can best instill morals in our children. Yet there is an important connection between education and moral life. Thus, the more specific issue at stake here is the connection between formal schooling and the transmission of moral values.

One position that has been widely supported by professional educators is that education should be value neutral. The "value neutrality" exponents try to guard against the indoctrination of students and to champion their right to make free choices. This view may have some validity in certain contexts, but many of its advocates operate on the fallacious assumption that there is a dichotomy between facts as objective truths and values as subjective preferences. They then insist that teaching must transmit only facts and must not impose the preferences of teachers on students. This idea was strongly reflected in the "values clarification" trend that was so popular in the 1970s and early 1980s. One popular technique, derived from the works of Jean Piaget and Lawrence Kohlberg, presented students with moral dilemmas in order to stimulate them to define and clarify their own values.[12]

Even though it is a familiar slogan for many educators, we must reject the education-as-value-neutral orientation. As John

Childs has stated, "Deliberate education is never morally neutral. A definite preference for certain values is inherent in all efforts to guide the experience of the young."[13] In fact, the very existence of formal schooling reflects the conviction that parents and society must rear their young in appropriate ways, conveying important information to them and encouraging certain patterns of behavior in them. It is inevitable, therefore, that the specific moral preferences of a school will permeate its activities: the subjects chosen for study, the way they are taught, the playground rules, codes of conduct, and countless teacher-pupil transactions. Of course, the whole issue of our schools and our values becomes quite complicated in a secular and pluralistic society, and I will explore some aspects of the problem of pluralism in the next chapter.

It seems that the pendulum has swung back now because some educators are again willing to recognize that values are more than merely private, subjective preferences.[14] There is, however, widespread disagreement over exactly what kind of objectivity values actually have and over the content of value education. In a sense, the debate is over the basis of moral knowledge. A healthy Christian theism, of course, provides a solid basis for moral ideals as well as the best methods for communicating them to our young. The sources of moral knowledge and moral ideals include the Scriptures of both the Old and New Testaments, the historical reflections of the believing community, and the common experience of humankind. The form in which moral insight is packaged may vary from New Testament parables to Aesop's fables, from historical narratives to biographies, from precepts to commandments. All such sources convey information related to how the morally mature person is liberated from the egocentrism of childhood and endeavors to live a life of respect and love for God, for other persons, and for nature.

Not everyone who considers the teaching of values in a public school setting believes that it is appropriate to consult religious sources. First Amendment activists, such as A.C.L.U. lawyers and National Education Association officials, insist that moral education in public schools be done without reference to religion. Their point is that there are some values that most people hold dear regardless of their religious preference and regardless of whether they are religious at all. In effect, they contend that there is a set of consensual values lying at the intersection of all religious and nonreligious preferences. For example, the Character Counts Coalition promotes the "Six Pillars of Character": trustworthiness, respect, responsibility, fairness, caring, and citizenship.[15] It contends that these values can be inculcated in students by incorporating them into classroom assignments, model teacher behavior, and the overall ambience of the school.

Even as Christians we know that certain values can be identified without directly consulting religious sources because God created persons with basic moral awareness. Teaching our students about such values will at least offer some resistance to society's moral decline. It remains to be seen, however, just how much this approach to moral education can accomplish and if its results can be lasting. The breakdown of the family, the corruption of some political leaders, the immorality portrayed in popular film and music media, and other factors in our culture raise serious concerns about whether the fabric of society is so badly torn that it cannot adequately reinforce the values taught in school. Furthermore, when curious students begin to raise even the most elementary questions about moral life, it is hard to see how the minimalist approach will provide them with satisfying answers. In fact, it is easy to imagine teachers having very different ideas about what each value means in practice, ideas as different as the conflicting political agendas and lifestyles in society at large. If students were to press teachers and ask why we should adopt, say, the six values, what could be said in reply? Suggesting that values are anchored in social consensus denies the possibility of an ultimate foundation of and motivation for morality. Perceptive students will detect the relativism that pervades so much of their learning and will raise serious objections to the apparent arbitrariness of their supposedly moral education.

Even if we grant, for the sake of discussion, that a secular or religious school could achieve sufficient agreement on the content of morality, it would still need a helpful theory about how to teach that morality effectively. Clearly, one of the great mistakes of modern educators who have at least tried to teach morality is that they have assumed that knowledge readily translates into action, that knowing what is right is a sufficient condition for doing it. They have been naive about the fact that some people knowingly do wrong. This, of course, takes us into the area of human life that the Bible calls sin. For those conducting moral education under the auspices of a religious institution, the problem of sin can be addressed more directly and the resources of divine grace for empowering moral life can be made available. For schools that are not officially Christian, what reasonable theory of moral education might we adopt that is compatible with Christian teachings and yet does not explicitly teach them?

There is no shortage of suggestions from the psychological community about how to conduct moral education. There are maturational theories (of Carl Rogers, Raths and Simon), which stress self-expression. There are the socialization theories (of Emile Durkheim and B. F. Skinner), which recommend conditioning the child to his or her social role. The cognitive-stage theories (of Jean Piaget and Lawrence Kohlberg) emphasize the increasingly complex patterns of moral reasoning through which a child advances (and thus probably qualify as a species of maturational theory). Christian theists should diligently seek advice from the best research available.

Nicholas Wolterstorff provides the broad outline of a reasonable theory of moral education.[16] He suggests that the root problem is how to get children to internalize correct moral standards and to act on them. This is the task of transforming children into moral agents. The "responsibility theory," as he labels it, calls for a balance between behavioral and cognitive domains. He believes that proposals for moral education miss the mark if they lose this balance. An overemphasis on the cognitive aspect runs the risk that strong behavior patterns may not be established. On the other hand, an overemphasis on moral education as the conditioning of students to behave rather automatically, as though operant conditioning were the key, risks the possibility that students may never come to be inwardly motivated and to own their own moral standards.

Moral education in the behavioral domain involves shaping the will and inculcating proper habits and dispositions in our young. Attention to the behavioral aspect is important because children are not born disposed toward moral comportment, nor are they susceptible to the rational persuasion that upholds it. Therefore, we must start very early in requiring behavioral conformity in children and in trying to instill in them correct attitudes. This function is particularly important because establishing patterns of behavior in children becomes increasingly difficult as they grow older. Thus, no reasonable form of education, whether in the school or in the home, can ignore the fact that shaping behavior is an important component of moral education.

Legitimate methods for shaping behavior include intelligent forms of discipline and correction as well as clear, rational explanation. It is paramount that discipline be administered with fairness and love and that reasons be given for it. Naturally, we must encourage children to greater moral maturity in ways that suit their level of mental and emotional development. In the elementary grades, for instance, a structured but loving environment coupled with an overt system of rewards and punishments is appropriate. By contrast, excessive reliance on extrinsic inducements becomes questionable at the college level, since such methods are associated with a lower stage of moral development. While I am certainly not ruling out consequences for inappropriate behavior in young adults, I believe we should make most of our appeals to college age students concerning moral behavior on grounds of the reasonableness and value of that behavior. The message must be consistently communicated to the young that their choices and actions have consequences and that this is simply the way the world works. Sometimes students may realize this by simply hearing about the results of certain types of actions or by observing them in the experiences of others. At other times, students may need to experience the natural results of their own choices before they can make the connection between action and consequence. Both naive permissiveness and authoritarian severity must be avoided, for between these two extremes we can lay a groundwork for healthy moral life.

Citing philosopher Michael Oakeshott's distinction between the "literature" and the "language" of a discipline, R. S. Peters says that moral education must first acquaint children with the forms of behavior, precepts, and principles of morality and then help them become ever more skillful in their application and evaluation.[17] Just as young students of geography must early learn the concrete locations of the continents and seas before they can grasp the more abstract concepts of space, time, and distance, they must first learn to go through the motions of ethical living before they can fully internalize its most cherished virtues and values.

The process of moral education is that of assisting the "outsider" to become an "insider." Aristotle explains:

> But the virtues we get by first exercising them, as also happens in the case of the arts as well. For the things we have to learn before we can do them, we learn by doing them, for example, men become builders by building and lyre players by playing the lyre; so do we become just by doing just acts, temperate by doing temperate acts, brave by doing brave acts. . . . It makes no small difference, then, whether we form habits of one kind or another from our very youth; it makes a great difference or rather all the difference.[18]

The door of the nursery is the gateway to moral education, and the school is the courtyard.

It is an interesting fact of our humanity that we so often come to *be* a certain way because of what we *do*. We do not have to understand all moral principles before performing morally good actions. We start out in life being helped by our parents and others to perform our initial moral actions, albeit in immature and halting ways. We progressively gain more understanding; small habits begin to form. Over time, we have the opportunity to develop fuller moral life, all due to the intricate connection between doing and being.

Of course, moral life cannot be confined to the behavioral domain, and moral education cannot be complete if it settles for mere behavioral conformity. Moral life ultimately depends on what we think, on what we understand about the content of morality; it also requires inward ownership of principles and values. This brings us to the second way in which education has an impact on moral life, according to Wolterstorff. Education engages the cognitive level and thus influences moral development by enlightening the mind and providing a rationale for our most cherished values. Consequently, we need effective strategies for dealing with moral ideas at the cognitive level. Somehow, some way, we need to regain a conscious appreciation of values and virtues. William Bennett, former U.S. Secretary of Education, claims that all civilizations use stories to communicate the virtues they prize. In *The Book of Virtues*, he shows that society has typically portrayed its moral ideals of character and virtue through a shared heritage of tales, fables, and sacred scriptures.[19] Traditional wisdom supports Bennett: there is nothing like an enthralling narrative or story to captivate the moral imagination, call forth our loftiest sentiments, and make us think about possibilities for our own lives.

There are other important facets of cognitive development that support moral education. For example, it is important to help the student to reason using general moral rules and categories. It is vital that students be given practice in reasoning from universal principles to specific applications, with an eye toward strengthening their ability to act upon the moral principles they accept. In the process of dealing with principles and applications, they will acquire an understanding of what is constant and what is variable in moral life. Of course, a complete moral education will invite students to discuss, question, and reflect upon the values they are taught. Even younger children should be encouraged to question and discuss these things. As students progress through their years of schooling, their developing abilities in cognitive examination and probing will continue in more complex forms. A true liberal education will invite students to do whatever it takes to satisfy their minds about the deeper nature and ground of moral values.

We now turn to the question of whether moral education should be a separate subject in school or be integrated as a dimension of all subjects. To be a place of real moral learning, the school must be a moral community. This means that people in the educational environment are consciously interested in moral improvement, both their own and that of their students. It means that moral behavior is encouraged in extracurricular activities and that moral issues are given serious consideration whenever they arise in any class. At times, it may be helpful to dedicate an instructional unit to ethical issues or even to design a whole course around them; but nothing can substitute for a whole environment permeated by opportunities for moral learning.

The ultimate goal of moral education is moral maturity. Moral maturity can be defined as good character constituted by the appropriate moral virtues, such as justice, benevolence, honesty, and so forth. A person who lives virtuously shows that he understands and honors the moral principles that correspond to the basic virtues. To be sure, moral virtues and principles are understood in slightly different ways among various cultures and throughout history. However, at base, morality is universal because our divinely created human nature is everywhere and at all times the same.[20] A healthy culture impresses upon its people, and especially upon its young, its ideals of character and virtue—and, traditionally, the school has been an important instrument in this process.

All mainstream Christian traditions respect the need for a person to appropriate for himself moral ideals for living. However, it recognizes that people must be helped along in this process of becoming mature moral agents, being allowed to ponder the principles they have been taught, to evaluate the kind of life which moral character implies, and to come to understand the unchanging basis of values from their various concrete expressions. This questioning and evaluating surfaces in the queries of children or young adults when the search for a healthy self-concept is very intense; hence, it is imperative that parents and educators be inviting and encouraging. It is important to nurture people so they will become responsible citizens and have solid moral character. We do this, in part, by helping the young invest themselves in moral life at deeper and deeper levels.

The modern crisis in our schools is caused, in part, by the loss of social consensus on the nature and foundation of moral life. Our schools simply reflect the value confusion within a morally conflicted society. In a commencement address, Charles Malik, noted statesman and former president of the United Nations General Assembly, pointedly describes the contemporary milieu: "They tell you there are no absolute values; it is all a matter of circumstances and custom and conditions." According to Malik, the whole "climate of modern thought" perpetrates the lie that nothing is really bad, that all morals and values are relative.[21] We must all hope that new movements in ethical education, both secular and religious, will help change this climate.

PEDAGOGY AND THE EDUCATIONAL ENTERPRISE

Clearly, education cannot be equated with formal schooling; learning can obviously take place apart from any deliberate instruction. Yet the role of the teacher is critical to a well-rounded concept of formal education. Whether teachers function in a secular or religious environment, Christian theism has much to say about their goals as well as their methods. The words of Philip Phenix provide a fitting preface to the topic:

> Teaching is an act of creation and thus falls within that aspect of religion concerned with beginnings. The teacher participates in a making of persons. . . . It is a sacred responsibility to have a hand in fashioning human personalities, the highest of all the orders of created beings. Linked with creation is also destiny, for upon the manner of the teacher's creating depends the future of mankind.[22]

Let us explore in more depth the importance of the role of the teacher.

Teaching is an art, and the teacher is something of an artist. But teaching does not resemble arts such as painting or sculpture. And if teachers are artists then they do not resemble painters or sculptors who impose a preconceived form on a passive medium, be it color or clay. The art of teaching might better be compared to the art of medicine. The teacher works with the inner principles of human nature in a way that resembles the way the physician works with the knowledge of the human body and its processes. Just as the physician works to bring the body to the point at which it can heal itself, the teacher helps to bring students to the point at which they can learn on their own.

Maritain refers to the teacher as a "ministerial agent" in the educational process.[23] This rich and suggestive terminology leads us to a Christian view of pedagogy in which teachers do not so much impart something of their own creation as they draw out the natural abilities of the learner. They are mediators of something that is higher than themselves, helping others to acquire not only facts and skills but also the dispositions and qualities suitable for rational beings in the image of God.

From a Christian perspective, the aims of teaching stem from the nature of reality, particularly the special reality that humanity is. The task of the teacher is linked to the right of students to develop their God-given capabilities. Instrumentalism's goal of socialization, existentialism's autonomous choice, naturalism's order of life, idealism's mental intensity, postmodernism's empowerment of the marginalized—none of these, as worthy as it might be, expresses the central aim of education as Christian theism envisions it. These other goals are included in but are subordinate to the larger, overarching goal of human liberation in the image of God, which must be the teacher's ultimate aim.

The teacher is the navigator in the young student's journey toward truth. It is not enough, however, for the teacher to point out incorrect opinions and refute false claims. In order to liberate students from falsehood, we must also help them relinquish those attitudes that incline them toward error and never give truth a fair chance: selfishness, prejudice, apathy, sloth. Such inner weaknesses affect our students' ability to think and make them susceptible to indoctrination and manipulation. Neither can teachers be content to have students dutifully memorize and recite accepted truths or favored points of view. We must help young learners acquire the ability to examine information on their own, judiciously weigh evidence, reason logically, display tolerance, and hold their emotions in check. This inner transformation of students into intellectually mature persons will substantially support the life of the mind, making education not just liberation *from* falsehood but also liberation *to* truth.

All of this has very clear spiritual significance. The biblical tradition teaches that we worship and serve God not simply from the depths of our spirits but with our bodies and minds as well. A holistic concept of humanity requires a very practical, realistic understanding of Christian spirituality. Therefore, the teacher, the one who guides the young mind, is in a strategic position to influence the spiritual life of the learner. The priority that Judaism has placed on being wise and imparting wisdom to others is an outgrowth of this basic principle.[24] Some Old Testament commentators observe that certain key social roles in ancient Israel—especially those of prophet, priest, and king—can be used to elucidate the meaning of Jesus.[25] Although Jesus himself never officially embraced any of these titles, in an important sense, he filled all of those roles. But there is another office, that

of *wise man*—a person consistently venerated in Jewish tradition. Interestingly, we find the New Testament saturated with
references to Jesus as "teacher," "wise man," *rabbi.*[26] Whatever
else Jesus was, he was a master teacher.

Spiritualizing the mission of teaching in this way does not
exaggerate its importance. Teaching deals with the very core of
one's being, one's mind and thoughts, motives and aspirations.
Insofar as the duties of teaching point the mind toward truth,
wholeness, and excellence, it is indeed a type of ministry or
sacred office, and learning is a kind of worship. Explicit worship involves the visible use of appropriate symbols and the
overt participation in acts familiar to a religious community;
seldom does teaching actually resemble explicit worship. However, in the classroom and other pedagogical situations, the
teacher as ministerial agent has the function of leading others in
what Phenix calls "implicit worship." The teacher is to lead students into study and contemplation as a reflection of their ultimate concern and religious devotion. Without the appearance
of any of the customary religious forms, the teacher has the opportunity to place students in a position in which their minds
are enlightened, their wills energized for good, and their spirits
suffused with new life. In these moments of true inspiration,
worship occurs: "Such worship need not wait for special times
and places, knows no difference of public or private school nor
law of separation, requires no approved formulae, and respects
no subject matter divisions."[27]

The recognition that such high moments are possible motivates us to try to define the teaching process as best we can. The
methods of teaching, according to B. P. Komisar, include
"sundry doings, showings, and sayings."[28] The list of intellectual acts involved in teaching is quite long: telling, drilling, explaining, demonstrating, reasoning, describing, questioning,
narrating, announcing, reporting, and so forth. But no single
one of these acts or any collection of them, when performed, is
necessarily teaching. What makes any of these intellectual acts
teaching is more than showing-and-telling. This "something

more" can seem elusive and mysterious, making the concept of teaching almost indefinable. What ingredient added to any one of a large number of intellectual acts makes it teaching? As traditional philosophers of science used to say, what is the particular "causal efficacy" of real teaching? Is it obvious subject mastery? Then we should strive for high levels of competency in our fields. Is it comprehension on the part of the students? Then we must seek to make ourselves transparent and credible so as to engage and open young minds. Since no final definition of the role of teacher has ever been formulated, we cannot expect to define it here. But ongoing reflection on it will yield fresh insights into this potentially life-changing activity.

In a day when computers and self-paced instruction promise "faster, more efficient" learning and when distance-education through the Internet offers quick, convenient credit and credentials, we must be careful not to forfeit a high view of teaching. There may indeed be certain types of factual material or performance skills that students can learn through online courses and other rather impersonal means. Each school and each educator will have to evaluate the extent to which these methods are appropriate in any given setting, and I offer some suggestions for doing this in the next chapter. However, what we must stress here is that the personal dimension of teaching, which comes through countless pedagogical transactions with students, is the fundamental quality we must refuse to relinquish. Wordsworth's description of the poet can be adapted to our description of the teacher: "He is a real live human being speaking to real live human beings."[29] There is something irreplaceable about the person-to-person contact between teacher and student. However education changes in the future, this must be kept at the center. The model of mature persons interacting with developing persons is indispensable to a complete philosophy of pedagogy.

Students do not simply need to learn facts and acquire skills; they need to witness well-integrated personalities manifesting strong intellectual capabilities. They need to see whole persons employing the fruits of education in dealing with issues, problems, and the basic realities of life. Students need to interact with positive, mature persons in teaching roles who are interested in how young people may progress in the human journey. The words of Abraham Joshua Heschel are exactly to the point: "What we need more than anything else is not text-books but text-people. It is the personality of the teacher which is the text that the pupils read, the text they will never forget."[30]

CHAPTER SIX

Issues in Educational Practice

Philosophical beliefs ultimately guide educational practice. These beliefs, combined with factual information, empirical research, and situational variables, give us the materials from which we draw conclusions that become the policies and procedures affecting the actual conduct of education.

Our Christian orientation can be applied to countless practical issues in education. Here we select five for close attention: public versus private education, academic rights and freedoms, multiculturalism, the new generation of student learners, and the impact of technology on the concept and delivery of education. Since there is room for diversity among those who fall within the scope of historic, orthodox belief, we cannot impose a strict, monolithic set of educational prescriptions. However, our present analysis of these matters can provide a model to illustrate how rigorous Christian thinking can be brought to bear on a host of educational issues.

PUBLIC AND PRIVATE EDUCATION

The long debate continues over the roles of public and private sectors in education. Historically, the issue closely parallels the question of state and church separation, but it is not identical to it. Although some issues in private education are not related to religion at all, we will focus on the state and church controversy as it pertains to education. Of course, the principles involved have a wider application.

One starting point for reflection is the nature of children as God's creation. Their inherent human nature is the foundation of their right to fulfill their capacities for responsible thought and action. Structured education is a vehicle through which these capacities can be nurtured and developed. Although education takes place in many areas of life and through the actions of many different mediators, formal schooling provides an important means of education.

The difficulty arises with the question of who may, or who should, provide formal schooling to our children and youth. Modern American society operates today on the firm conviction that the state has the right, even the duty, to support all levels of education.[1] Most Western democracies hold similar views concerning the rights of the civil state. Schools exist not simply for the mental, moral, and spiritual growth of the individual but also for the overall good of civil society. If democracy is going to work, there must be adequate preparation of the populace for responsible citizenship. Since the enlightened principles of justice and liberty that undergird constitutional democracy mirror some themes in a wholly Christian vision of society, we could say that a Christian view thereby supports the idea that the government has the right to educate its citizens.

Controversy arises, however, when the role of government is misinterpreted. Compulsory school attendance laws are justified, for example, but it is not fair for the government to require that all children attend public or state schools. When the Oregon legislature passed a law in 1922 requiring every child between the ages of eight and eighteen to attend public school, this issue became heated. In 1925, the United States Supreme Court struck down the Oregon law as unconstitutional, recognizing the right of parochial and other private schools to function alongside public or state schools. In recent decades, home schooling movements have grown and are winning similar legal protection. States have reserved the right to inspect all schools according to fair educational standards. Yet even the state's regulatory power has been questioned as those who run private schools as well as those in home school organizations sense that this prerogative is too often exercised in the service of state political agendas. In Holland, for example, a level of protection from government intrusion exists, and there is a strong emphasis on private schooling.

Actually, a long string of court decisions regarding the relation of public and private involvement in the schooling of our young people has followed after that early Supreme Court decision. These cases involve everything from released time for religious instruction to prayer in school, from Bible and religious clubs using school facilities to the posting of the Ten Commandments in public school buildings. Many of these decisions reflect how the constitutional doctrine of separation of church and state is understood. Since the public role in education has expanded from very local community control to increased supervision by the state and even by federal agencies, the controversies have become quite complex.

Additional complications stem from the sheer diversity of modern American and Western European life in moral, religious, and other areas. While the political consensus about the need for public education once mirrored a significant religious and moral consensus among the populace, now cultural pluralism exerts new and conflicting pressures on education. This pluralism will later be discussed in depth, but it is very clear that thinking Christians must find responsible ways of understanding and living in a society in which homogeneity of belief and lifestyle will probably never again exist.

Church/state issues must be carefully analyzed, including those that influence education. To be sure, there are many forces at work in this arena. At one extreme, some advocates for pure secularism urge that the government regulate and tax churches and other private educational organizations in the same way non-religious organizations are taxed and regulated, a move which would erode their independence. Religious zealots, at the other extreme, insist that public forms of education recognize that America is traditionally a "Christian nation" and that schools must teach in accord with that tradition, with the eventual result of creating a Christian environment within which all must receive their education. Parallels to these ideas exist in England among some Conservatives.

Neither extreme position is reasonable, and neither is faithful to the original meaning of the First Amendment to the Constitution of the United States: "Congress shall make no law respecting an establishment of religion, or prohibiting the free exercise thereof."[2] The ultra-secularist, in effect, wants the state to wield the power to banish religion from public life. The religious crusader wants the state to advance a particular religion. However, the American political doctrine of separation of church and state declares that the state will have no power either to inhibit or to promote religion.[3]

The constitutional doctrine reflects the wisdom of the founding fathers, who thought that government and church function best when they are not entangled with one another. It also protects the religious liberty of those who wish to practice a given religion. Naturally, Christians will not want the state to monitor the expression of their faith, but they will err, perhaps unconsciously, in expecting government to favor their religion over others.

Although governmental favor may initially seem desirable, it sets a perilous precedent. One danger is that official recognition of a religion by a public agency (federal, state, or local) tends to become purely perfunctory and rote. Psychological research shows that nominal public agreement with a religious position, whether displayed by the meaningless recitation of prayers or other routine exercises, tends to hinder personal spiritual growth.[4] Hence, it makes good sense for Christian believers to desire for themselves and their particular church the exclusive religious instruction and nurture of their children.

In *The Idea of a Secular Society and Its Significance for Christians*, D. L. Munby explores alternative models for the state and society. He concludes that a neutral posture on the part of government conforms more closely to a Christian view of social organization than any other pattern.[5] Our God-given humanity includes the right to judge what is true and good without the state telling us what to think. Because of our finitude and fallibility in areas legitimately left to reason, conscience, and taste, the principle of not imposing the preference of some on others is valid. Besides, truth itself may be more fairly treated when diverse opinions are allowed to flourish. If our reasons for our religious beliefs are correct, let them stand in the midst of dynamic interchange with competing beliefs. In secular society, then, what Christians should want is a level playing field.

To limit the practice of giving specific religious guidance to private organizations is not to denigrate all displays of civil religion. It is surely wise and proper for Christians to endorse the public acknowledgment of the fact that the founding documents of the United States, its monetary currency, and even the oaths taken in courts of law presuppose the existence of a Supreme Being. The Declaration of Independence asserts that all human beings are created equal and endowed by their Creator with certain intrinsic rights, a statement that connects the dignity and worth of persons to God.[6] In a culture that lives increasingly as if there were no God and no moral norms, it is not unreasonable for Christians to work toward restoring at least minimal recognition of religion in the public square.

Decisions people make about what kind of school to attend or to send one's children to attend are based on many factors.[7] In some cases, parents may choose the public educational system. They may deem it important, all other things being equal, for their child to rub shoulders with a diverse group of people. Other parents may become aware of aspects of their local public school that move them to think that it is not an appropriate place to send their children. Such aspects include the risks that the child's faith and morals might be undermined by both subtle and overt anti-Christian ideas. These parents may opt instead for private and religious education, which may be conducted in either an institutionalized or home school format.

In fact, as American public education continues to struggle with declining academic standards, increased drug traffic and violence, and other serious problems, forms of private education will become increasingly attractive to parents. Of course, since alternatives to public education tend to be expensive, cost becomes one more variable affecting a decision that is already complicated.

In other circumstances, the reasons for choosing some form of private schooling may be not the perceived disadvantages of public schooling but rather the positive attributes of a private religious education. Of course, especially protective parents may want their children to be in a "pure" environment from a religious point of view. But many parents will make a private school decision based on convictions that learning is enhanced within a context that acknowledges Christian truths as well as the great spectrum of other discovered truths. This kind of total educational context, which sees all truth in whatever field of study we encounter it as a divine gift, is found only in a private institution or home school.

A reasonable Christian view, then, supports the establishment of public or state schools while it seeks to protect the rights of religious and other private schools to offer alternatives. Regardless of whether children attend public or private schools, Christian parents and churches have the clear duty of communicating to them a sound understanding of Christian faith. They would also serve their children well if they communicated a Christian vision for education. This vision—drawn from concepts of God, humanity, and the world—can support and strengthen them morally and spiritually, regardless of where they attend school.

ACADEMIC FREEDOMS AND DUTIES

The educational enterprise rests on certain conceptions of the rights and responsibilities of the members of the academic community. These concepts shape and support teaching and learning at the elementary level, university level, and any level of education in between. Academic freedom and intellectual responsibility are among the most important of these concepts.

Although many American educational experts contend that the doctrine of academic freedom is derived straightforwardly from the First Amendment, its original source is more ancient and much less political.[8] Teachers are obviously protected by the same constitutional guarantee of freedom of speech that protects every United States citizen. However, the doctrine of academic freedom implies that an institution of learning is endowed with certain rights which may not be appropriate, for example, in a business enterprise or government agency. We could say that the fundamental doctrine of academic freedom had its ultimate origin in Socrates' eloquent defense of himself against the charge of corrupting the youth of Athens by his teaching.[9] We could also say that it has had a continuous history from the beginning of universities in the twelfth century to the present day.[10]

Concern for academic freedom is based on the assumption that the search for truth has inestimable value and therefore must be diligently protected. There should be appropriate honor for the scholars who commit themselves to this search and for the teachers who lead others in it, and there should also be a system of protections for their endeavors. In both medieval and modern times, tenure has been intimately joined to the preservation of academic freedom. Tenure is intended not to promote job security among one class of professionals but to guard the fragile nature of the academic enterprise.[11] Since the search after truth can be hindered by those wielding political power, the positions of established scholars and teachers who hold unpopular views must be shielded from administrators and pressure groups.[12] Neither is tenure meant to prevent the removal of a teacher who has flagrantly debased the academic mission through either incompetence or immorality. When dealing with teachers subjected to such charges, each educational institution must follow its own rules of due process and conduct itself according to the highest ethical and legal principles. Tenure, properly serving academic freedom, will protect the excellent teacher whose views may differ from the views of those in power.

The traditional concept of academic freedom involves the mystique of liberty and honor.[13] It is the affirmation of the teacher's freedom to study and do research and to speak and write about the results of that study and research. With some qualification, the idea applies in much the same way to students. The learned scholar has the full academic authority and rights that accrue to one who possesses expertise; the callow student merely has the right of exploration. In both cases, academic freedom may be defined as the freedom to think for oneself, to consider ideas, to make errors and correct them, to communicate the results of one's study, and to disagree with others on reasonable grounds. Although Christian theism unequivocally affirms the dignity of all people and the value of all legitimate work, it assigns a very high value to knowledge and wisdom, and it cherishes the role of those who seek it.

The rights of the teacher or scholar are necessarily intertwined with those of the student. The academic freedom of teachers is not the privilege of espousing just any opinion they please or of teaching views outside their spheres of competence. Educators must bear the responsibility of trying to determine truth in their fields and seeking to transmit it fairly to students. The commitment to truth also includes the right of students not to be indoctrinated, misled, or incompetently taught. As Lord Acton remarked, "at the root of all liberty is the liberty to learn." None of this, of course, precludes possible diversity of judgments about facts and values; it simply upholds the dignity of the mind in the search for truth.

Historically, the principle of academic freedom has been threatened by parties at two extremes: those who pressure for restrictive legalism and those who crusade for unbridled license. The former group includes people who often do not understand the nature of an academic community: citizen censorship committees who know little about the value of reading, lay boards of trustees who panic when controversial subjects are discussed on campus, administrations who attempt to abolish tenure, and government agencies that prohibit the intellectual discussion of religious and ethical topics in the name of separation of church and state. Limiting thought and discussion endangers academic freedom and injures the educational enterprise.

Intellectual liberty is also threatened by the opposite orientation. Those who strenuously demand that any opinion or action whatever should be protected under the canopy of academic freedom are equally unreasonable and dangerous. Immoral actions, subversive practices, and false positions produced by fraudulent or sloppy scholarship have been protected under the guise of academic freedom. This amounts to stretching the very precise idea of academic freedom until it becomes a *laissez-faire* concept that promotes an environment in which all views, and perhaps all behaviors, must be uncritically protected. Those who hold a lofty view of human dignity under God, a high view of education, and a deep concern for the moral fabric of society cannot afford to be naive or timid about this perversion of the idea of academic freedom.

Humane, enlightened societies and their educational institutions must wrestle with difficult issues in determining a legitimate range of freedom. In order to find a balance, faculties and administrations must work to build a structure of freedom for inquiry and expression, regardless of whether their school is public or private, secular or religious. We cannot forget that all freedom—First Amendment freedom as well as academic freedom—exists only within structure: all meaningful freedom is bounded freedom. Outside the bounds, there is not more freedom; there is only havoc. There will virtually always be a great variety of opinion among the faculty and students of any public school or university, but a greater range of opinion does not mean that there is more academic freedom. Truth does not have a fair chance in the midst of chaos. So, it may well be that religious schools—for example, those with a Christian commitment to responsible inquiry—actually exercise at least as much academic freedom as their secular counterparts. As secular culture relinquishes more and more of its grasp of any classical or Christian ideals of our humanity and its noble intellectual endeavor, it loses its compass for thinking about academic freedom and the conditions which foster it.

Intellectual liberty is not automatically forfeited and academic freedom is not necessarily abridged when an institution seeks to perpetuate its historic identity or subscribes to a particular creed.[14] Academic freedom promotes honesty and integrity in the search after truth, not neutrality. It makes little sense to foster total neutrality as an ideal, since all genuine searching for truth begins with some basic precommitments. At the very least, there is a prior commitment to the laws of logic so that our thoughts about truth may be consistent, coherent, and systematic. There may be other prior commitments to ethical and theological principles—such as the ethics of honest inquiry or even the sense of divine calling in the search after truth. Any individual or group that claims to be searching for truth but to have no assumptions is simply naive. However, the fact that we bring our prior assumptions to our search does not destroy its objectivity. It simply tempers our understanding of the kind of objectivity we can have. We can strive for proper objectivity by being honest and open, by trying to be aware of the initial assumptions we bring to our tasks, and by being willing to evaluate and change those assumptions when there is sufficient reason to do so. This sort of modest objectivity retains belief in a stable, intellectually accessible reality to which the mind has access.

Problems frequently arise when an educational institution defines its identity too narrowly or dictates restrictive criteria for student and faculty loyalty. When a school policy fails to acknowledge that responsible people can interpret or apply the same basic beliefs in different ways, it mistakes conformity for safety. The notorious "monkey trial" (Scopes v. State) is a clear example of confusing a scientific opinion with theological heresy. Equally harmful mistakes are made in private religious institutions when intelligent and dedicated professors are censured or dismissed for expressing views that do not echo a narrow "party line."

To be sure, truth occasionally needs a helping hand in the support of institutional identity.[15] Sometimes faculty members espouse views inconsistent with their school's mission or conduct themselves in ways that threaten their school's integrity. But before coercive measures are taken, all of an institution's constituency must clearly distinguish grievous abuse of academic liberty from desirable diversity of opinion. The principle of academic freedom demands that as much diversity be allowed as is consistent with the mission and aims of the institution, even an institution with a well-defined religious identity.[16] It is generally wise to allow errors in belief and unpopular opinions to exist because the evil of suppressing errors is almost always greater than the evils they present. Building a monolithic climate of opinion not only stifles the minds of those living within it but also robs any tradition of positive input and constructive criticism from those who are often most committed to it.

A sound version of Christian theism endorses the venerated ideal of academic freedom. It acknowledges the dignity of the mind in the image of God and the reality of a knowable world. However, since we are fallible and limited, we understand that no scholar or teacher or student can have infallible knowledge or a perfect grasp of truth. That is why legitimate forms of free inquiry must be honored and attempts to compel conformity of belief must be denounced. Belief, intellectual assent, is like worship and faith: it cannot be coerced but must be freely given.[17] Christian theism concurs with the best traditional wisdom on this important educational matter: there is simply no acceptable alternative to academic freedom.

MULTICULTURALISM IN EDUCATION

Celebration of diversity—as well as denunciation of racial, gender, and ethnic prejudices—is ubiquitous in current educational circles. Throughout the last two decades of the twentieth century, no other single topic has stirred more vigorous debate and discussion than "multiculturalism." It remains a serious issue. The objective of the multiculturalist position is the acknowledgment that every person's cultural heritage is valuable, the empowerment of those who have been marginalized, and the elimination of various sorts of oppression. I will analyze multiculturalism in three basic phases. First, I try to illustrate the main ideas of multiculturalism as they are revealed in its practical educational manifestations. Second, I will place multiculturalism in a larger conceptual context by tracing it to postmodernist philosophy. Third, I will evaluate multiculturalism in light of basic Christian and theistic themes.

Perhaps no image more vividly captures the expression of multiculturalism than that of demonstrating Stanford University students in 1988. Dressed in their Lakers T-shirts, Levi jeans, and Reeboks (an irony that needs no comment), students chanted: "Hey, hey, ho, ho, Western culture's got to go!" Their point was that the standard texts of higher education—as well as texts at all levels of education—are mainly works of Western civilization. These texts are generally written by Dead White European Males (DWEMS), such as Aristotle, Aquinas, Kant, Milton, and Shakespeare. However, in the eyes of multiculturalists, these Eurocentric texts do great harm to the different minorities compelled to study them. The damage supposedly ranges from diminished self-esteem to continued alienation from American economic and political life.

Stanford students and the radical faculty who inspired them were able to effect a sea change at that prominent academic institution. Stanford's required course on Western culture was replaced by a course requirement called Cultures, Ideas, and Values (CIV), which includes texts that are representative of various groups of people. This shift toward "multiculturalism," which has occurred on virtually every campus in America, aims at correcting the perceived monocultural bias in teaching and texts and at creating an environment that validates every minority group. The aggressive multiculturalist movement is, however, not limited to the citadels of higher education.

In an effort to make their public schools more multicultural, the Educational Task Force of the State of New York issued the following statement:

> African Americans, Asian Americans, Puerto Ricans/Latinos, and Native Americans have all been the victims of intellectual and educational oppression that has characterized the culture and institutions of the United States and the European world for centuries.[18]

The document goes on to explain that Eurocentric oppression is "the reason why children of non-European descent are not doing as well as expected." These children have had to compete in a school environment in which the knowledge base is created and protected by specific groups in power. Multiculturalists are not simply trying to prevent the imposition of religious preference or artistic taste on students; they are recommending that anything which passes for traditional knowledge—including the facts of world history and the rules of English grammar—not be imposed upon students.[19]

Multiculturalism has now profoundly affected all levels of education from elementary through undergraduate and graduate study. Virtually every aspect of today's educational environment is touched by multicultural concerns: curriculum design, text book selection, pedagogical technique, financial assistance, promotion, tenure, and grant funding. All of this is supposed to be the educational remedy for the longstanding "insensitivity" to and "oppression" of minorities in our society. The objective is to break power dichotomies that reinforce dominance of one group over others: male/female, white/nonwhite, heterosexual/homosexual, and so forth. According to multiculturalists, these dichotomies are the underlying basis of what has been accepted as "official knowledge" in every academic field and thus have led to the maldistribution of power.

The most famous multiculturalist project is the trenchant critique of the great texts—what is known as the "canon" of the Western world. These books are charged with perpetrating a worldview that supports the interests of white European males. Stanley Fish is one of the leaders in "canon busting." He and other canon busters are portrayed as wanting to eliminate the great books of Western culture from the university curriculum or to place on a par with them just any piece of literature that happens to be a passing fad. Fish insists, however, that his point is more complicated and subtle than that. He contends that the traditional allegiance to a fixed, universal set of literary standards— as well as to the works deemed excellent by those standards—is fallacious. His argument for this position is instructive.

The canon has emerged over time, according to Fish, not because it measures up to some transcendent values, but because it was fashioned through the interplay of historical forces. This is the crux of the debate between "fundamentalists" and "historicists." Do we read the accredited texts of the Western world because they are the best according to some timeless criterion or do we read them because the vicissitudes of history have worked to favor them? Fish argues that our values and the texts we select accordingly are conditioned by political ideologies, social agendas, economic interests, and gender relations. Had these historical variables been different, we would be reading a different canon. Fish does not reject the canon in a wholesale way; in fact, he thinks that many of its approved works are good. What he does is to reinterpret the source of our judgments of literary value. Thus, it is theoretically possible that historicist Fish and a fundamentalist such as Mortimer Adler would agree on the very same list of great books. However, Adler would think that their greatness reflects timelessness and universality, while Fish would maintain that they have persisted because of the accidents of history.

This conceptual shift—from unchanging, global standards to standards that are specific to different traditions, regions, and cultures—is an important aspect of the multiculturalist movement. The literature of different groups and different cultures can now be deemed just as valuable as that of white, European, male culture. In addition to Western world literature, we can have African-American literature, Asian-American literature, Appalachian literature, feminist literature, gay/lesbian literature, and so forth. The crucial point is that these different cultures will have their own standards for what counts as good literature. According to multiculturalists, the supremacy of Eurocentric standards can be rejected. Americans can now, in Fish's words, "embrace their ethnic or racial differences and make of them a point of personal identification, rather than attempting to have those differences absorbed in the larger American culture."[20]

Interestingly, multiculturalism is rooted in the philosophical soil of postmodernism. Not surprisingly, the multiculturalist enterprise of canon busting is conducted largely through the method of deconstruction—that is, through exposing the power relationships involved in the establishment of the traditional canon. When we factor in the postmodern assumptions that reality has no inherent structure and that the mind cannot make cognitive contact with it anyway, we see why multiculturalists do not regard the deconstruction of the canon as the destruction of enduring insights into the nature of reality and the human condition. Truth for them is the truth of cultures and groups; it is not an expression of the way things really are. Of course, since the multiculturalist approach rests on postmodern philosophy, it becomes subject to the same criticisms already leveled against postmodernism, and there are other criticisms as well.

Christian theism clearly affirms the dignity and equal worth of all human beings. Our God is infinitely creative, and the vast array of cultures, colors, customs, and historical journeys reflect the wonderful diversity of his human creation. Major biblical themes speak of the importance of caring for the marginalized and seeking justice for disenfranchised peoples.[21] But this does not mean that today's multiculturalist proposals are justified. Concern for the downtrodden must be guided by sound thinking. This is why certain methods used by multiculturalists in attempting to correct alleged wrongs are alarming. The presumption that any story but one's own—or any story but that of one's group—is oppressive is very damaging to constructive social interaction and progress. We are reverting with accelerating speed to a new form of tribalism as various ethnic and cultural groups pursue their own identities in ways that cut them off from a larger society. Neil Postman observes that we are now producing a populace of "hyphenated Americans": African-Americans, Asian-Americans, Latin-Americans, and so on. Consequently, we are in grave danger of creating a people whose predominant mode of consciousness is determined by race or gender or some other trait that separates them from the whole. We will ultimately become a nation in which many groups of people will prefer to be known and identified primarily by their differences rather than by our common heritage and current lives as Americans. This fragmentation of the public mind and soul poisons public discourse and makes a national consciousness impossible.

The key to avoiding the errors of multiculturalism lies in a more inclusive concept of diversity. Let us call the kind of multiculturalism that is bred in a postmodern climate "particularistic multiculturalism" or "particularism." Particularism contends that there are ethno-specific, gender-specific, and class-specific ways of knowing. Each group has its own truth, so to speak. We can no longer speak of timeless truths, transcendent truths, truths that can be recognized by all. Curricula, texts, examinations, and teaching styles must take this new "multiplicity of truth" into account. The particularist vision of American culture is that of a conglomeration of nonassimilating group traditions.

There is, however, an alternative concept of multiculturalism that is faithful to our highest historical ideals as a nation and to our best understanding of Christian teachings. "Pluralistic multiculturalism" or "pluralism" recognizes the differences among ethnic and other cultural groups but also attests to deeper, underlying commonalities. Three important areas form common ground here: our mutual American heritage, our divinely created human nature, and our equal standing as believers in the household of faith.

First, as a nation the United States has a historically multi-ethnic character. American culture as we know it has always been shaped by immigrants from many lands. In addition to Native Americans, America has been influenced and forged by people of European heritage, Africans (slave and free) and their descendants, Asians, and many others.[22] The contributions made by various ethnic groups, which add variety and texture to the American experience, have traditionally been considered part of a shared and shareable heritage. This is what was meant by the phrase, "the Great Melting Pot." We even inscribe on our currency the poignant Latin phrase: *E pluribus unum* ("in many, one"). The hope for America to find cultural wholeness and solidarity lies not in the factionalization of many ethnic groups, each demanding their rights and accenting their differences, but rather in recovering our historic pluralistic dream and in correcting our failings in living up to it.

A second place in which we can find unity in diversity is the Judeo-Christian view of our divinely created human nature. The Christian doctrine that persons are made in the image of God contains an indispensable insight for discussions of multi-culturalism: human beings are more alike than they are different. Differences in ethnicity, taste, dress, cuisine, religion, and other matters do not diminish our commonality in our fundamental human traits. We are rational-moral-social-physical beings. We all must be born, grow, struggle, experience joy as well as pain, relate to our fellow human beings, and try to live productive lives upon this earth. We will do these distinctively human things regardless of the location of our birth, color of our skin, or language of our ancestors. Even before the Judeo-Christian doctrine of the *imago Dei*, thinkers in Greek antiquity recognized that education must address what is universal in our humanity. This ancient idea has motivated interest in diverse beliefs and cultures throughout the history of liberal arts education. Honest exploration of this diversity simply reveals the many ways in which our common humanity interacts with the variables of history and experience. Here we find the basis for a more adequate pluralistic vision for a culturally diverse world than that of the factionalist multiculturalists.

A distinctively Christian perspective points us to a third kind of commonality that we may also consider. Christian theology teaches that those who have found salvation through the work of Jesus Christ are unified in him. In the book of Galatians, the Apostle Paul writes:

> For in Christ Jesus you are all children of God through faith. As many of you as were baptized into Christ have clothed yourselves with Christ. There is no longer Jew or Greek, there is no longer slave or free, there is no longer male and female; for all of you are one in Christ Jesus.[23]

While acknowledging legitimate diversity among its members, Paul stresses the deeper unity of persons in the body of Christ. Of course, there are still Jews and Greeks, males and females, whites and non-whites, and there are other differences as well. What deserves primary emphasis—and indeed celebration—is our spiritual unity, not our contrasts and divergences. Proper understanding of Christian community, then, justifies a wholesome pluralism that overcomes particularism.

With this greater understanding of the issues of multiculturalism, we can now revisit the debate concerning the Western canon. The Western tradition is not the result of a monolithic, oppressive conspiracy of white male elites, but rather it traces its origins to the clashes of diverse peoples and ideas whose intellectual descendants continue in vociferous debate. Dissent from a received orthodoxy is as old as Western civilization itself, whether that dissent manifests itself in theological heresy, skeptical philosophy, or political disagreement. In fact, it has frequently been in the face of dissent that the enduring tenets of Western thought have been forged, clarified, and strengthened. It has historically been Western intellectual activity that has shown such keen interest in other lands, peoples, cultural contexts, and ideas. Western culture has not always lived up to its highest ideals: the dignity of the individual, the value of a humane social order, the integrity of rational debate and discussion. Yet the moral and spiritual resources found in the Western tradition itself provide the basis for the most incisive and helpful critique of its own errant practices. It is clear that the Western tradition rests on a profound multiculturalism, which has always been the source of its intellectual vibrancy.

As the postmodernist and multiculturalist attacks on Western culture have mounted, defenders have offered two broad responses. Both endorse the Western canon in subtly different but important ways. First of all, E. D. Hirsch, Jr., argues in his best-selling book, *Cultural Literacy*, that there is a specifiable body of information—including the themes contained in the great books—that everyone in America should know. Acquiring basic information, according to Hirsch, makes one able to participate in public discourse and to partake in activities in the American marketplace.[24] This rationale is essentially progressivist, activist, and utilitarian, since it revolves around economic and other practical factors extrinsic to the truths and principles learned. Interestingly, such an approach lends itself to list making, and Hirsch himself has devised an extensive list of the sorts of things one should know in order to be culturally literate in America. It is important to know, for example, that *Moby Dick* is about a whale, that a quark is thought to be the fundamental, irreducible unit constituting protons and neutrons, and that the Amazon is a large river in South America. Although learning items on a list may be done by rote memorization, the acquisition of that knowledge still gives one the cultural background to navigate more effectively in society.

Linda Chavez has offered a similar argument about the utilitarian value of a common learning for public school students. She points out that immigrant groups that come to the United States frequently want two very closely connected things: "economic opportunity and political freedom."[25] In order to facilitate their pursuit of these legitimate goals, she proposes several thoughtful suggestions for a common learning in the schools. At the very least, advises Chavez, school children must be taught

1. the same basic skills of reading, writing, and speaking standard English
2. basic math and science to function in a complex technological society
3. a broad understanding of our form of government and its institutions, appreciation for our heritage of American liberty, including the duties and responsibilities of being a citizen in a democracy
4. the history of the United States, including the English antecedents of our political and legal institutions as well as many who built this nation who were neither English nor white nor male
5. a better understanding of the world, including some of the history of other nations, the geography of the globe, and perhaps a second language (in which some immigrant children will naturally have an advantage)[26]

This or any other sane proposal for a common learning is entirely compatible with the desire of any ethnic group to remember and revere the particularities of its own heritage. However, we as a nation need to strive for an appropriate and workable vision of a common national life amid otherwise great diversity.

Historically, the American school system was inspired by the ideal of requiring a common schooling of children at all levels and of funding a variety of public post-secondary institutions. We have sometimes fallen short of our ideal. Educational quality varies widely; discrimination and other problems have marred our efforts. We must continue to try harder because education is a very important key to a better life. Education has been the ladder out of poverty for countless immigrant groups who have come to the United States. So, we dare not fail people of any color, creed, sex, or age by allowing American education to succumb to a new tribalism that does not value a common base of knowledge. Those who will be hurt the most will be the minorities. On pragmatic grounds alone, multiculturalism as it is currently envisioned and practiced must be resisted.

A second defense against multiculturalism—found in the ideas of Josef Pieper, Mortimer Adler, William Bennett, and others—is both realist and traditional. While acknowledging the clear utilitarian value of a common learning, these authors make a special point of explaining the deeper significance of the Western tradition. That significance lies in the search for self-transcendence. Whatever else we say about the great books of the Western world (their style, their evocative quality, and the like), we must say that they are works that have proved over time to do a particularly good job of including us in the ongoing discussion of our own humanity. There might have been other ways of drawing us out of ourselves, keeping us from being prisoners of our place in time and space, letting us see through other peoples' eyes, and escaping the passing, pedestrian attractions of popular culture; but the Western canon is the best we have.

The very notion that we can seek to identify with what is universal in humanity assumes that there is such a thing as an enduring, unchanging human nature. By identifying with this ontological reality called human nature, we can be enlightened, uplifted, and transformed. Aristotle wisely counsels that we

> must not follow those who advise us, being men, to think of human things, and, being mortal, of mortal things, but must, so far as we can, make ourselves immortal, and strain every nerve to live in accordance with the best thing in us; for even if it be small in bulk, much more in power and in worth does it surpass everything. This would seem, too, to be each man himself, since it is the authoritative and better part of him. It would be strange, then, if he were to choose not the life of this self but that of something else.[27]

This incredible passage is the great proclamation that our fundamental humanity is everywhere and at all times the same.

The Western cultural tradition provides an avenue for discovering the knowledge most worth having: self-knowledge. Genuine self-knowledge is ultimately found through proper identification with our humanity. Thus, liberal learning and its great books must be defended because our common humanity must be defended. Multicultural particularism places excessive emphasis on differences, on what is peculiar to a given group or culture, on what empowers a certain minority. Linking one's most fundamental identity to a cultural group inevitably results in separation from others. While this seems "relevant" and "empowering" and even "politically correct," it is actually narrow absorption in lesser details. What is really most timely and most relevant—our very humanity—is missed. Perhaps C. S. Lewis said it best: "Whatever is not eternal is eternally out of date."[28]

The New Generation of Learners

Our conventional wisdom on how to teach and how to learn effectively may be facing its toughest challenge in the new generation of students. Of course, many children born from 1965 to 1981, the Generation X, have already completed college and are moving into the social mainstream. The group of children called by some the Baby Boomlets, born from 1981 to 1999, is now in elementary and secondary schools, and some of them are even matriculating at colleges and universities. Sociologists and psychologists tell us that this generation of students is different from any we have seen before. Because of these differences, which we will explore, many educational experts contend that today's students will learn differently from the way past generations learned and that we will need to teach them differently, too. Although we cannot afford to ignore any reasonable recommendations for educating our young people, a sound educational philosophy based on enduring principles will be applicable to every new situation. If our emerging educational perspective is valid, it will serve us well as we seek to

teach the upcoming generation. Let us first sketch a profile of
today's youth, citing the educational and sociological trends related to them. The statistics are alarming, but I will venture
some suggestions concerning how Christians might think about
educating the young people who are now entering our educational system.

A number of statistics from both scholarly studies and government reports may be indicators of what is to come.[29] First,
there has been a dramatic increase in the student population.
The number of college students tripled between 1960 and 1975,
leveled off and moderated a bit and then surged upward in the
1990s. The percentage of high school graduates (ages 16–24)
enrolled in college rose from 46.6% in 1973 to 65% in 1996.
The total number of bachelor's degrees awarded grew 26% between 1980 and 1994. Second, these population increases are ac-
companied by shifting demographics. By the year 2030, the
percentage of non-Hispanic white high school students will
drop to 50%. College students 25 years of age and older were
28% of the total in 1974 but were 44% in 1995. Enrollment of
women and ethnic minorities in higher education is increasing.
Between 1985 and 1995, the number of college men rose 9%
while the number of women increased by 23%. Enrollment of
ethnic minorities in higher education rose from 15.7% in 1976
to 25.3% in 1995. In elementary and secondary schools, students from minority groups increased from 29.6% in 1986 to
35.2% in 1995.

Do the numbers and demographics tell us that education is
improving? That is unclear. SAT and ACT data from the mid-
1960s to the early 1980s show a decline in skill levels for basic
academic tasks. Paradoxically, high school teachers are award-
ing more "A" grades than ever (31.6% in 1997 compared with
12.5% in 1969). High school students report spending less time
per week studying (3.8 hours per week average in 1997 compared to 4.9 in 1987). High school teachers report that tardiness
and absenteeism are increasingly serious problems. Despite relatively low levels of preparedness, student attitude studies show

that they tend to be highly confident of their abilities. Could this signal an increasing disconnection between performance and outcome, between effort and reward? Educational fads intended to enhance student self-esteem seem blind to the fact that real self-esteem is built through real work and accomplishment.

Although educational changes in America are significant, they pale in comparison to the psychological and sociological shifts affecting the emotional life of students. Clearly, children are receiving less emotional support from parents. In 1970, about 39% of children of two parent families with children had mothers in the workforce. That figure rose to 61% in 1990. During the twenty-year period between 1976–1996, the proportion of mothers of college freshmen who were full-time homemakers dropped from about one-third to one-tenth. A number of trends in contemporary life strongly suggest the serious effect of parental absence and inattentiveness throughout childhood and teenage years. We have every reason to believe that children naturally need all sorts of emotional transactions with both mother and father. It is time to expose as myth the idea that parents can simply spend infrequent "quality time" with otherwise neglected children and still produce healthy adults.

Even more disturbing is the fact that the percentage of two-parent families is rapidly decreasing every year. Family breakup is a fact of life for too many students. In the twenty-five-year interval from 1972 to 1997, the proportion of college freshmen coming from divorced families tripled to 26%. During the 1980s and 1990s, the number of households with children under 18 years of age that are headed by single mothers increased by almost 40%. In 1997, about one-third of all children lived with only one parent—and the numbers keep increasing. It is no surprise that emotional scars, anxiety, and cynicism seem to characterize so many youth.

Parental commitment is markedly down; family solidarity is seriously weakening. Predictably, violent crime and suicide rates are increasing among children and adolescents. In the United States, between 1976 and 1993, the annual number of murders committed by 14- to 17-year-olds rose from 4.6 in

100,000 to 12.3. In 1995, 14.3% of males in grades 9–12 carried a weapon (knife, gun, club) on school property at least one day per month. The number of public school teachers who were physically threatened or attacked by a student increased from 10% to 15% between 1991 and 1994. Suicide is now the second-leading cause of death of 15- to 19-year-olds.

Further statistics document an alarming incidence of drug and alcohol abuse. The percentage of 10th graders who reported that someone offered to sell or give them an illegal drug at school during the previous year rose from 18% in 1992 to 32% in 1996. A study done in 1993 by the University of Michigan states that "[i]mmoderate drinking has long been a distinguishing element of college and university culture."[30] A 1997 study showed that 42.7% of college students qualified as binge drinkers and 20.7% as frequent binge drinkers. The binge drinkers reported forgetting where they were or what they had done while drunk. One report links 95% of all violent crime on campus (rape, assault, vandalism, etc.) to alcohol. Although the statistics regarding male drinking on campus have always been high, some recent studies suggest a growing percentage of women binge drinkers.[31]

Another disconcerting fact is that young people are increasingly consumers of mass media. By 16 years of age, the average adolescent who watches 35 hours of television programming per week has seen 200,000 acts of violence. Violence fills the screen in most popular video games. Sex is the other major theme. In the last two decades of the twentieth century, MTV was the fastest growing channel. Its contents are typically provocative, and it often portrays women as objects for men to use. A University of Michigan survey showed that 76 percent of women were sexually active, averaging four partners during their college experience. A mere 64 percent used some sort of protection in their first relationship; the number fell to 49 percent by the time they had had sexual relations with their fifth partner.

No doubt, violence and sex supply too much media content and are extremely influential in the development of today's youth. Furthermore, the very form in which mass media communicates may also be reason for concern. Just about everything that young people experience through the media is brief, amusing, and sensational: half-hour television programs in which all elements of a (usually trivial) plot get settled, sound bites as news, commercials that bombard the senses. Youth have to do little cerebral work and seem to be getting habituated into a passive state of mind in which they expect everything they encounter intellectually to be quick, easy, and entertaining.

Inundated with a culture that is entertainment-crazed, sex-saturated, and materialistically oriented, today's youth express a deep sense of meaninglessness. How can self-esteem develop when accountability is low and possibilities for cheap, instant gratification are everywhere? Youth are reflecting the spiritual, moral, and social crisis of our society at large. We have let them down and abandoned them in many ways. A study conducted by the American Medical Association and the National Association of State Boards of Education concludes: "Never before has one generation of American teenagers been less healthy, less cared-for or less prepared for life than their parents were at the same age."[32] Today's students are indeed different from their predecessors. We now see some of the major reasons for the differences, and we see that the differences are more cultural than academic. But the cultural differences are having major repercussions in education.

A realistic Christian position places utmost importance on family. Family is the primary society, the first training ground for our intellectual, moral, and spiritual responses to the world. No legislative measures and no educational proposals can positively influence our schools as much as healthy family life. "Family" here, according to the Christian ideal, is an organic social circle built around a monogamous, heterosexual couple and their offspring.[33] Even in the great variety of cultures around the globe, with nuclear families and extended families and other kinds of family structures, this primary social unit is at the core. Family is the basic building block of civilization. Concerned Christians who understand this profound truth must be constantly vigilant against attempts in our schools and in our society to redefine and distort the essential meaning of family. We must do everything possible to strengthen and encourage the well-being of families while recognizing that a fallen world will contain broken families in need of compassion and guidance.[34]

COMPUTER TECHNOLOGY AND EDUCATION

"Education must keep up with technology!" We hear this chorus from politicians as well as educational experts. Most proposals for technological progress are motivated by radical changes that the computer revolution is making in contemporary life. We do a great many things with computers— everything from flying planes to transacting business, from fighting wars to balancing checkbooks. Champions of computers in education announce that this is the "information age" and urge the "education industry" to upgrade their ability to educate accordingly. The growth in the use of computers to produce, collect, manipulate, analyze, synthesize, transform, report, share, and exchange information is phenomenal. Computer-education advocates are pushing schools to become faster and better "delivery systems" of information to students and to give them up-to-date technical skills for making their way in the fast-paced, computer-dominated world.[35]

To be sure, technology deeply affects culture. The clock, telescope, printing press, cotton gin, steam engine, telephone, automobile, and countless other inventions have forever changed the way we live. But for every benefit that new inventions bring, they also bring about unpredictable consequences, some positive and some negative.[36] Commenting on the cultural impact of technology, Sigmund Freud said, "If there had been no railway to conquer distances, my child would never have left his native town and I should need no telephone to hear his voice. . . ."[37] This comment is not an argument for blind knee-jerk resistance to the development, introduction, or improvement of technology. It is a caveat that we must carefully weigh the possible liabilities as well as the possible benefits of each new technology for the whole realm of human affairs and particularly for the educational process.

Over the years, we have incorporated many technologies into the educational endeavor: the phonograph, the speed-reading machine, closed-circuit television, and 16-millimeter films. With computer-based technology, we now have encyclopedias on CD-ROM, virtual reality software, distance learning via the Internet, and the manifold possibilities of the computer age. In *School's Out*, Lewis Perelman argues that the latest information technology makes the conventional school setting completely irrelevant since vast amounts of information can be obtained outside the formal classroom.[38] As more powerful computers are designed, more impressive instructional programs written, and greater Internet access provided, more and more enthusiasts will herald the end of traditional education and the obsolescence of the teacher.[39] How should we think about all the passionate claims for computer technology? Does it lay the basis for an educational revolution? Will it significantly enhance learning? Let us look briefly at both sides of these questions.

We can readily cite some positive results of computer use and computer-based instruction. The obvious advantages for the academic environment include the speed and ease of creating and manipulating information with word processing, spreadsheet, database, and other programs. In terms of research, large amounts of material are becoming available that can be searched more efficiently by computer than by handling paper and books. Computers can enhance classroom presentations of both textual and graphic materials. All of this is certainly beneficial. There is even evidence to show that learning-disabled students and students with below-average intelligence grasp packaged information better with computers than with traditional methods. But the clear explanation for this is that the computer can be programmed to be a tireless administrator of drill and repetition. Some studies also indicate that computers can offer a large body of practice material to assist students in certain phases of learning in mathematics. Again, additional drill and repetition is important, but doing drills by computer is hardly a revolution in the way students do math.

If schools exist simply for the purpose of conveying and managing information, then conventional education might well become outmoded. However, in spite of much discussion of how computers improve the way students learn, we have almost no hard evidence proving that they actually do so and some good reasons to think that they do not. This suggests that the computer cannot be a panacea. As computer usage in schools is expanding, national tests show our children are increasingly deficient in essential skills. Consider the fields of mathematics and English. We now have grade school children as well as high school teens who cannot solve even simple addition and subtraction problems in their head and do not know the multiplication table. The computer is now a crutch that calculates for them. Computer advocates in education are unable to point to rising national math scores on the SAT or ACT to substantiate their claims that computers are indispensable to math instruction.

Many English and writing classes also integrate computer technology into classroom work. While there are computer programs that take students through elementary rote exercises in grammar, we have no hard statistical evidence that proves the new technologies actually enhance the learning of language skills among our young. We have some anecdotal evidence that these technologies can create a climate in which students—at various levels—are encouraged to "publish" their pieces on the Internet. One may strongly suspect that revising and perfecting the written work is secondary to seeing it on the Internet. But this just confirms that there is no intellectual quality control in this new technological arena and should deter us from giving students the impression that publishing their work "online" quickly is part of an educationally significant experience.

The whole idea of doing "research" on the Internet seems to be another problem in our schools. Are we equipping students with the intellectual standards as well as the moral values for sifting through material they find on the Internet? Are we somehow communicating to students that searching the Internet is a substitute for traditional library research? Will they also be exposed to the excellent library resources that are simply not available on any web site? Internet research simply cannot become the *only* form of research taught in schools.

The widespread use of CD-ROMs for instruction and research also raises questions. Interactive encyclopedias and other collections contain impressive amounts of textual material, photographs, sound recordings, film clips, and the like. Companies producing these materials call them "child-friendly" and promote them as superior to bland, traditional textbooks. They quote teachers who say that children can now go into more depth in their studies, that they can dig "beneath the surface." For example, a child might watch a film clip of Martin Luther King, Jr., giving his famous "I Have a Dream" speech or see the launch of the space shuttle Columbia. In spite of the obvious benefits of these materials, they are unbalanced: there are far more pictures than text, more sensational thrills than careful analysis. Yet they are often marketed as offering all students need for complete, well-rounded study. Are we not developing a bias against reading in our schools? Should history students be told that they are studying "in depth" by using audio-visual media to see and hear recorded excerpts of Dr. King's oratory? Can this compare to having students read *My Life with Martin Luther King, Jr.* by Coretta Scott King—a book that recounts her personal experiences with the civil rights hero? Or why not study a biography of Dr. King that is appropriate to the children's grade level? If simply seeing and hearing the speech is considered "in depth" study, what used to count as superficial? One is inclined to wonder how the great works of history were written and many discerning commentaries produced when the authors did not have computer-assisted learning available to them.

Computer reformers in education seem intent on convincing students that school should be fun and easy. Parents' hopes are bolstered by assurances that technology will allow their children to have a better life, to achieve more. I am reminded of humorist Garrison Keillor's description of fictional Lake Wobegon, Minnesota, "where all the children are above average." Although there are indeed things computers can do to improve learning, we must be careful not to expect more from the tool that is technology than it can deliver. We must still be cautious, though not paranoid, about revolutionary methods that promise to make our children smarter but may subtly hasten the "dumbing down" process that is so painfully obvious in American schools. What began looking like a boon to education may prove to be something that perpetuates and even accelerates the decline of our students' essential academic skills. We harm our children by substituting shallow stimulation for a transformative educational experience. The burden is on the computer education advocates to address the many legitimate concerns and questions that can be raised along these lines.

The emergence of the computer in our culture has been impressive, and no one should take it lightly. Computer technology will inevitably continue to influence education, forcing us to try to enhance its positive role while reducing its negative effects. We must never forget that the pencil as well as the dictionary, the chalk board as well the computer, are simply tools. They must be used in the service of our loftier understandings of life and the world. The higher our view of humanity and its prospects, the more diligently we should put our best tools to their most productive use. This includes the computer and all related technology. Let us do with computers in education all that we can possibly do that serves our proper ends.

As Thoreau said, we tend to become tools of our tools. In the case of computer technology, let us not be slow to grasp the particular power of this tool to spellbind us and, ultimately, to make us in its image. In Plato's *Phaedrus*, Socrates tells a story to his friend Phaedrus about Thamus, the king of a great city in Upper Egypt. Thamus had entertained the god Theuth, who was the inventor of many helpful things: number, calculation, geometry, astronomy, writing, and more. The god displayed his wonderful inventions to King Thamus, stating that they should be made widely available to the Egyptian subjects. Socrates proceeds to finish the story:

> Thamus inquired into the use of each of them, and as Theuth went through them expressed approval or disapproval, according as he judged Theuth's claims to be well or ill founded. It would take too long to go through all that Thamus is reported to have said for and against each of Theuth's inventions. But when it came to writing, Theuth declared, "Here is an accomplishment, my lord the King, which will improve both the wisdom and the memory of the Egyptians. I have discovered a sure receipt for memory and wisdom." To this, Thamus replied, "Theuth, my paragon of inventors, the discoverer of an art is not the best judge of the good or harm which will accrue to those who practice it. So it is in this; you, who are the father of writing, have out of fondness for your offspring attributed to it quite the opposite of its real function. Those who acquire it will cease to exercise their memory and become forgetful; they will rely on writing to bring things to their remembrance by external signs instead of by their own internal resources. What you have discovered is a receipt for recollection, not for memory. And as for wisdom, your pupils will have the reputation for it without the reality: they will receive a quantity of information without proper instruction, and in consequence be thought very knowledgeable when they are for the most part quite ignorant. And because they are filled with the conceit of wisdom instead of real wisdom they will be a burden to society."[40]

This charming legend reveals the error of thinking that technology can only be a blessing. Theuth is an archetype of the technophiles of today who do not consider the full effect of innovation. The history of technology and culture reveals many unintended and undesired social consequences of innovation.[41] However, the discerning Thamus also commits an error. He believes that writing will be nothing but a burden on his people, clearly underestimating the benefits which writing could produce. The lesson we should draw here is that technological innovation may be both a benefit and a burden, a blessing and a curse. It is almost never exclusively one or the other. Therefore, each society must negotiate its way between the positive and negative effects of technology.

Noting that technology has both positive and negative aspects is not equivalent to asserting that technology is intrinsically neutral and that the good or ill associated with it are due solely to how it is used. There is a certain degree to which the harm or good of technology can be linked to its particular use—the use of nuclear power, for example. There have been important philosophical questions raised about the applications of technology. But there is also a more elusive question: to what extent is the use of technology largely determined by the very structure of the technology itself? Does function follow form here? Technology is a part of culture but, as it changes quickly, its new forms may exert pressure on us. New technologies do what they are designed to do, and the effects unfold in our lives. The movie *Avalon* powerfully depicts how the television changed American family life, from lively, intimate talk around the dinner table to eating in mute silence over TV trays while watching a favorite program. Television technology placed certain demands on us, and it shaped us in its image. Rapidly proliferating computer technology must be considered with this example in mind.[42]

We must ultimately grapple with the issues created by the computer in the realm of education. A Christian and theistic perspective places high value on the dignity of persons and regards education as a vehicle for fulfilling some of our most profound human potential. Broadly speaking, education is a human awakening. All children, all young persons, deserve significant exposure to this process because they are created in God's image. This is the overarching goal of quality education, a goal toward which all else should contribute. In this light, we can begin to see that all the chatter about the delivery of information and the need for technical skills and the prospect of better jobs assumes that schooling is by nature about preparing for specialized or professional jobs. We know, however, that education is much more about making a life than about making a living.

This fundamental insight provides a context for our thinking about the need for specialized skills and the legitimate need to earn a living in today's world. It also relates to a healthy, realistic recognition of the fact that human beings are tool-making creatures, inventors of technology, and that our tools must be controlled and managed to serve our noblest purposes. Unfortunately, these are exactly the insights that seem absent in today's educational circles. Thus, while we must incorporate technology into our educational endeavors, we cannot uncritically accept all the promises about the possible benefits of computers in the classroom.

When we have our philosophical bearing, we understand that the only adequate education is a holistic one that shapes the whole person.[43] Student proficiency with computer-based technology is only one facet of a complete education. At best, this skill is complementary to the host of other real skills that are necessary for students to acquire in order to become competent adults or effective professionals. At worst, computer usage may become excessive; it may become a detriment rather than an asset to our fundamental humanity. That is why the ideal of the whole person must serve as the basis for all educational discussions.

As I have argued, the most vital educational experiences for our young are mediated directly through person-to-person contact with teachers and mentors. Information can sometimes be delivered through mechanical means; instructional drill and practice can be conducted through clever, interactive software programs; computers can be of amazing assistance; the Internet can be a vehicle for bringing academic courses into our homes. Proper, balanced use of any of these tools is always the key. But if we glimpse the larger Christian vision of education and of what it takes to become a well-developed person, we will not allow computers or any other form of technology to usurp the important relationship between teacher and pupil.

CHAPTER SEVEN

Christianity and
the Pursuit of Excellence

Wh, hat is excellence? Aristotle tells us that excellence is doing the right thing well.[1] In
our own day, best-selling books by Stephen
Covey and others expound theories of personal and corporate excellence.[2] A Christian worldview also beckons
us to the pursuit of excellence in all things, and this call
has several sources. Our divinely created human nature
seeks fulfillment and a measure of perfection in earthly
life. Also, our witness to the world is enhanced by the
care and integrity reflected in our activities. Further, it is
our duty to God to offer humbly our best efforts back
to him. These compelling themes form the basis of a
distinctively Christian vision of excellence, providing
added depth and perspective to our emerging philosophy of education.

    The Christian quest for intellectual excellence, which
drives the pursuit of educational quality, rests on both
the intrinsic and extrinsic values of knowledge. A Christian philosophy recognizes the inherent worth of
knowledge and personal improvement. Since education
deals with matters of the human mind and spirit, it
touches a part of our nature that is like God. The eloquent words of the Apostle Paul address this: "whatever
is true, whatever is honorable, whatever is just, whatever
is pure, whatever is pleasing, whatever is commendable,

if there is any excellence and if there is anything worthy of praise, think about these things."³ Of course, education has practical value as well. The practical use of the knowledge we gain through education can greatly aid in communicating the faith. A solid education gives students a greater understanding of people, provides them with insight into their deepest concerns, and presents methodologies which they may use for advancing the gospel. More generally, knowledge helps us manage our lives in God's world.

There are several angles from which we may consider the Christian ideal of excellence in education. I will explore four of them here: the idea of education as a dynamic process, the Christian intellectual presence in our culture, the need for personal wholeness and integration, and our call to be "salt and light" in the world. The first two topics pertain to the nature of learning and the life of the mind. The second two place our intellectual endeavors within a comprehensive understanding of the benefits and purposes of Christian life.

Education as Product or Process?

To think of education exclusively in terms of curriculum structure, course content, and methods for the delivery of information is to treat knowledge as a product for consumption. Some educational programs, such as those teaching vocational and technical courses, tend to handle knowledge exactly this way. However, when our concept of education is broadened to include human liberation and fulfillment, we can no longer consider knowledge simply as a product. Authentic liberal education assumes that knowledge is active, dynamic, processive. The sheer acquisition of data—through rote memorization, recitation of answers, or repetitive computer drill—is not enough. From a liberal arts perspective, to speak of the learning *process* is to speak of the search for truth, the energetic exploration of ideas, and the careful refinement of mental skills. Learning in this sense is active, not passive.

An educational institution, whether Christian or not, cannot merely disseminate what it accepts as the truth. Neither can any real educator simply seek to replicate his beliefs in his students. Liberal education is concerned with the impact of truth upon the student's mind. *How* we pursue truth is as important as the fact that we seek it. Truth is properly sought through honest, critical thinking. The thinking abilities of students are most effectively enriched when students are directed to great ideas and important issues and are held to high intellectual standards within a community of other truth seekers.

The integrity of the intellectual process is so important that some thinkers try to protect it by specifying conditions under which a person is rationally justified in holding a belief. Philosophers differ about the exact conditions, and we cannot treat all the details here. However, the general idea is clear: our beliefs should be rationally warranted, and the process of forming our beliefs should conform to proper rational standards. Some thinkers even attach ethical responsibility to the intellectual process, saying that we have an ethical obligation to follow rational standards and that we are ethically culpable when we do not.

Nineteenth-century philosopher W. K. Clifford argued that no person has a right to hold any belief unless it is based on evidence. Clifford's definition of rationality is austere, but it helps us begin to think about the issue. To illustrate his point, Clifford tells the tale of a shipowner who ignored reports that his old and deteriorating vessel was unsound. The shipowner told himself that his ship was seaworthy because it was originally well-built and had survived many previous journeys. He thus maintained the belief that the ship was still sound and allowed it to carry many immigrant families on a transatlantic voyage. The ship "went down in mid-ocean and told no tales."[4]

Clifford asks rhetorically what we should say about the shipowner. Clearly, we should say that he is responsible for the deaths of those people. While the shipowner "sincerely" believed in the soundness of the ship, he formed the belief in an irrational manner, by stifling doubts and avoiding close scrutiny of available facts. Thus, he violated the ethics of intellectual life.

As Clifford says, "He had no right to believe on such evidence as was before him."[5] Even if we alter the story a bit and suppose that the ship was not unsound after all, the shipowner is still just as responsible. The question of intellectual duty here pertains not to the actual truth or falsity of the belief in question but to the way it is attained and held. John Stuart Mill makes this same point in his classic essay *On Liberty*, stating that even truth may reside in the mind as a prejudice, a superstition, and that this is beneath the dignity of a rational being.[6] If we have been intellectually irresponsible in forming a belief, even if the belief happens to be true, we are not justified in holding it.

Clifford's formulation of the ethics of belief is overly stringent, resting on a naturalistic model of rationality that allows only empirical evidence for all beliefs and is predisposed against religious belief.[7] It dismisses scores of common beliefs that we commonly take to be perfectly rational but for which we have no evidence—such as perceptual beliefs ("I see a tree") and memory beliefs ("I remember eating oatmeal this morning"). Moreover, Clifford's view favors those with high intelligence and thus tends to be elitist. However, none of these weaknesses constitutes grounds for dismissing the underlying conviction that we are rationally, and perhaps ethically, accountable for how we form our beliefs. The basic emphasis on intellectual responsibility is consistent with Christian theism and is especially relevant in the educational enterprise. However, we should not feel pressure to allow anti-theistic and anti-Christian assumptions to dictate the norms for rational belief. We also should be careful not to erect artificially high standards of rational belief that promote intellectual elitism.

Thoughtful Christians need to work out a conception of the rational process that acknowledges the need for intellectual responsibility in religious belief and still makes sense of the way many intellectually unsophisticated people come to God. The epistemological writings of Christian philosopher Alvin Plantinga provide assistance here.[8] For Plantinga, a good argument that cites appropriate evidence can provide rational warrant for a given belief. However, human beings also hold some beliefs that are not accepted on the basis of discursive argument but instead are formed directly through the operation of mental powers, such as perception. Plantinga maintains that these types of beliefs have rational warrant if they are the result of cognitive faculties functioning properly in an environment designed to accommodate the search for truth. This theory about how our beliefs acquire rational warrant is readily compatible with all we have said about a Christian worldview. Whatever the details of our Christian theory of rational belief may be, they will, at the very least, have to make sense of our divinely created need to see our beliefs as being true, justified, and reasonable. We are simply not made so as to think that our beliefs have no warrant. This is the case for both the uneducated person and the intellectual. An adequate concept of rational belief will also remind us of our stewardship of the mind, inviting us to employ our mental abilities to the fullest, regardless of the extent of our formal education.

To give the human intellect its proper due, we must seek a general theory of responsible, rational belief. To give Christian belief its due, we need this theory both to answer critics and to tutor the faithful. Clifford and other critics accuse religious believers of violating the ethics of intellectual life. Therefore, believers who seek to engage intellectual culture must come to an understanding of what really constitutes legitimate grounds for belief, particularly belief about the ultimate questions of life. Plantinga and others rightly point out that Clifford's empiricist and evidentialist approach accepts only certain tangible evidence. Thus, it is clearly prejudiced against any inquiry into nonempirical matters; it does not give Christian truth a fair chance. Unfortunately, some who embrace Christian faith make themselves vulnerable to the charge of irresponsible believing. They appear to be credulous persons, defending themselves by saying that their religious belief is a purely private matter which is not subject to any rational or ethical constraints. It is no wonder that nonbelievers sometimes characterize Christians as believing on fancy, ignoring all doubts, and filling their minds with comfortable and familiar ideas.

Christians cannot allow themselves to acquiesce in the comfortable and the familiar, thereby fostering a provinciality that precludes a wider understanding of Christianity and the world at large. If all truth is God's, and if the human mind is a precious gift from God, then Christians have nothing to fear from rigorous and thorough intellectual investigation. We must abandon easy answers that do not address the tough problems and must confidently launch open-ended exploration; we must also be willing to tolerate some ambiguity as we search for deeper insight. These are simply the risks of free, honest inquiry. Although avoiding uncomfortable questions and the intellectual work they demand may seem the safer strategy, it is actually extremely dangerous. If we hide intellectually, we do not do justice to God's creation whose truths exist for us to discover, and we fail to use our minds for his glory.

I will illustrate this with an example that is quite common. We all know that one's religious beliefs are sometimes challenged during college. Suppose a college student is exposed to new ideas that seem threatening to her religious understanding, and she experiences a crisis of faith. Her crisis cannot be completely resolved by urging her to have more faith. Eventually, she must deal with her doubts. If the doubts arose by *thinking* about certain issues, they will ultimately have to be dispelled by *thinking* further about those matters. No amount of spiritual devotion, firm resolve, or sheer willpower can eliminate them. No neat, prepackaged answers will provide a satisfying solution. Instead, the student should be encouraged to work through the various intellectual problems in a way appropriate to her level of intellectual development. Although this process involves ambiguity and risk, it is essential if she is to develop the intellectual strength and confidence to face other challenging issues that will inevitably arise.[9]

St. Paul's poignant directive to "take every thought captive to obey Christ" underscores the importance of relating everything we know to our faith. But we now know that thoughts cannot be brought into captivity, so to speak, by just any means; intellectual honesty must govern the methods we use.

Obviously, there are inappropriate means of inducing belief: peer pressure, propaganda, hypnosis, and drug therapy merely begin the list of ways to seduce the minds of others. Unfortunately, some religious groups seem willing to secure belief at any cost, either by disseminating propaganda, which ensures conformity, or by exerting social pressure, which discourages candid questioning.

Madeleine L'Engle illustrates the importance of intellectual integrity in *A Wrinkle in Time*. Her well-known children's story is about two children whose father, a scientist, has been taken captive on a distant planet by a cosmic evil force. The children have discovered their father's method of traveling through space and time called "wrinkling." The adventuresome children, six-year-old Charles Wallace, ten-year-old Meg, and her friend Calvin embark on a rescue mission that involves wrinkling through time to the planet where their father is imprisoned. During their odyssey, they learn that the whole universe is under attack by a sinister force and that some planets have already succumbed to it.

When they arrive to save their father, they find that the emissary of evil on the planet is called "the man with red eyes." The children know that they must confront him. As they make their way to the large metallic building in the center of the capital city, they observe that all the people are organized and useful, but stiff and unresponsive. All the tots simultaneously bounce their balls up and down on the sidewalks in front of their homes; all the mothers simultaneously pop their heads out the front doors of all the homes to call them in for supper; all the business people in town are dressed alike and look straight ahead as they walk. Without taking time to ponder the curiously uniform behavior, the children go to the building and find their way to the man with red eyes:

> Meg stared at the man in horrified fascination. His eyes were bright and had a reddish glow. Above his head was a light, and it glowed in the same manner as the eyes, pulsing, throbbing, in steady rhythm.

Charles Wallace shut his eyes tightly. "Close your eyes," he said to Meg and Calvin. "Don't look at the light. Don't look at his eyes. He'll hypnotize you."

"Clever, aren't you? Focusing your eyes would, of course, help," the soothing voice went on, "but there are other ways, my little man. Oh, yes, there are others ways."

"If you try it on me I shall kick you!" Charles Wallace said. It was the first time Meg had ever heard Charles Wallace suggesting violence.

"Oh, will you, indeed, my little man?" The thought was tolerant, amused, but four men in dark smocks appeared and flanked the children.

"Now, my dears," the words continued, "I shall of course have no need of recourse to violence, but I thought perhaps it would *save you pain* if I showed you at once that it would do you no good to try to oppose me. You see, what you will soon realize is that there is no need to fight me. Not only is there no need, but you will not have the slightest *desire* to do so. For why should you wish to fight someone who is here only to *save you pain and trouble?* For you, as well as for the rest of all the *happy, useful people* on this planet, I, in my own strength, am willing to assume all the pain, all the responsibility, all the burdens of thought and decision."

"We will make our own decisions, thank you," Charles Wallace said.

"But of course. And our decisions will be one, yours and mine. Don't you see how much better, how much *easier* for you that is?"[10]

My interpretation of this encounter is fairly obvious. I take the "man with red eyes" to be a type of *false Christ*. He demanded that the children relinquish the burden of thought and decision to him—what Michael Cain calls "psychic surrender."[11] After all, did not the man promise to make them just like "all the happy, useful people" on the planet? However, Christian theism cautions against directing one's mind to anything just because it is supposed to make us happy or useful or comfortable or anything else. It endorses believing something only because one genuinely sees it as true. The *real Christ* does not promise an end to intellectual hard work; he calls us right back to it. Thinking hard is a deeply spiritual matter.

In C. S. Lewis's *The Screwtape Letters*, uncle Screwtape, an experienced demon, advises his nephew Wormwood not to employ logical argument to try to lead his victim to hell:

> The trouble with argument is that it moves the whole struggle onto the Enemy's own ground [here "Enemy" refers to God]. He can argue too; whereas in really practical propaganda of the kind I am suggesting he has been shown for centuries to be greatly the inferior of Our Father Below. By the very act of arguing, you awaken the patient's reason; and once it is awake, who can foresee the result? Even if a particular train of thought can be twisted so as to end in our favor, you will find that you have been strengthening in your patient the fatal habit of attending to universal issues and withdrawing his attention from the stream of immediate sense experiences. Teach him to call it "real life" and don't let him ask what he means by "real."[12]

The message is clear: God is the Lord of truth and argument, the Master of giving reasons. Because intellect is an ally of genuine faith rather than a nemesis, Christians should not fear the intellectual process.

Let us examine St. Paul's words: "We destroy arguments and every proud obstacle raised up against the knowledge of God, and we take every thought captive to obey Christ."[13] Taking thoughts captive involves "destroying arguments." *Arguments*, of course, are simply *reasons for beliefs*, premises marshaled in support of a conclusion. When we accept a belief as true on the basis of reasons, we are embracing an argument. Argument in this sense is the only legitimate way to take a thought captive. There is no way to destroy an argument but on its own grounds; we must come up with stronger reasons and superior logic—in short, a better argument. We cannot close our eyes to an adverse argument or have faith enough to ignore it. Such responses allow the troublesome argument stand; they let it win.

There is absolutely no inconsistency between Christian commitment and the process of sincerely and openly seeking the truth. In fact, each activity draws life from the other; they are inseparably bound together. Commitment to Christ provides a focus for truth, and concern for truth keeps us from accepting fraudulent substitutes for Christ. In *The Drama of Atheist Humanism*, Henri de Lubac suggests that one great fallacy of the modern age is not simply that it has rejected Christ but that it has abandoned Socrates.[14] He cites Socrates, of course, as a symbol of the *love of truth*. De Lubac argues that when regard for objective, rational truth declined in our age, the possibility of maintaining Christianity as a *true* religion was undermined. Consequently, commitment to Christ has come to be characterized as stemming from personal bias, or driven by political agendas, or rooted in psychological needs. In this new environment, we may even call Christianity "true" as long as we relegate truth to the subjective realm ("what is true for me") or to the intersubjective ("what is true for my group"). Until our age recovers the high regard for real truth, calls to genuine religious commitment may fall on deaf ears.

Part of our role as Christians involved in education is to help restore the love of truth and the earnest search for it. We must not even breathe the slightest hint that there is a dichotomy between the intellectual life and the life of faith.[15] Indeed, because of our devotion to Christ, we should endeavor not merely to *know* and *teach* the truth in whatever area it may be found, but to *love* the truth and inspire others to love it too. After all, people are impelled not so much by what they know as by what they love. To love truth is to love something of Christ.

The Possibility of a Christian Mind

The Christian love of truth must have an impact on the intellect itself. If truth is important, then the mind is important because it is our instrument for seeking truth. We may actually speak of a *Christian mind* and define it as the ability to think within a Christian framework. Our ideal is to "think Christianly." Of course, to have a Christian mind is not merely to think about Christian matters, for the range and diversity of topics to which distinctively Christian thought applies is as broad and complex as reality itself. Neither is a Christian mind manifested by just any Christian who happens to think about a various problems and issues, since he or she may not be using Christian categories of thought. What I mean by the term "Christian mind" is a mind marked by the very way it processes information—its fundamental perspective, its guiding ideas, its overall aims. In a day when secular thinking is both strong and pervasive, we need to develop a lively awareness of what it means to think like a Christian.

Christians in our culture demonstrate their faith through many practical actions: feeding the hungry, caring for orphaned and at-risk children, assisting Third World countries in agricultural and medical endeavors, and so forth. While these projects are legitimate, they are not necessarily the result of penetrating intellectual reflection. There are also issues in high culture—the arts, the sciences, politics, philosophy, and other areas—that need to be addressed by Christians who think as Christians. Orthodox Christian thought contains unique insights into morality, society, nature, and other important realities—insights which would contribute wisdom and balance to countless issues in intellectual culture. Yet we see few Christian inroads into the ongoing cultural discussion. If we were to develop strong Christian thinking, it would greatly enhance our ability to exert intellectual influence on a number of prominent and pressing social problems: war and nuclear weapons, social and domestic violence, gender and ethnic concerns, aging, euthanasia, and many more.

My point is that Christian thinking—what I call a Christian mind—is desperately needed as a participant in constructive cultural discussions. Let me clarify the idea of a Christian mind by considering three questions. First, exactly what is the Christian mind? Second, to what degree has the Christian mind already been realized? Third, what are the main features of a Christian mind?

The concept of a Christian mind may be understood in two distinct senses. Perhaps the most obvious sense locates the Christian mind at the individual level. We definitely need many Christian individuals who spend their intellectual energies on important issues, making contributions at the highest levels in all fields of study: scientific research, economics, literature, music, and so forth. Although their numbers are relatively small, there are in fact a few Christians doing some of these things.[16] But these Christian scholars mainly work as isolated persons with no vital connection to a supportive intellectual community. Also, in spite of their degree of dedication, they typically function without an acute understanding of how Christian faith relates conceptually to their respective fields.

This brings us to the second sense in which we may speak of a Christian mind. A Christian mind can be understood as a collective phenomenon, a pool of discourse among thinkers operating within a shared frame of reference.[17] In its public dimension, a Christian mind would be an identifiable cultural presence that would play a significant role in our society's intellectual life. At this level, it is not an exaggeration to say that the Christian mind is almost nonexistent. The deep structures of modern intellectual life are essentially unaffected by any ideas that could be labeled Christian; instead they are almost completely influenced by the works of non-Christian and anti-Christian thinkers. The Jacques Derridas and the Stephen Hawkings of our times frame the high-level cultural discussions. The set of assumptions that are commonly taken for granted in cultural debate simply rule out the tenets of Christianity. Reasons for the marginalization of Christian ideas are legion, some tracing back to the Enlightenment and some to postmodern views concerning the relativity of truth and the political nature of speech.

In spite of the public absence of a Christian mind, there actually have been times when most major voices in intellectual and cultural discussions assumed the truth of Christian claims. Historian Mark Noll reminds us in *The Scandal of the Evangelical Mind* of two historical examples that demonstrate the reality of a collective Christian mind: one pertains to the various thrusts toward reform within the monastic movement during the Middle Ages and the other to the Protestant Reformation. Reviewing these two examples is both instructive and encouraging.

Noll first explains that the monastic movement within Catholicism during the Middle Ages was a key cultural influence, manifesting itself in St. Benedict in the sixth century, the monks at Cluny in the tenth, and the Dominicans and Franciscans in the thirteenth. Indeed, the work of St. Thomas Aquinas, a Dominican friar, eventually became the foundation of much intellectual endeavor in the Catholic Church.[18] Noll astutely observes that the intellectual impulses emanating from the monastic tradition were responsible for almost everything of lasting Christian value from the fourth to the fifteenth centuries.[19] These monks emphasized inward contemplation of the mercies of Christ, promoted aid for the disenfranchised, and encouraged energetic missionary efforts. Interestingly, their consecrated intellectual activity kept learning alive during the epoch now called the Dark Ages. They protected and passed on scriptural texts; they promulgated the learning of logic, languages, and other disciplines of the ancient liberal arts. Noll concludes: "Monks, in short, preserved the life of the mind when almost no one else was giving it a thought. By so doing, by God's grace, they preserved the church."[20]

According to Noll, the intellectual vitality surrounding the Protestant Reformation provides a second example of the very significant Christianizing influence in past culture. Many predicted that the Reformation would kill off the life of the mind that was rooted in the early church and had survived through the Middle Ages.[21] However, Martin Luther issued strong statements about the need to understand both the word of Scripture and the nature of the world.[22] Maintaining that the realm of the world was created by God to be studied, John Calvin undertook to educate the mind as well as to inspire the heart.[23] Although it is possible to find fault with aspects of the Reformation, as we may with monasticism, it contained a strong impulse toward distinctively Christian thinking about the whole range of human experience. Its influence on culture was profound.

Based on these two examples alone, we see that Christianity can and will have a considerable impact on culture when it involves thinking at the most fundamental levels. However, frequent neglect of—and sometimes outright hostility toward—intellectual activity has been a scandal in many wings of the church.[24] Those who hope to see Christianity affect culture in America and elsewhere must work toward the development of a strong public Christian mind. A very ambitious ideal indeed, but it is an important way we can bear fruit for Christ and his kingdom.

The present situation is not terribly encouraging for the future establishment a Christian mind. A Christian viewpoint is generally ignored in contemporary intellectual and cultural debates. We may, however, detect a few signs of hope. Evidence of serious intellectual discourse taking place within a shared frame of reference is easier to detect among Roman Catholics than among Protestants, but we can find evidence in both groups. The intellectual intensity of the medieval period continued throughout the centuries among Catholic academics. John Tracy Ellis treats this theme in *American Catholics and the Intellectual Life*.[25] Also, among contemporary Catholics, we simply find more visible public figures, such as Richard John Neuhaus and William Bennett, who project their voices into current cultural debates.[26] Protestant Christianity in America, on the other hand, does not seem to enjoy a common intellectual heritage which consistently nurtures sophisticated and critical thinking. Instead there are only pockets of serious intellectual activity, as we find, for example, with the Dutch Calvinists. A case in point is the Calvin College Center for Christian Scholarship, which has produced a number of fine scholarly studies on the relationship of Christianity to various intellectual issues. We can also gain a sense of hope for serious Christian intellectual expression in specific academic fields. In my own field of philosophy, the Society of Christian Philosophers is having a profound influence.[27]

None of these indicators of rigorous intellectual endeavor has yielded anything resembling a pervasive cultural influence. The secularizing influences in contemporary culture will almost certainly keep Christian thinking from ever being a dominant force again. Yet serious Christians should still strive to make a Christian mind a potent force, one that makes its presence felt and must be reckoned with in all debates. Therefore, the ideal of the Christian mind—one which engages other mentalities at work in the world, critiques them, and brings worthwhile insights into the mutual discussion—must still be pursued. Efforts toward this goal will meet with apathy in some sectors of the church universal and with outright hostility in others. Nevertheless, it is an important objective for the church to pursue as it attempts to penetrate culture intellectually.

If we are ever going to be able to sustain what I call a Christian mind, we must have a realistic understanding of its role in our social milieu. A Christian intellectual presence will undoubtedly be small and thus will have to win assent by rational and moral persuasion rather than by sheer majority of numbers. William Hull perceptively observes that "Christianity seems to work best from a modest position. That posture keeps its advocates humble, which is the paradoxically powerful servant stance. Furthermore, informed dissent keeps the dialogue honest and delivers the Christian apologist from the twin perils of complacency and authoritarianism."[28] I personally believe that this is the way God is opening for educated Christians in our day. It is up to us, then, to be faithful stewards of the intellectual credentials of the faith so that we may move ever closer to the reality of a public Christian mind.

What is the nature of distinctively Christian thinking? The initial response to this question is that the Christian mind sees things as a totality, as a unified whole. It does not suffer from the intellectual schizophrenia that besets many contemporary Christians who think about religious matters in Christian categories but think about almost everything else in secular terms. For the Christian intellectual, this too frequently means a kind of divided mental life with little or no connection between Christian truths, on the one hand, and the knowledge commonly accepted in one's discipline, on the other. A sound Christian view of intellectual life, and particularly a sound philosophy of education, echoes St. Paul's admonition: "Do not be conformed to this world, but be transformed by the renewing of your minds."[29] Christians need to allow the intellectual side of faith—its principal concepts and essential themes—to guide the way they think about everything. George Marsden admonishes Christian scholars to let their belief in God be relevant to their respective academic fields.[30] The ramifications of "transformed thought" will be far-reaching.

Of course, the sheer fact that we have a comprehensive, integrated view of things does not in itself constitute a uniquely Christian way of thinking, since some other worldviews, as we have already seen, offer a holistic vision as well. Their organizing principles are simply different and not related to Christian faith at all, although they still provide a high degree of intellectual integration and coherence for those who embrace them. Distinctively Christian thinking is integrated around Christian assumptions. These assumptions cannot provide ready answers for every problem but do provide reference points for thinking seriously about all issues that we face.

A Christian mind, first of all, assumes a *theistic and supernaturalistic frame of reference*. Although it endorses both nature and history as valuable and meaningful, it places them in the larger context of God's care and providence. It refuses to see nature as ultimate or the affairs of human history as the whole story. There is a transcendent, eternal, personal source of all, and in relation to it our true significance is understood. In this respect alone, the Christian mind differs radically from the pantheistic mind, the dualistic mind, and the secular mind.

A second characteristic of Christian thinking is that it is *creational in outlook*. It understands that reality is divided into two broad domains: the Creator and the creation. God brought everything else into being. The doctrine of creation implies that everything which exists is real, rational, and good. Being creaturely, however, means being dependent, contingent, and not self-sufficient. It means being finite and fallible but also possessing positive potentials that may be actualized through time and effort. When we realize that everything is a creature, it opens our minds to the fact that everything has the capacity to teach us something about God, the Creator.[31] This perspective implies that we have the responsibility to treat all aspects of creation as divine gift.

Third, the Christian mind possesses an *incarnational perspective*. A fundamental motif in Christian theology is that God identifies himself intimately with humanity. The unfolding theme of the Bible is that Christian life is more than living a religious life and being assured of heaven. It is participating in the quality of the life of God; it is being wonderfully transformed. The crowning expression of this is the incarnation of God in the man Jesus of Nazareth. The Christian thinker extends the incarnational viewpoint to all realms of creation, such that culture, scholarship, the arts, work and productive labor, and a host of other created realities are understood as needing to be penetrated and inhabited by the divine.

A fourth feature of the Christian mind is its *sacramental orientation toward life*. Augustine defined "sacrament" as a "visible sign of an invisible reality." Each Christian tradition has its own theological understanding of the rites through which partakers receive God's grace. The Roman Catholic and

Eastern Orthodox churches accept seven formal sacraments (baptism, confirmation, marriage, ordination, penance, the Eucharist, and annointing of the sick), and the Protestant denominations generally accept two (baptism and the Eucharist).[32] But an overall understanding of life as sacramental envisions many other created realities as potential channels of grace. Only the mystics claim to meet God directly in an unmediated experience. However, the rest of us, who live a more ordinary existence, must be able to recognize that a multitude of mundane objects, activities, and relationships can mediate God's grace to us. The ordinary can be sacramental.[33] Although any mundane thing may in some way become an avenue of grace (such as the starry heavens, the majestic grandeur of the Vermont Mountains, the lovely music of a Bach concerto, and even the sustaining discipline of work), the best candidates are human relationships—family and friends.

A *deep regard for the human person* is the fifth item on our list of ideas that constitute Christian thinking. "The Christian conception of the human person," observes Harry Blamires, "is a high one."[34] After all, God at creation pronounced human beings "very good." In the Incarnation, did he not take on our human nature and thereby exalt it beyond our comprehension? God's plan through the ages is to redeem and restore the wounded and fallen human creature. So, it is an essential trait of the Christian mind to place a value on personhood incommensurate with all other values. People today have lost sight of who God is and so cannot figure out who they are; they cannot comprehend the value and dignity of their own humanity. That is why the Christian mind must work diligently against the multitude of cultural forces that cheapen human life.

A sixth hallmark of Christian thinking is its *concept of truth*. Judaeo-Christian theism teaches that truth is based on the way things are—the way things are with God and with the created order. The connection between reality and truth is essential. Bernard of Clairvaux says it this way: "A wise man is one who savors all things as they really are."[35] Articulating a longstanding principle of Western metaphysics, St. Thomas states that "all things are true."[36] To have the ability to know truth is, for us, to exist in and be immersed in all that is; it means having a kinship with other things in the universe and thus an intellectual home.[37] The conviction that there is such a thing as truth and that the search for it is not futile serves as an anchor in our society's unsettled sea of skepticism and relativism.

A seventh feature of the Christian mind is its *recognition of evil*. While it acknowledges the supreme goodness and absolute power of God, and while it affirms the intrinsic goodness of the creation, Christian theism regards the world as being under the shadow of evil. Human beings, individually and collectively, cause evil in many forms. Distinctively Christian thinking does not hesitate to identify actions and programs as evil. It traces the root of evil to the perverse use of creaturely freedom: "The heart is deceitful above all things, and desperately wicked."[38] Consequently, Christian thinkers are not shocked by the presence of evil in a world that has largely turned away from God. In fact, they fully expect that there will be combat in the moral sphere as Christians stand against evil in our experience. The Christian recognition of evil is not self-righteous but is humbly accepting of our common guilt. It is we humans who have done this awful thing, turning God's world into a place where adultery, addiction, murder, slavery, war, and innumerable other horrors are prevalent.

The subject of evil is intimately connected to the fact of human suffering. The eighth element of the Christian mind, then, is its keen *sensitivity to the sufferings of others*. Clearly, human beings do not simply commit evil acts; they also suffer evil of various sorts. Injustice, disease, deformity, natural disaster, and death just begin the endless list. The Christian theist knows that in this world we are all vulnerable to pain and loss. These evils follow no predictable patterns. The story of the biblical patriarch Job illustrates that there is indeed undeserved suffering, a theme amplified in the New Testament in the teachings and ministry of Jesus.[39] Understanding the fragility of our

earthly existence is a precursor to genuine compassion that motivates our efforts to alleviate the suffering of others. I personally could not fathom calling any mentality truly Christian if it
lacked this perspective.

The eight characteristics above provide a good start for
thinking about the constitution of a Christian mind. More extensive discussion would include other characteristics as well:
faithfulness to revelation (the idea that God has made himself
known), *commitment to community* (including our connection
to the historic Christian community through tradition), and
appreciation of sacrifice (both that sacrifice which made possible
our redemption and the inherently sacrificial nature of all redemptive human efforts in cooperation with God). The more
completely we define the shape of Christian thinking, the more
we will see just how distinctive it is in contrast to secular thinking and to other religious ways of thinking as well.

THE CALL TO WHOLENESS

To speak of a Christian mind in purely intellectual terms is too
reductive. The use of the intellect is just one aspect of our created human nature, and Christian intellectual endeavor is but
one dimension of a total Christian life. Consider the poignant
New Testament passage dealing with the giving of the two great
commandments:

> When the Pharisees heard that he had silenced the Sad-
> ducees, they gathered together, and one of them, a lawyer,
> asked him a question to test him. "Teacher, which com-
> mandment in the law is the greatest?" He said to him, "'You
> shall love the Lord your God with all your heart, and with
> all your soul, and with all your mind.' This is the greatest
> and first commandment. And a second is like it: 'You shall
> love your neighbor as yourself.' On these two command-
> ments hang all the law and the prophets."[40]

The point of the first great commandment is not to propose that we are made of distinguishable parts which are individually and severally directed toward God. Actually, the Greek words for "heart" (*kardia*), "soul" (*psychē*), and "mind" (*dianoia*) function together in this passage to make just one key point: that there is a single, essential core to human personhood, a center which contains all our thoughts, motives, attitudes, and choices. It is this conscious center, in its totality, that we must yield to God.

I have argued throughout that we must be good stewards of the divinely created gift of intellect. That in itself is a high calling. But Jesus establishes an inestimably high ideal of loving God completely, thoroughly, with our whole being. The idea that the intellect and its endeavors must be dedicated to God is, therefore, placed in the wider perspective of a complete life that is wholly devoted to God. This use of intellect makes best sense in light of the holistic model of a Christian person: a person who is yielding every aspect of life to God.

Paul's letter to the Romans approaches this idea from an interesting perspective: "I appeal to you therefore, brothers and sisters, by the mercies of God, to present your bodies as a living sacrifice, holy and acceptable to God, which is your spiritual worship."[41] In describing the essence of spiritual worship, Paul says, "present your bodies as a living sacrifice." Paul does not use words such as "heart" or "soul" or "mind" in this passage. His use of the term "body" (*sōma*) implies an all-encompassing view of our human nature. The ancient Gnostic heresy and its modern variations—all of which downplay the importance of the physical in the name of spirituality—are immediately dispelled. Although Jesus' answer to the Pharisees emphasizes that spirituality involves the entirety of the inner life, Paul's statement here stresses that spiritual commitment also includes the outer life, bodily existence, and ethical behavior. The totality of life is encompassed. To put it simply: God wants all of us.

We are to surrender all aspects of the inner life (thoughts, intentions, decisions) and all aspects of the outer life (actions, relationships, life path) to God in love. This concept of personal wholeness and well-being is as profound as it is radical. The Christian ideal is one of integration and health in human personality, which would otherwise be broken and fragmented. Although none of us is completely whole, and none of us can claim perfection, we must proclaim that the Christian life is a journey into precisely this kind of life—what Dallas Willard calls the "transformation of the self."[42] All Christian philosophizing about the value and conduct of education must be done in light of this overarching vision of a total life.

A person's intellectual adoration of God and intellectual service to God must be rendered within the context of a whole life devoted to God. Similarly, any public Christian mind we achieve must itself be embedded within a vital, complete Christian community. This is simply the holistic principle applied at the corporate level. If a collective Christian intellectual presence does not abide within a dynamic, healthy Christian community, what ultimate impact can it have? Whatever truths we declare, whatever verities we defend, would lack full conviction and be devoid of persuasive power in a culture bristling with ideas vying for attention. Our culture needs to hear words of truth that speak of life, real life. But those words are meaningful only if the speakers share in real life themselves.

Jesus, that Life which is the True Life, instituted a redemptive society. He gathered a handful of rather unpromising men and women, infused his life into theirs, and built them into an intensive fellowship of worship, work, service, and love. The disturbing fact is that there is no substitute for the tiny redemptive society within larger society. If it fails, all is failure. Our lofty theorizing about a collective Christian mind is futile if Christian community is not taken seriously. The Christian community has been entrusted with sharing the divine life with all others, but its attempts to do so in the intellectual arena will not be effective unless it actively exhibits that life in all other areas. If we are to have genuine influence as God's people in the world, we need to be, as Elton Trueblood says, "A society of loving souls, set free from the self-seeking struggle for personal prestige and from all unreality."[43]

Admittedly, the church in the world is not always a loving community and does not consistently manifest the life of God. It is all too frequently ingrown, unloving, and indifferent toward social needs. Moreover, it has often neglected or disparaged intellectual efforts on behalf of Christ's kingdom. Yet the church in various guises does perform deeds of mercy, work against injustice, and give direction and healing to many. That is simply the paradox of the imperfect church representing a perfect Savior in an imperfect world. Dietrich Bonhoeffer warned against becoming disillusioned with the Christian community when it fails to match our romantic dreams of what it should be. For him, Christian community is not a wish or a fantasy but a divine reality "created by God in Christ in which we may participate."[44] Understanding this high privilege helps us see ourselves and other Christians within the fellowship as Christ sees us all.

Although the temporal church will always be imperfect, we must still strive to improve it. What we must work toward is the church functioning well as the whole body of Christ in the world: directing worship, strengthening families, engaging in evangelism, comforting the afflicted and oppressed, resisting forces of individual and collective evil, and addressing the influential intellectual movements of our day. When intimately connected to all the other legitimate operations of the body of Christ, the Christian intellectual pursuit of truth should properly flourish.

SALT AND LIGHT

Our love of truth is an expression of our love of God, and our complete love of God will overflow into love of the world he created. Our stewardship of the mind is diminished if it does not have the redemption of the world as its aim.

You are the salt of the earth; but if salt has lost its taste, how can its saltiness be restored? It is no longer good for anything, but is thrown out and trampled under foot.

You are the light of the world. A city built on a hill cannot be hid.

No one after lighting a lamp puts it under the bushel basket, but on the lampstand, and it gives light to all in the house.

In the same way, let your light shine before others, so that they may see your good works and give glory to your Father in heaven.[45]

Thus, we are salt, meant to permeate culture. We are the light, and our house is the whole world.

The church must come to grips with its relation to culture, being wary of total antagonism toward culture, on the one hand, and complete absorption into culture, on the other. It must find a way of being in the world that penetrates, uplifts, and transforms culture through Christ's power operating in all our thoughts, words, and deeds. In the words of Robert Briner, we need to be "roaring lambs."[46]

All of this should heighten our sensitivity to all the different ways in which Christians encounter culture. If Christ is not only the Head of the Church but also the Redeemer of the World, then the body of believers must represent him in the world. Unfortunately, criticisms of the church's actions in the larger society resemble the criticisms of its internal affairs. We can be unforgiving, judgmental, and isolationist. Just as we must strive for greater harmony within the body of believers, we must also be healthier in how the church encounters the contemporary world. We must *be changed* as we attempt *to change*. In order to represent God to others, we must cultivate attitudes that genuinely reflect the character of God. This same principle applies to Christians as they work to represent God in their intellectual endeavors.

What attitudes and virtues are appropriately Christian and particularly relevant in this regard? In his book *Habits of the*

Heart, Robert Bellah and his coauthors investigate the question of whether we can foster a meaningful civility. They use the term "civic friendship" to describe what they think can be a positive force in our fragmented and individualistic culture.[47] Author Richard Mouw admonishes the body of believers to display what he calls "Christian civility."[48] He suggests several positive ways for people to relate to each other, among them, the stance of humility over triumphalism. Humility includes flexibility, modesty in what we expect of others, and patience in waiting for God to work. This is an excellent place to start, as this posture implies that a fundamental level of respect is due to others simply because they are human beings. Authentic Christian civility is rooted in this creational concept.

There must, of course, be more to the Christian way of being in the world than displaying even the highest form of civility. Respect and fairness are both necessary traits, but we must also find within ourselves deeper levels of empathy and compassion that are not included in the idea of civility. The Vatican II statement on the church in the modern world eloquently addresses this theme:

> The joy and the hope, the grief and anguish of the men of our time, especially of those who are poor or afflicted in any way, are the joy and hope, the grief and anguish of the followers of Christ as well. Nothing that is genuinely human fails to find an echo in their hearts.[49]

We identify with the wounded side of humanity, not because we ourselves are self-sufficient and capable of offering a remedy but because we too are wounded and have found the Source of all healing. Christians need this attitude in all their transactions in our culture. Christians seeking to bear intellectual witness must exhibit this attitude as well.

Our call to be salt and light relates to both the structure and aims of education. Because of the premium placed on our rational powers, we cannot think of learning as merely the acquisition of information or the refinement of job skills. Ultimately, education must develop our divinely created abilities to think logically and to evaluate matters wisely. The concept of a Christian mind is that of an intellect that considers everything from a distinctively Christian frame of reference. The idea of a Christian mind must, in turn, be understood within the wider ambit of Christian life. Intellectual vitality should be but one expression of the energy radiating from that Life in which we participate. The principles of balance, integration, and holistic health are also part of this concept, both for individual Christians and for Christian communities. I believe that it is our sense of wholeness and spiritual health that makes our words ring true and makes our actions attractive to the world. All attempts to develop a complete Christian philosophy of education must take this larger perspective into account.

The call to be salt and light should prompt Christian scholars to examine their relationship to their fields and to our larger intellectual culture. Christians have an obligation to listen to and learn from the broader intellectual community. Moreover, they should master the concepts and techniques of their respective disciplines while displaying diplomacy, finesse, and mutuality to the highest reasonable degree. Salt is flavorful; it is an enhancer.

Does this mean that the Christian thinker and researcher must embrace all the presuppositions that prevail in his discipline or in the intellectual world at large? Must the Christian scholar base his thinking and research on assumptions that secular thinkers would also accept? Must he validate any relevant Christian insights by appeal to the criteria commonly accepted among secular thinkers? In some cases, the answers to these questions might be "yes." However, it is time for Christian scholars and thinkers seeking to penetrate and transform culture to formulate incisive critiques of assumptions that are accepted in their fields and to treat important subjects in ways that are informed by a decidedly Christian understanding. Plantinga declares that Christian academics need to display more "Christian courage" or "Christian boldness"; they need to think *as* Christians.[50] This kind of intellectual forthrightness stands a fighting chance at correcting serious distortions of reality that have become entrenched in various academic disciplines. There is, for instance, behavioral psychology's deeply rooted assumption that "personality is not a real thing" but only an aggregate of responses,[51] which needs to be challenged by Christian psychologists. There is also the longstanding position of many philosophers that there is not sufficient rational evidence for the existence of God, which must be stringently challenged by Christian philosophers.[52] Further examples can be found throughout the intellectual disciplines.

In addition to making efforts at being "salt and light" in their own disciplines, Christian intellectuals also have a duty to Christ's church, the body of believers. They actually have an obligation to do some of their thinking on behalf of the Christian community itself. This may mean channeling their expertise into specifically Christian causes or undertaking research projects of significance to Christians, which their professional peers could not envision. In this way, Christian academics could make the intellectual resources of this world available to the church. Furthermore, it is not only Christian intellectuals who have an obligation to put their professions to work for the church. Educated Christians in any profession whatsoever have an obligation to make their expertise and talents available in meaningful ways to the whole body of Christ. In so doing, we help give light to all who are in the house.

It is clear that for Christians education is not a badge or credential or a ticket into the job market; it is, rather, our reasonable service. We cannot acquiesce in the ultimate truth of Christianity but avoid seeking truths about the world it seeks to penetrate. If our mission is to help Christ save the world, we must take seriously the enormity and complexity of the task. Bringing redemption to human existence involves more than direct evangelization; it includes the search after truth and goodness in every sphere of life.

This mission may seem unrealistically visionary. However, every person and every educational community must have an ideal toward which to strive. We may not always live up to our ideals, but their presence in our lives is of supreme importance. There is no ideal more exhilarating or more worthwhile than that of education in the service of Christ. It deserves the best that is in us: stewardship of our talents, honor and virtue in all of our dealings, quality in our performances, honesty and rigor in our thinking. We need the ideal because it helps us to focus clearly on what it means to love God with all our minds.

Notes

CHAPTER ONE   What Is Philosophy of Education?

1. Dionysius of Halicarnassus, *Aristotle* xi.

2. Abraham Lincoln, "To the people of Sangamon Co.," March 9, 1832.

3. Charles Silberman, *Crisis in the Classroom: The Remaking of American Education* (New York: Vintage Books, 1970), p. 11.

4. Lawrence Cremin, *The Genius of American Education* (New York: Vintage Books, 1965), p. 30.

5. Neil Postman, *The End of Education: Redefining the Value of School* (New York: Vintage Books, 1996), pp. 3–7.

6. Proverbs 29:18 (KJV).

7. Three very helpful books that seek to express the core of Christian belief and experience are C. S. Lewis, *Mere Christianity* (New York: Macmillan, 1952); G. K. Chesterton, *Orthodoxy* (New York: Image Books, 1959); and John Stott, *Basic Christianity* (Grand Rapids, Mich.: Eerdmans, 1958).

8. For a list of the great historical councils, see *The Documents of Vatican II*, Walter M. Abbot, general ed., Joseph Gallagher, translation ed. (New York: The America Press, 1966), p. 740.

9. Vincent of Lérins, *The Commonitory*, trans. T. H. Bindley (London: Society for Promoting Christian Knowledge, 1914), p. 26. This is the location for the Vincentian rule.

10. Even before the great ecumenical councils were held, the text of the creed was assembled, probably around the year 150 A.D. Reaching its final, accepted form by about 700 A.D., the Apostles' Creed was considered a "symbol of the faith" (*symbolum apostolorum*). Also, by the second century, the three-fold structure of the creed was visible in questions asked of new Christians at their baptism. The Apostles' Creed in its entirety reads:

I believe in God the Father Almighty, maker of heaven and earth;

And in Jesus Christ his only son our Lord; who was conceived by the Holy Spirit, born of the Virgin Mary, suffered under Pontius Pilate, was crucified, dead, and buried; the third day he rose from the dead; he ascended into heaven, and sitteth at the right hand of God the Father Almighty; from thence he shall come to judge the quick and the dead.

I believe in the Holy Spirit, the holy catholic Church, the communion of saints, the forgiveness of sins, the resurrection of the body, and the life everlasting.

Amen

11. A brief anthology of sources on the beliefs of the early church is Henry Bettenson, ed., *Documents of the Christian Church* (New York: Oxford University Press, 1963).

12. *Anglican Thirty-Nine Articles*, art. 34, in *Subscription and Assent to the Thirty-nine Articles* (London: Society for Promoting Christian Knowledge, 1968), p. 64.

13. 2 Corinthians 5:19 (KJV).

14. *Catechism of the Catholic Church* (Liguori, Mo.: United States Catholic Conference, 1994), p. 7.

15. I follow tradition and the scriptures in using masculine pronouns throughout to refer to God. I am not implying in any sense that God possesses sexuality or a specific gender. Christian orthodoxy clearly teaches that God is not a sexual being.

16. 1 Corinthians 15:1–8 (RSV).

17. *The Westminster Confession*, art. 26. See the complete *Confession* included as the appendix in Paul Smith, *The Westminster Confession: Enjoying God Forever* (Chicago: Moody Press, 1998), p. 229.

18. Thomas Oden, *After Modernity—What?* (Grand Rapids: Zondervan, 1990), p. 177.

19. For a more complete discussion of issues in metaphysics, see William Hasker, *Metaphysics: Constructing a World View* (Downers Grove, Ill.: InterVarsity Press, 1983).

20. For a more complete discussion of basic issues in epistemology, see Roderick Chisholm, *Theory of Knowledge*, 2nd ed. (Englewood Cliffs, N.J.: Prentice-Hall, 1977).

21. For a more complete discussion of basic issues in ethics, see William Frankena, *Ethics* (Englewood Cliffs, N.J.: Prentice-Hall, 1973).

22. For a more complete discussion of the creation of a worldview, see Arthur Holmes, *Contours of a World View* (Grand Rapids, Mich.: Eerdmans, 1983).

23. Robert Beck, ed., *Perspectives in Philosophy: A Book of Readings*, 3rd ed. (New York: Holt, Rinehart and Winston, 1964), p. 3.

CHAPTER TWO   Traditional Philosophies of Education

1. It is important to understand how I use the concept of a worldview in this book. I am not investing it with the same meaning as did nineteenth-century German philosophers such as Hegel, Schopenhauer, and others. Their *Weltanschauung* meant a coherent and comprehensive viewpoint that is imposed on our experience in order to give it meaning and order. This *Weltanschauung* is essentially a product of mind ordering its experience and does not conform to my themes. Neither am I employing "worldview" in the way twentieth century sociologists of knowledge do. Asserting that historical and cultural factors shape and condition all knowledge, these thinkers maintain that all worldviews are relative to a given group at a given time. In this vein, Thomas Kuhn's term "paradigm" has become common for expressing the notion that human beings "project" mental constructs onto the world. By contrast, my use of "worldview" is more realistic, designating a set of ideas about the way the world really is. Of course, people can and do differ in their worldviews, and disputes along these lines are very difficult to settle. But this fact alone does not prove that worldviews are merely subjective or even intersubjective projections, constructs, models, or paradigms that tell us more about the persons holding them than they do about the world itself.

2. For a more complete discussion of the extent to which educational conclusions may be deduced from philosophical premises, see Harry S. Broudy, "How Philosophical Can Philosophy of Education Be?" *Journal of Philosophy* 52 (October 1955): 612–22; Hobart Burns, "The Logic of Educational Implications," *Educational Theory* 12 (January 1962); 53–63: Joe Burnett, "An Analysis of Some Philosophical and Theological Approaches to Formation of Educational Policy and Practice," *Proceedings of the Seventeenth Annual Meeting of the Philosophy of Education Society* (1961). See also Burnett, "Some Observations on the Logical Implications of Philosophical Theory for Educational Theory

and Practice," *Proceedings of the Fourteenth Annual Meeting of the Philosophy of Education Society* (1958): 51–57.

3. William Hocking, *Types of Philosophy*, 3rd ed. (New York: Scribner's, 1959), p. 152.

4. George Berkeley, *Principles of Human Knowledge*, in *The Empiricist* (Garden City, N.Y.: Anchor Books, 1974), p. 152.

5. Immanuel Kant, *Critique of Pure Reason*, B edition, trans. Norman Kemp Smith (London: Macmillan, 1929), pp. 1–2.

6. Immanuel Kant, *Foundations of the Metaphysics of Morals*, trans. Lewis White Beck, in *Kant: Foundations of the Metaphysics of Morals*, ed. Robert Paul Wolff (Indianapolis: Bobbs-Merrill, 1969), pp. 38–39.

7. In keeping with my microcosmic/macrocosmic model, I note that Kant wrote of the "systematic union of different rational beings by means of common laws." Immanuel Kant, *The Fundamental Principles of the Metaphysic of Ethics*, trans. Otto Manthey-Zorn (New York: Appleton-Century-Crofts, 1938), pp. 50–51.

8. Immanuel Kant, *The Critique of Pure Reason*, trans. Norman Kemp Smith (New York: St. Martin's Press, 1961), chap. 3, sec. 7, especially pp. 525–27. Also see the translation by Lewis White Beck (Chicago: University of Chicago Press, 1960), chap. 14.

9. For example, the orthodox Christian doctrine of original sin may simply be interpreted as a statement about the radical evil in human nature, which is the source of moral failing. Immanuel Kant, *Religion within the Bounds of Reason Alone*, trans. T. M. Greene and H. H. Hudson (New York: Harper and Row, 1960), especially bk. 1.

10. The realm of art is not merely the sensory world but the world of intellect in which genius and talent apply rules of practice to the work at hand. See Immanuel Kant, *Critique of Judgment*, trans. J. Bernard (London: Macmillan, 1982).

11. Herman H. Horne, "An Idealistic Philosophy of Education," in *Philosophies of Education: National Society for the Study of Education, Forty-first Yearbook*, part 1 (Chicago: University of Chicago Press, 1942), pp. 156–57.

12. See William Frankena, *Three Historical Philosophies of Education: Aristotle, Kant, Dewey* (Glenview, Ill.: Scott, Foresman, 1965), pp. 83–97.

13. J. Donald Butler, *Idealism in Education* (New York: Harper and Row, 1966), pp. 91–92.

14. Immanuel Kant, *Critique of Practical Reason*, trans. T. K. Abbot (London: Longmans Green, 1927), part 1, bk. 2, chap. 2, pp. 220–22.

15. G. E. Moore, "The Refutation of Idealism," *Philosophical Studies* (1922), reprinted in Morris Weitz, ed., *Twentieth-Century Philosophy: The Analytic Tradition* (New York: Macmillan, 1966), pp. 15–36.

16. Immanuel Kant, *Education*, trans. A. Churton (Ann Arbor: University of Michigan Press, 1960), pp. 15–36.

17. Kant, *Religion within the Bounds of Reason Alone*, p. 3.

18. Carl Sagan, *Cosmos* (New York: Random House, 1980), p. 4.

19. Ernest Nagel, "Naturalism Reconsidered," in Robert Beck, ed., *Perspectives in Philosophy* (New York: Holt, Rinehart and Winston, 1975), p. 191.

20. Some develop the idea that freedom is the unpredictability of human choices within an otherwise determined system, which I consider to be a kind of pseudo–free will. Physicist Edward Friedkin holds this position. See Robert Wright, *Three Scientists and Their God* (New York: Harper and Row, 1988), p. 67. Some philosophers argue for compatibilism, which is the position that freedom is compatible with determinism. See, for example, W. T. Stace, "Compatibilism," in Louis Pojman, ed., *Philosophy: The Quest for Truth* (Belmont, Calif.: Wadsworth, 1999), pp. 341–47.

21. Jacques Monod, *Chance and Necessity*, trans. Austryn Wainhouse (New York: Alfred A. Knopf, 1971), p. 146.

22. Nagel, "Naturalism," p. 196.

23. Nagel, "Naturalism," p. 193.

24. Julian Huxley, "The Uniqueness of Man," in *Man and the Modern World* (New York: Mentor, 1948), pp. 7–28.

25. Nagel, "Naturalism," p. 193.

26. Peter Singer, *Practical Ethics*, 2nd ed. (Cambridge: Cambridge University Press, 1993), p. 13.

27. "Humanist Manifesto II," in Richard Purtill, ed., *Philosophical Questions: An Introductory Anthology* (Englewood Cliffs, N.J.: Prentice-Hall, 1985), p. 341.

28. B. F. Skinner, *Science and Human Behavior* (New York: Macmillan, 1953). See also Skinner, *The Technology of Teaching* (New York: Appleton-Century-Crofts, 1968). Skinner's philosophical views are expressed in *Beyond Freedom and Dignity* (New York: Knopf, 1971).

29. Harry Broudy, *Building a Philosophy of Education* (Englewood Cliffs, N.J.: Prentice-Hall, 1954), p. 405.

30. Karl Marx, *Das Kapital*, vol. 1 (New York: Modern Library, n.d.), pp. 436–40.

31. Karl Marx, *Communist Manifesto*, in K. Marx and F. Engels, *Selected Works*, vol. 1 (Moscow: Foreign Languages Publishing House, 1962), pp. 33–69.

32. 32. Mortimer Adler, *The Difference of Man and the Difference It Makes* (New York: Fordham University Press, 1993).

33. C. S. Lewis, *Miracles* (New York: Macmillan, 1946), chap. 3.

34. For a more complete discussion of this kind of problem, see Nicholas Wolterstorff, *Educating for Responsible Action* (Grand Rapids, Mich.: Eerdmans, 1980), especially chap. 5.

35. See Armand Mauer's introduction to Thomas Aquinas, *On Being and Essence*, 2nd ed. (Toronto: Pontifical Institute of Medieval Studies, 1968), p. 10.

36. The heart of this philosophical position is found in Aquinas, *On Being and Essence*, 2nd ed. (Toronto: Pontifical Institute of Medieval Studies, 1968).

37. "And God said unto Moses, I AM THAT I AM: and he said, Thus shalt thou say unto the children of Israel, I AM hath sent me unto you." Exodus 3:14 (KJV).

38. Mortimer Adler, "In Defense of Philosophy of Education," in Nelson B. Henry, ed., *Philosophies of Education* (Chicago: National Society for the Study of Education, 1942), part 1, p. 211.

39. Etienne Gilson, *The Philosophy of St. Thomas*, trans. Edward Bullough (New York: Dorset Press, 1948), p. 311.

40. William McGucken, "The Philosophy of Catholic Education," in Henry, ed., *Philosophies of Education*, part 1, chap. 6.

41. St. Thomas Aquinas, *Summa Theologica*, q. 61, art, 1, in Anton C. Pegis, ed., *Introduction to St. Thomas Aquinas* (New York: Modern Library, 1948), pp. 586–89.

42. Jacques Maritain, *Creative Intuition in Art and Poetry*, Bollingen Series 35, no. 1 (New York: Pantheon Books, 1953), p. 161.

43. Ibid.

44. There was, in fact, interaction between ecclesiastical and lay Thomists. Hutchins prodded the ecclesiastical Thomists to make good on their promises of an integrative liberal education and they, in turn, took heart in the success of Hutchins's program at the University of Chicago. See Philip Gleason, *Contending with Modernity: Catholic Higher Education in the Twentieth Century* (New York: Oxford University Press, 1995).

45. Jacques Maritain, *Education at the Crossroads* (New Haven, Conn.: Yale University Press, 1943), pp. 1–2.

46. Jacques Maritain, *The Education of Man*, ed. D. Gallagher and I. Gallagher (Notre Dame, Ind.: University of Notre Dame Press, 1962), pp. 111–12.

47. For an explanation of the disintegration of the Thomistic synthesis by the middle of the twentieth century, see Gleason, *Contending*, pp. 297–304.

48. See the work of Ralph McInerny in communicating Thomism to contemporary culture: *A First Glance at St. Thomas: A Handbook for Peeping Thomists* (Notre Dame, Ind.: University of Notre Dame Press, 1990).

49. See Maritain, *Education at the Crossroads*, pp. 10–12, 23, 29–38.

50. Clark Pinnock, et al., *The Openness of God: A Biblical Challenge to the Traditional Understanding of God* (Downers Grove, Ill.: Intervarsity Press, 1994), pp. 86–87. Other books advocating an "open" God, somehow a moderate position between process and predestination views, include David Basinger, *The Case for Freewill Theism: A Philosophical Assessment* (Downers Grove, Ill.: Intervarsity Press, 1996), and John Sanders, *The God Who Risks: A Theology of Providence* (Downers Grove, Ill.: Intervarsity Press, 1998). Also, contemporary process philosophy offers a trenchant critique of the substantialist metaphysics of Aristotle and Aquinas in that they yield a static concept of deity. For a discussion of process thought, see Ronald Nash, ed., *Process Theology* (Grand Rapids, Mich.: Baker, 1987).

CHAPTER THREE   Contemporary Philosophies of Education

1. From the seventeenth century onward, the traditional confidence in formulating a worldview has seriously eroded. René Descartes showed that humankind's most basic beliefs about the existence of the external world, the reliability of sense perception, and even the existence of God can be subjected to extreme doubt. David Hume concluded that our basic beliefs are not supportable by argument and thus recommended skepticism about them. Immanuel Kant proposed that metaphysics is a kind of mental projection and does not constitute a true knowledge of reality. It is not surprising that philosophical positions that developed in this intellectual environment make no pretense to being comprehensive worldviews. Instead, each position limits itself to its own particular insights or approaches to specific intellectual problems.

2. John Childs, *Education and the Philosophy of Experimentalism* (New York: Century, 1931), pp. 50–51.

3. See John Dewey, *How We Think*, rev. ed. (Boston: D. C. Heath, 1933).

4. John Dewey, *Experience and Nature* (Chicago: Open Court, 1929), pp. iii.

5. John Dewey, *Art as Experience* (New York: Minton-Balch, 1934), p. 244.

6. Van Cleve Morris and Young Pai, *Philosophy and the American School: An Introduction to the Philosophy of Education*, 2nd ed. (Boston: Houghton Mifflin, 1976), p. 92.

7. John Dewey, *Democracy and Education* (New York: Macmillan, 1916), p. 257.

8. Morris and Pai, *Philosophy and the American School*, p. 280.

9. William James, *Pragmatism* (New York and London: Longmans, Green, 1959), p. 201.

10. Avrum Stroll and Richard Popkin, *Introduction to Philosophy*, 2nd ed. (New York: Holt, Rinehart and Winston, 1972), p. 373.

11. For a further discussion of enjoyable and admirable beauty, see Mortimer Adler, *Six Great Ideas* (New York: Macmillan, 1981), chaps. 15 and 16.

12. There is a piece of traditionalist humor which envisions a child approaching an experimentalist teacher as the school day begins, asking, "Mrs. Simpson, do we have to do what we want today?" The potential tyranny of wants and needs is all too clear in this scenario.

13. Morris and Pai present this experimentalist agenda in *Philosophy and the American School*, p. 283.

14. Jean Paul Sartre, *Existentialism and Human Emotions*, trans. Bernard Frechtman (New York: Philosophical Library, 1957), excerpted in Beck, ed., *Perspectives in Philosophy*, 3rd ed. (New York: Holt, Rinehart and Winston, 1975), p. 447.

15. Sartre, *Existentialism*, in Beck, pp. 501–3.

16. George Kneller, *Existentialism and Education* (New York: Philosophical Library, 1959), p. 59.

17. N. J. Blackham, *Six Existentialist Thinkers* (London: Routledge and Kegan Paul, 1952), pp. 155–56.

18. For a discussion of an existentialist theory of art, see E. F. Kaelin, *An Existentialist Aesthetic: The Theories of Sartre and Merleau-Ponty* (Madison: University of Wisconsin Press, 1962).

19. See Martin Buber, *I and Thou*, trans. W. Kaufmann (New York: Charles Scribner's Sons, 1970), and *Between Man and Man*, trans. R. G. Smith (New York: Macmillan, 1965).

20. Van Cleve Morris, *Existentialism in Education* (New York: Harper and Row, 1966), pp. 117–18.

21. See Robert Ulich, *Crisis and Hope in American Education* (Boston: Beacon, 1951), chap. 3. Ulich points out that education of the emotions is crucial for eventual self-actualization.

22. Kneller, *Existentialism and Education*, p. 133.

23. Jean Paul Sartre, *The Psychology of Imagination*, trans. B. Frechtman (New York: Philosophical Library, 1948), especially pp. 273–82.

24. See Robert Lloyd, *Images of Survival* (New York: Dodd, Mead, 1973). Lloyd portrays the inner dynamics of teaching and learning art from a rather existentialist point of view.

25. Ludwig Wittgenstein, *Tractatus Logico-Philosophicus*, trans. Pears and McGuinness (London: Routledge and Kegan Paul, 1961), p. 49, proposition 4.112.

26. For a presentation of the central concerns of logical positivism, see A. J. Ayer, ed., *Logical Positivism* (New York: Free Press, 1959).

27. For a presentation of general analytic philosophy, see Morris Weitz, ed., *Twentieth-Century Philosophy: The Analytic Tradition* (New York: Free Press, 1966).

28. R. S. Peters, *Ethics and Education* (London: George Allen and Unwin, 1966), p. 15.

29. Peters, *Ethics*, p. 15.

30. Arnold Levison, "The Uses of Philosophy and the Problems of Educators," in Joe Park, ed., *Selected Readings in the Philosophy of Education*, 4th ed. (New York: Macmillan, 1974), p. 17.

31. This example is found in Samuel Shermis, *Philosophic Foundations of Education* (New York: D. Van Nostrand, 1967), p. 266.

32. William Frankena, *Philosophy of Education* (New York: Macmillan, 1965), pp. 7–9. Also see Frankena, "A Model for Analyzing a Philosophy of Education," in Joe Park, ed., *Selected Readings in the Philosophy of Education*, 4th ed. (New York: Macmillan, 1974), pp. 139–44.

33. William Frankena, "Toward a Philosophy of the Philosophy of Education," *Harvard Educational Review* 26, no. 2 (Spring 1956): 95.

34. Frankena, *Philosophy of Education*, pp. 7–9.

35. Frankena, "A Model for Analyzing a Philosophy of Education," in Park, ed., *Selected Readings*, p. 143.

36. Frankena, *Philosophy of Education*, pp. 9–10.

37. Frankena, "A Model for Analyzing a Philosophy of Education," in Park, ed., *Selected Readings*, p. 141.

38. Jonas Soltis makes this point rather poetically in *An Introduction to the Analysis of Educational Concepts*, 2nd ed. (Reading, Mass.: Addison-Wesley Publishing, 1978), p. 82.

39. An excellent book that makes this point by its very title is James Sennet, ed., *The Analytic Theist: An Alvin Plantinga Reader* (Grand Rapids, Mich.: Eerdmans, 1998).

40. For example, see Alvin Kimel, Jr., and Donald D. Hook, "Calling God 'Father': A Theolinguistic Anlysis," *Faith and Philosophy* 12, no. 2 (1995): 207–22; also see Patricia Altenbernd Johnson, "Feminist Christian Philosophy," *Faith and Philosophy* 9, no. 3 (1992): 320–34.

41. William Alston, *Divine Nature and Human Language* (Ithaca, N.Y.: Cornell University Press, 1989).

42. For a survey and evaluation of the linguistic analysis of religion, see Michael Peterson, "Theology and Linguistic Analysis in the Twentieth Century," *Wesleyan Theological Journal* 15, no. 1 (1980): 19–33. See also Janet Soskice, "Religious Language," in Philip Quinn and Charles Taliaferro, eds., *A Companion to Philosophy of Religion* (Oxford: Blackwell Publishers, 1997), pp. 197–203.

43. Jean-François Lyotard, *The Postmodern Condition: A Report on Knowledge,* trans. Geoff Bennington and Brian Massumi (Minneapolis: University of Minnesota Press, 1999); also Brian Massumi, *Theory and History of Literature* (Minneapolis: University of Minnesota Press, 1984), 10:xxiv.

44. The modern mentality considered itself to have superseded a premodern mentality, which employs superstition, myth, and religion to interpret the world.

45. Dave Robinson, *Nietzsche and Postmodernism* (New York: Totem Books, 1999).

46. In de Saussure's terms, the bond between the "signifier" (word) and "signified" (thing) is purely arbitrary. The term "dog" (as a signifier) and the dog (as signified) have no special relationship.

47. Michel Foucault, see the attribution in "The Political Function of the Intellectual," in E. D. Klemke et al., *Philosophy: Contemporary Perspectives on Perennial Issues,* 4th ed. (New York: St. Martin's) p. 601.

48. Ronald Beiner, "Foucault's Hyper-liberalism," *Critical Review* (Summer 1995): 349–70.

49. Stanley Fish, *Is There a Text in This Class? The Authority of Interpretive Communities* (Cambridge and London: Harvard University Press, 1980).

50. Christine E. Sleeter, ed., *Empowerment through Multicultural Education* (Albany: State University of New York Press, 1991), pp. 20–21.

51. Postmodern historian Keith Jenkins writes: "In the post-modern world, then, arguably the content and context of history should be a generous series of methodologically reflexive studies of the makings of the histories of post-modernity itself. History becomes reflection on histories of reflection." Keith Jenkins, *Re-Thinking History* (London: Routledge, 1991), p. 70.

52. Gertrude Himmelfarb, "Where Have All the Footnotes Gone?" in *On Looking into the Abyss* (New York: Alfred Knopf, 1994).

53. Lyotard, *The Postmodern Condition: A Report on Knowledge*, p. 29.

54. Stanley Grenz, *A Primer on Postmodernism* (Grand Rapids, Mich.: Eerdmans, 1996), p. 130.

55. Richard Rorty, *The Consequences of Pragmatism* (Minneapolis: University of Minnesota Press, 1982), p. xiii.

56. E. D. Hirsh, *Innocence and Experience* (New Haven and London: Yale University Press, 1964), pp. 244–52.

57. Derrida calls this "playing with the text" or "troping." See *Glas* (1974) or *The Post Card* (1980). Of course, Stanley Fish argues that what a critic sees in a text depends on his point of view, and that his interpretation is an attempt to persuade others to share his perspective. See Stanley Fish, "Demonstration vs. Persuasion: Two Models of Criticism," in P. Hernadi, ed., *What Is Criticism?* (Bloomington: Indiana University Press, 1989), pp. 30–37. This essay is reprinted in *Is There a Text in This Class?*.

58. We could continue here with more questions: Is postmodernism's full-scale rejection of meta-narratives—with its story about how all cultures reflect power hierarchies, etc.—itself just another meta-narrative? Is postmodernism's account of how certain narratives seek illegitimately to suppress other narratives and become the dominant narrative simply an attempt at creating a new, dominant narrative?

Alan Sokal, a physicist at New York University, exposed the pretense of postmodernist scholarship in an article entitled "A Physicist Experiments with Cultural Studies." The article, intentionally riddled with inanities from the point of view of both physics and sociology, was published by the postmodernist journal *Social Text* (Spring/Summer

1996): 217–52. Sokal then announced in *Lingua Franca* that the article was a hoax, thus underscoring the shoddiness and insubstantiality of much postmodernist scholarship. In fact, it is reasonable to conclude that *Social Text* editors published his article because it was in line with their own views. This is shoddy scholarship published in the service of obvious political agendas.

For discussion on this hoax, see Sokal, "Transgressing the Boundaries: An Afterword," *Dissent* (Fall 1996): 93–97; Sokal, "Mystery Science Theatre," *Lingua Franca* (July/August 1996): 54–64; Bruce V. Lewenstein, "Science and Society: The Continuing Value of Reasoned Debate," *Chronicle of Higher Education* (June 21, 1996): B1–2; Liz McMillan, "The Science Wars," *Chronicle of Higher Education* (June 28, 1996): A8–9; Steven Weinberg, "Sokal's Hoax," *New York Review of Books* (August 8, 1996): 11–15; "Sokal's Hoax: An Exchange," *New York Review of Books* (October 3, 1996): 54–56; "Footnotes," *Chronicle of Higher Education* (November 22, 1996): A8.

59. C. S. Lewis, *The Abolition of Man* (New York: Macmillan, 1970), p. 91.

60. Merold Wesphal, for example, argues that the haughty spirit of modernism is met by the much more humble—and thus "biblical"—spirit of postmodernism. See "The Ostrich and the Boogeyman: Placing Postmodernism," *Christian Scholar's Review* 20, no. 2 (December 1990): 114–17. Westphal uses the term "epistemic humility" in regard to postmodernism. My argument here is not simply that faith under a radical postmodern description is arbitrary, but that it actually lacks a quality of humility that biblical faith has, which is an acceptance of and compliance with a Reality that one did not create.

61. Michel Foucault, *The Order of Things* (New York: Random House-Pantheon, 1971), pp. 342–43.

62. Psalm 8:3–8 (NRSV).

CHAPTER FOUR   Toward a Christian Perspective on Education

1. Tertullian, *On the Prescription against Heretics*, in *Tertullian: Apologetical and Practical Treatises*, trans. C. Dodgson (London: Oxford, 1854), chap. 7.

2. See E. G. Bewkes et al., *The Western Heritage of Faith and Reason*, 2nd ed. (New York: Harper and Row, 1963).

3. Daniel O'Connor and Francis Oakley, eds., *Creation: The Impact of an Idea* (New York: Charles Scribners' Sons, 1969), p. 7.

4. Lucretius, *On the Nature of Things,* in Richard Purtill, Michael MacDonald, and Peter Kreeft, eds., *Philosophical Questions: An Introductory Anthology* (Englewood Cliffs, N. J.: Prentice-Hall, 1985), pp. 70–79; Ernest Nagel, "Naturalism Reconsidered," from *Logic without Metaphysics* (New York: Free Press, 1956), excerpted in Harold Titus et al., eds., *The Range of Philosophy* (New York: D. Van Nostrand, 1975), pp. 326–33; Stephen Hawking, *A Brief History of Time* (London and New York: Bantam Press, 1998).

5. The passage reads as follows:

> And God said, Let us make man in our image, after our likeness: and let them have dominion over the fish of the sea, and over the fowl of the air, and over the cattle, and over all the earth, and over every creeping thing that creepeth upon the earth.
>
> So God created man in his own image, in the image of God created he him; male and female created he them.
>
> And God blessed them, and God said unto them, Be fruitful, and multiply, and replenish the earth, and subdue it: and have dominion over the fish of the sea, and over the fowl of the air, and over every living thing that moveth upon the earth.
>
> Genesis 1:26–28 (KJV)

6. The argument for a Christological focus for ontology could be mounted from numerous New Testament passages, such as the assertion that in Jesus Christ we live and move and have our being (Acts 17:28). There is also the wonderful passage from Colossians 1:15–17 (NRSV):

> He is the image of the invisible God, the firstborn of all creation; for in him all things in heaven and on earth were created, things visible and invisible, whether thrones or dominions or rulers or powers—all things have been created through him and for him.
>
> He himself is before all things, and in him all things hold together.

7. The idea of noetic powers that form beliefs in us has antecedents in Aristotle, Thomas Aquinas, Thomas Reid, and others. The Christian philosopher Alvin Plantinga presents this idea in the terminology of contemporary analytic philosophy. He shows that this view provides an

adequate account of how some beliefs can have rational warrant. See Alvin Plantinga, *Warrant and Proper Function* (New York: Oxford University Press, 1993).

8. See Arthur Holmes, *All Truth Is God's Truth* (Grand Rapids, Mich.: Eerdmans, 1977).

9. Thomas Aquinas, *Summa Theologica*, trans. Fathers of the English Dominican Province (Westminster, Md.: Christian Classics, 1911), q. 16, art. 5, part 1.

10. John 1:1–2; Col. 2:2–3; Col. 1:16–17; Acts 17:28.

11. Pope John Paul II, *On the Relationship between Faith and Reason: Fides et Ratio* (Washington, D.C.: United States Catholic Conference, 1998).

12. I think immediately of emotivism, which bases morality on subjective attitudes and reactions, situation ethics, which links moral decision to variables of the situation, and postmodernist ethics, which equates moral norms with the manipulation of power.

13. For further discussion of this point, see Keith Yandell, *Christianity and Philosophy* (Grand Rapids, Mich.: Eerdmans, 1984), p. 175. The reader may find helpful the appendix in C. S. Lewis, *The Abolition of Man* (New York: Macmillan, 1970). Lewis assembles examples of the universal moral law from all cultures and traditions—Buddhist, Hindu, Muslim, Christian, Jewish, etc.

14. A Christian ethical position rejects moral theories that are subjectivist or relativistic; it also rejects various versions of ethical egoism and utilitarianism.

15. I note that some theists have tried to establish a foundation of moral value by opting for a version of divine command ethics. This is the theory that the basis of moral obligation is the will of God. See Janine Marie Idziak, ed., *Divine Command Morality* (Toronto: Edwin Mellon Press, 1979). See also Idziak, "Ethics Is Based on Divine Commands," in Michael L. Peterson, ed., *Contemporary Debates in Philosophy of Religion* (Oxford: Blackwell Publishers, forthcoming). However, a theory of divine command ethics encounters a number of difficulties (e.g., the problem of how sheer willing, whether human or divine, can itself be ethically normative). Thus, whatever else may be said for divine command ethics, at the very least we must take into account the kind of being who is addressed by the commands, which brings us to our ontological grounding for ethics in human personhood created in the image of God.

16. For a more complete exploration of the ontological basis of morality in the structure of our personhood, see Henry Veatch, *For an Ontology of Morals* (Evanston, Ill.: Northwestern University Press, 1979).

17. Yandell, *Christianity and Philosophy*, p. 266.

18. We can contrast this Christian view I am developing with Immanuel Kant's view of the subjective side of morality. Kant realizes that simply conforming our behavior to the objective demands of duty is not sufficient for an action to be fully moral. One must obey the laws of duty with the right motive. For Kant, desire for praise, pleasure, gain, or anything else destroys the moral quality of an action. Kantian ethics recognizes the only truly moral motive as sheer respect for duty. Kant's quite stringent view is noble in its own way, for he realized that moral life cannot be reduced merely to acting in accord with duty; one's motives are an essential consideration. Yet his proposal that respect for duty is the sole moral motive is unduly restrictive. Ironically, Kant argued that we can never know the natures of things (things-in-themselves). This implies that we cannot have full knowledge of human nature. The result is that Kantian ethics developed without an investigation into the nature of humanity itself! It is not so surprising that we are left with a highly rationalistic approach to moral life that can accept only the rational apprehension of duty coupled with the motive of respect for duty.

19. Christian moral theory, therefore, cannot agree with the utilitarianism of John Stuart Mill. Mill states: Society cares not what manner of man obeys, just so he obeys (*On Liberty*). We must care deeply about the inward quality of the person, in addition to his or her obedience to objective ethical principles. On the other hand, Christian moral theory must reject the Kantian view that a moral agent performs an act of ethical obedience through the single motive of sheer respect for duty. A Christian perspective places moral life in a much larger perspective, recognizing a number of morally relevant motives and dispositions to act.

20. St. Thomas Aquinas, *Summa Theologica*, q. 91, art. 2 in *Treatise on Law*, ed. Stanley Parry (Chicago: Regnery Gateway, 1949), p. 16.

21. C. S. Lewis, *The Abolition of Man* (New York: Simon and Schuster, 1996).

22. The Greek word for blessed that recurs throughout Matthew 5:1–12 is *makarioi*. Interestingly, *makarioi* is related to the word *eudaimonia*, which Aristotle used. Both words can be translated as happy, blessed, or fulfilled. In both the New Testament and in Aristotle's writings, the words used denote the fulfillment of our human nature that

comes through morally virtuous activity. I am grateful to my colleague Gerald Miller for his advice on how to translate these Greek words in the contexts in question.

23. Claude Tresmontant, *Christian Metaphysics*, trans. Gerard Slevin (New York: Sheed and Ward, 1965), pp. 95–97.

24. Psalms 19:1 (NRSV).

25. Cited in Mortimer Adler, *Six Great Ideas* (New York: Macmillan, 1981), pp. 112–13.

26. See Maritain, *Education at the Crossroads* (New Haven, Conn.: Yale University Press, 1943), p. 24.

27. *Heidelberg Catechism* (Philadelphia and Boston: United Church Press, 1962) and *Westminster Shorter Catechism* (New York: M. W. Dodd, 1856).

28. See Niel McCluskey, S.J., ed. *Catholic Education in America: A Documentary History* (New York: Columbia University Press, 1964); and James Michael Lee, ed., *Catholic Education in the Western World* (Notre Dame, Ind.: University of Notre Dame Press, 1967). For those particularly interested in the impact of Vatican II, see *Vatican Council II: Its Challenge to Education*, ed. George Donovan (Washington, D.C.: The Catholic University of America Press, 1967).

29. See the discussion in Kerry L. Morgan, *Real Choice, Real Freedom in American Education: The Legal and Constitutional Case for Parental Rights and against Governmental Control of American Education* (Lanham, Md.: University Press of America, 1997).

30. Holmes, *All Truth Is God's Truth.*

31. Jerome Bruner, *The Process of Education* (Cambridge: Harvard University Press, 1960). Bruner is not a realist who believes that the structure of knowledge is based in the nature of things instead he believes that the structure that knowledge takes is imposed on it by the human mind.

32. George Miller, "The Magical Number Seven, Plus or Minus Two," *Psychological Review* 64 (1956): 81–97.

33. It is well worth taking a close look at the studies cited by Hirsch as he builds his argument for cultural literacy. Particularly see chapters 1 and 2 in E. D. Hirsch, Jr., *Cultural Literacy: What Every American Needs to Know* (Boston: Houghton Mifflin, 1987).

34. Hirsch, Jr., *Cultural Literacy.*

35. For example, by age thirteen, Catholic children are confirmed, Jewish children have a bar or bat mitzvah, and many tribal children expe-

rience various sorts of rites of passage into adulthood. Also, in many Asian cultures, the children are required to do extensive memorization of sacred scriptures, cultural narratives, and the like.

36. Robert Paul Wolff, *The Ideal of the University* (Boston: Beacon Press, 1069), p. 8.

37. Josef Pieper, *Living the Truth* (San Francisco: St. Ignatius Press, 1989), p. 80.

38. This is a basic theme in Philip Phenix, *Education and the Common Good: A Moral Philosophy of the Curriculum* (Westport, Conn.: Greenwood, 1977).

39. Arthur Chickering, *Education and Identity* (San Francisco: Jossey-Bass, 1969). A description of this overly optimistic and romantic movement in education is found in Robert Glaser, "Education and Thinking: The Role of Knowledge," *American Psychologist* 39 (January 1984): 93–104.

40. Mortimer J. Adler, *The Paideia Proposal* (New York: Macmillan, 1982), p. 22.

41. The first edition of *Great Books of the Western World* appeared in 1952 and had fifty-four volumes. The second edition, appearing in 1990, added six more volumes. Both sets contained an extremely helpful topical index to discussions of the great ideas contained in the great books, the *Syntopicon*. Now, the topics and related essays on them in the *Syntopicon* are gathered in Mortimer Adler, *The Great Ideas of Western Thought* (New York: Macmillan, 1992).

42. Two typical biblical passages that support the view that knowledge of moral law is part of natural revelation are Romans 1:18–20 and Romans 2:14–15.

CHAPTER FIVE   Issues in Educational Theory

1. This ideal is connected to the classical understanding of "human flourishing." The flourishing of anything is the proper fulfillment of its unique nature; and this is true happiness. Thus, from the perspective of education, there has to be significant exposure to those subjects that help us understand what it means to be human. Although Aristotle expressed this position in the *Nicomachean Ethics,* St. Thomas Aquinas develops it from a Christian point of view. See Aquinas, *Treatise on Happiness,* trans. John A. Oesterle (Notre Dame, Ind.: University of Notre Dame Press, 1983).

2. Philip Gleason traces the threads of Catholic discussion on integration in *Contending with Modernity: Catholic Higher Education in the Twentieth Century* (New York: Oxford University Press, 1995). See also Robert Hutchins, "The Integrating Principle of Catholic Higher Education," *College Newsletter, Midwest Regional Unit* (May 1937).

3. The most widely read work on this subject among Protestants in higher education, originally published in 1975, is Arthur F. Holmes, *The Idea of a Christian College* (Grand Rapids, Mich.: Eerdmans, 1994).

4. To cite but one example, the journal *Faculty Dialogue* was founded in 1984 by the Institute for Christian Leadership in order to advance the discussion among evangelicals in higher education.

5. Hughes and Adrian contend that different Christian traditions have different ideas about what they consider integration to be. See Richard T. Hughes and William B. Adrian, eds., *Models for Christian Higher Education: Strategies for Success in the Twenty-First Century* (Grand Rapids, Mich., and Cambridge, U.K.: Eerdmans, 1997).

6. Holmes, *The Idea of a Christian College*, especially chap 4. For a discussion of various aspects of the Christian concept of the integration of truth, see Holmes, *All Truth Is God's Truth* (Grand Rapids, Mich.: Eerdmans, 1977).

7. Robert Paul Wolff, *The Ideal of the University* (Boston: Beacon Press, 1969), pp. 76–79.

8. For a fascinating proposal along these lines (called a trilinear curriculum), see Warren B. Martin, *College of Character* (San Francisco: Jossey-Bass, 1963), chap. 7.

9. E. Harris Harbison, "Liberal Education and Christian Education," in Edmund Fuller, ed., *The Christian Idea of Education* (New Haven, Conn.: Yale University Press, 1962), p. 60.

10. See Edward L. R. Elson, "Life's Single Vocation," in Michael L. Peterson, ed., *A Spectrum of Thought* (Wilmore, Ky.: Francis Asbury Press, 1982), chap. 1.

11. See Mortimer Adler, *The Paideia Proposal* (New York: Macmillan, 1982).

12. In contemplating and resolving the moral dilemma with which she is presented, the student employs a pattern of moral reasoning. It is this pattern of reasoning that educators use as an indicator of her stage of moral development: pre-conventional (based on rewards and punishments), conventional (based on conformity to rules), or post-conventional (based on autonomous choice). For a summary of how the Piaget-Kohlberg strategy

is used, see Brian Hall, *Value Clarification as Learning Process: A Sourcebook of Learning Theory* (New York: Paulist Press, 1973).

While there are some benefits in the Piaget-Kohlbert approach to moral education, it suffers from serious problems. First, it and many other contemporary moral development strategies fail to recognize any objective standard of morality. They all elevate either the individual or society to the status of supreme arbiter of values. Second, it and other current theories fall remarkably short on the matter of teaching responsible moral action. This weakness is due largely to the fact that they fixate on cognitive and developmental factors. The view of human nature that we have been developing here requires that sound moral education address both volition and behavior, on the one hand, and cognition, on the other.

13. John Childs, *Education and Morals* (New York: John Wiley and Sons, 1967), p. 17.

14. We could chart a theoretical position at the other extreme, although it has few active proponents in educational philosophy. This second extreme position virtually identifies knowledge and virtue. Proponents of this position believe that theoretical knowledge translates readily into practical action: that is, that really knowing what is right is a sufficient condition for doing it. This approach reduces moral instruction to conveying correct moral information, with the assumption that simply telling students what they ought to do will tend to result in their doing it. Although the first position is too weak, this position is too strong. Moral education cannot be confined to the transmission of moral teachings. Doing so ignores the fact of life that some people knowingly and willingly do wrong. Thus, it lacks a recognition of what the Bible calls sin. It also overlooks other matters relevant to moral performance, such as the need to habituate the young to behavioral patterns of moral conduct. Of course, even though we reject the notion that correct moral knowledge automatically yields proper conduct, we still insist that moral knowledge must be clearly articulated and discussed in the education of our youth.

15. Rachel Smolkin, "Educators Say You Can Teach Morals without Religion," story carried by Scripps Howard News Service, June 25, 1999.

16. Nicholas Wolterstorff, *Educating for Responsible Action* (Grand Rapids, Mich.: Eerdmans, 1980).

17. Richard S. Peters, "Reason and Habit: The Paradox of Moral Education," in *Moral Education in a Changing Society*, ed. William Niblet (London: Faber and Faber, 1963), pp. 46–65.

18. Aristotle, *Nicomachean Ethics*, bk. 2, chap. 1, in *Introduction to Aristotle*, ed. Richard McKeon (New York: Modern Library, 1947), pp. 331–32.

19. William J. Bennett, *The Book of Virtues: A Treasury of Great Moral Stories* (New York: Simon and Schuster, 1993). Also see William Bennett, *The Moral Compass: Stories for Life's Journey* (New York: Simon and Schuster, 1995).

20. Consider the case made by C. S. Lewis that the Moral Law, or the Chinese Tao, is common to all humanity. See *The Abolition of Man* (New York: Macmillan, 1965). Also note his remark that our differences "never amounted to anything like a total difference." See *Mere Christianity* (New York: Macmillan, 1952), p. 71.

21. Charles Malik, *Wheaton College Bulletin*, "Fallacies of the Age" (July 1981): 6. See also Robert Hutchins, *The Conflict in Education in a Democratic Society* (Westport, Conn.: Greenwood Press, 1972), pp. 71–72.

22. Philip Phenix, *Religious Concerns in Contemporary Education: A Study of Reciprocal Relations* (New York: Teachers College of Columbia University, 1959), pp. 60–61.

23. Jacques Maritain, *Education at the Crossroads* (New Haven, Conn.: Yale University Press, 1943), p. 39.

24. Ben Witherington, *Jesus the Sage: The Pilgrimage of Wisdom* (Philadelphia: Fortress Press, 1994).

25. Note that the Jewish attitude toward learning parallels that toward teaching. The book of Proverbs states: "Keep hold of instruction, do not let go; guard her for she is your life" (4:13 RSV). The Talmud warns that "an ignorant man cannot be a pious man," indicating that intellectual apathy and neglect is spiritual suicide (quoted from Morris Kertzer, *What Is a Jew?* [New York: Collier Books, 1960], p. 73). For further discussion of the Jewish attitude toward education, see Marvin Wilson, "The Jewish Concept of Learning: A Christian Appreciation," *Christian Scholar's Review* 5, no. 4 (1976): 350–63.

26. Jesus was also called *rabbonni*, which is the heightened form of *rabbi*. It means "my lord, my master."

27. Phenix, *Religious Concerns*, p. 80.

28. B. P. Komisar, "Teaching: Act and Enterprise," in C. J. B. Macmillan and T. W. Nelson, eds., *Concepts of Teaching* (Chicago: Rand McNally, 1968), p. 77.

29. Wordsworth's exact words are: "What is a Poet? To whom does he address himself? And what language is to be expected from him?—He

is a man speaking to men: a man, it is true, endowed with more lively sensibility, more enthusiasm and tenderness, who has greater knowledge of human nature, and a more comprehensive soul, than are supposed to be common among mankind." William Wordsworth, *Preface to Lyrical Ballads.*

30. Abraham Joshua Heschel, "The Spirit of Jewish Education," *Jewish Education* 24, no. 2 (Fall 1953): 19.

CHAPTER SIX   Issues in Educational Practice

1. See R. Freeman Butts, *A Cultural History of Education: Reassessing Our Educational Traditions* (New York: McGraw-Hill, 1947), p. 624.

2. *The Declaration of Independence and The Constitution of the United States* (New York: Bantam Books, 1998), p. 78.

3. For further reading on the separation of church and state, see Robert Cord, *Separation of Church and State: Historical Fact and Current Fiction* (New York: Lambeth Press, 1982).

4. See C. D. Batson, P. Schoenrade, and W. C. Ventis, *Religion and the Individual: A Social Psychological Perspective* (New York: Oxford University Press, 1993); A. E. Bergin, K. S. Masters, and P. S. Richards, "Religiousness and Mental Health Reconsidered: A Study of an Intrinsically Religious Sample," *Journal of Counseling Psychology* 34 (1987): 197–204; J. Gartner, D. B. Larson, and G. D. Allen, "Religious Commitment and Mental Health: A Review of the Empirical Literature," *Journal of Psychology and Theology* 19 (1991): 6–25; I. R. Payne, A. E. Bergin, K. A. Bielema, and P. H. Jenkins, "Review of Religion and Mental Health: Prevention and the Enhancement of Psychosocial Functioning," *Prevention in Human Services* 9 (1991): 11–40; P. S. Richards, "Religious Devoutness in College Students: Relations with Emotional Adjustment and Psychological Separation from Parents," *Journal of Counseling Psychology* 38 (1991): 189–96.

5. D. Munby, *The Idea of a Secular Society and Its Significance for Christians* (London: Oxford University Press, 1963).

6. "We hold these truths to be self-evident, that all Men are created equal, that they are endowed by their creator with certain unalienable rights, that among these are Life, Liberty, and the Pursuit of Happiness. . . ." The Declaration of Independence, by the action of the

Second Continental Congress, July 3, 1776 (in *The Declaration of Independence and The Constitution of the United States*, p. 53).

7. For a common-sense discussion of relevant factors, see Barbara Thompson, "The Debate over Public Schools: The View from the Principal's Office," *Christianity Today* 7 (September 1984): 19–23.

8. It is worth quoting Amendment 1 in its entirety: "Congress shall make no law respecting an establishment of religion, or prohibiting the free exercise thereof; of abridging the freedom of speech, or of the press; or the right of the people peaceably to assemble, and to petition the government for a redress of grievances." The Bill of Rights, in *The Declaration of Independence and The Constitution of the United States*, p. 78.

9. Plato, *The Apology*, in *The Trial and Death of Socrates*, trans. G. M. A. Grube (Indianapolis: Hackett Press, 1975).

10. See Hastings Rashdall, *The Universities of Europe in the Middle Ages*, 3 vols. (Oxford: Clarendon Press, 1936).

11. For a fascinating discussion of the medieval origins of the concept of academic freedom and its link to tenure, see Robert Nisbet, *The Degradation of the Academic Dogma*, part 2 (New York: Basic Books, 1971), p. 62.

12. Robert Hutchins is a noteworthy representative of this point of view. In a memorable address, he declared, "A university is a community of scholars. . . . Freedom of inquiry, freedom of discussion, and freedom of teaching—without these a university cannot exist. . . . The university exists only to find and to communicate the truth. If it cannot do that it is no longer a university." Quoted in David Fellman, "Free Teachers—The Priesthood of Democracy," in H. Ehlers and G. Lee, eds., *Crucial Issues in Education*, 3rd ed. (New York: Holt, Rinehart and Winston, 1966), pp. 17–18.

13. Nisbet, *Degradation*, p. 64.

14. One interesting discussion regards the relation of *Ex Corde Ecclesiae* to academic freedom as conceived under the norms expressed in the American Association of University Professors (AAUP) 1940 *Statement of Principles on Academic Freedom and Tenure. See Ex Corde Ecclesia: A Conversation "From the Heart of the Church,"* September 18, 1999 (Washington, D. C.: The Catholic University of America, 1999), pp. 49–58.

15. For an interesting discussion regarding the ways in which truth can need a helping hand, see William F. Buckley, *God and Man at Yale*, 2nd ed. (South Bend, Ind.: Gateway Editions, 1977), p. 64.

16. The case of Father Curran triggered an important and fascinating debate over the nature and extent of academic freedom within an academic setting with a confessional stance. See, for example, John F. Hunt

and Terrence R. Connelly, *The Responsibility of Dissent: The Church and Academic Freedom* (New York: Sheed and Ward, 1969).

17. See Philip Phenix, *Religious Concerns* in *Contemporary Education* (New York: Teachers College, 1959), pp. 96–99; Arthur F. Holmes, *The Idea of a Christian College* (Grand Rapids, Mich.: Eerdmans, 1994), pp. 62–64.

18. Quoted in A. Schlesinger, Jr., *The Disuniting of America: Reflections on a Multi-cultural Society* (Knoxville, Tenn.: Whittle Direct Books, 1992), p. 33.

19. One example of this was the push for "ebonics" or AAL (African American Language). See Selase Williams, "Classroom Use of African American Language: Educational Tool or Social Weapon?" in Christine Sleeter, ed., *Empowerment Through Multicultural Education* (Albany: State University of New York Press, 1991), pp. 205–7. See also Judith Renyi, *Going Public: Schooling for a Diverse Democracy* (New York: New York Press, 1993), p. 122.

20. Stanley Fish, *National Forum: Phi Kappa Phi Journal* (Summer 1989): 14.

21.

> Ah, you who make iniquitous decrees, who write oppressive statutes,
>
> to turn aside the needy from justice and to rob the poor of my people of their right, that widows may be your spoil, and that you may make the orphans your prey!
>
> Isa 10:1–2 (NRSV)
>
> As for the Levites resident in your towns, do not neglect them, because they have no allotment or inheritance with you.
>
> Every third year you shall bring out the full tithe of your produce for that year, and store it within your towns;
>
> The Levites, because they have no allotment or inheritance with you, as well as the resident aliens, the orphans, and the widows in your towns, may come and eat their fill so that the LORD your God may bless you in all the work that you undertake.
>
> Deut 14:27–29 (NRSV)

Also consult Deut 26:11–13. See also Nicholas Wolterstorff, *Until Justice and Peace Embrace* (Grand Rapids, Mich.: Eerdmans, 1983).

22. Who could deny that the English language is the most multicultural of all languages, with words borrowed or derived from German, French, Italian, Arabic, Swedish, Greek, and many other languages?

23. Galatians 3:26–28 (NRSV).

24. E. D. Hirsch, Jr., *Cultural Literacy: What Every American Needs to Know* (Boston: Houghton Mifflin, 1987).

25. Linda Chavez, "Should America Foster Cultural Diversity?" *Special Report*, no. 66 (Grove City College, January 1993): 3.

26. Chavez, "Should American Foster Cultural Diversity?" p. 4.

27. Aristotle, *Nicomachean Ethics*, 1177b32–1178a4, trans. W. D. Ross, in *Introduction to Aristotle*, ed. Richard McKeon (New York: Random House, 1947), p. 534.

28. C. S. Lewis, *The Four Loves* (New York: Harcourt, Brace, and Co., 1960), p. 180.

29. Unless otherwise noted, all data to follow is found in Edmund J. Hansen, "Essential Demographics of Today's College Students, *American Association of Higher Education Bulletin* 51, no. 3 (November 1998): 3–5.

30. Cited in Henry Wechsler et al., "Too Many Colleges Are Still in Denial about Alcohol Abuse," *Chronicle of Higher Education*, April 14, 1995, p. B1. See also Joseph A. Califano, Jr., "Rethinking Rites of Passage: Substance Abuse on America's Campuses," *New York Times*, June 11, 1994.

31. Cited in W. H. Willimon, *Abandoned Generation: Rethinking Higher Education* (Grand Rapids, Mich.: Eerdmans, 1995), p. 11.

32. Quoted in T. H. Naylor, W. H. Willimon, and Mr. R. Naylor, *The Search for Meaning* (Nashville, Tenn.: Abingdon, 1994), p. 12.

33. Genesis 2:24 indicates that the marriage bond between a man and a woman creates a new reality, or "one flesh." Song of Songs celebrates the beauty and purity of romantic, heterosexual, monogamous love. Jesus blesses marriage in the New Testament with his first miracle (John 2:1–10). Various New Testament documents, such as Ephesians, directly address the importance of marriage and family.

34. See Elton Trueblood, *The Recovery of Family Life* (New York: Harper and Row, 1953).

35. In an article posted on the Global SchoolNet (a Microsoft-sponsored site for computer education), Al Rogers writes: "Large segments of our society use [computers] to collect, produce, manipulate, analyze, synthesize, transform, and report information in a variety of contexts and formats. With the advent of the Internet in the academic and research community, we now add the ability to collaborate, communicate, share, exchange . . . in ways that are now truly transforming our economy and, increasingly, our culture. . . . Unfortunately, these tasks

are exactly what most schools and most teachers are not equipped to accomplish, since the educational industry today requires teachers to 'deliver' a prescribed body and sequence of knowledge."

36. On the impact of technology itself on culture, see Gene I. Rochlin, *Trapped in the Net: The Unanticipated Consequences of Computerization* (Princeton, N.J.: Princeton University Press, 1997); see also J. R. Beniger, *The Control Revolution: Technological and Economic Origins of the Information Society* (Cambridge, Mass., and London: Harvard University Press, 1986).

37. Sigmund Freud, *Civilization and Its Discontents* (New York: W. W. Norton, 1961), p. 39.

38. Lewis Perelman, *School's Out: Hyperlearning, the New Technology, and the End of Education* (New York: William Morrow, 1992).

39. Diane Ravitch writes of a world of "pedagogical plenty" made available at home over the television at the child's convenience. See Ravitch, "When School Comes to You," *The Economist* (September 11, 1993): 45.

40. Plato, *Phaedrus and Letters VII and VIII*, trans. Walter Hamilton (New York: Penguin Books, 1973), p. 96.

41. For examples of undesired and unpredictable consequences of technology on culture, see Lewis Mumford, *Technics and Civilization* (New York: Harcourt Brace Jovanovich, 1963), and S. Geidion, *Mechanism Takes Command: A Contribution to Anonymous History* (New York: W. W. Norton, 1948).

42. Mark Slouka argues that computer-technology amounts to a kind of assault on reality, making it harder to distinguish real life from virtual reality and even making virtual reality more attractive. Slouka fears that new computer technology may even redefine what it means to be human. See Slouka, *War of the Worlds: Cyberspace and the High-Tech Assault on Reality* (New York: Basic Books, 1995).

43. This shaping is what Aristotle called *paideia*.

CHAPTER SEVEN   Christianity and the Pursuit of Excellence

1. In the *Nicomachean Ethics*, Aristotle argues that the morally virtuous person has a kind of excellence of soul. Excellence is determined by the end that any given thing is meant to fulfill by nature. When human beings fulfill their proper end, they are achieving excellence.

2. Stephen R. Covey, *The Seven Habits of Highly Effective People: Powerful Lessons in Personal Change* (New York: Simon and Schuster, 1989); Thomas J. Peters, *In Search of Excellence: Lessons from America's Best-Run Companies* (New York: Harper and Row, 1982).

3. Philippians 4:8 (NRSV).

4. W. K. Clifford, *Lectures and Essays* (1879), reprinted in M. Peterson et al., eds., *Philosophy of Religion: Selected Readings* (New York: Oxford, 1996), p. 66.

5. Ibid.

6. John Stuart Mill, *On Liberty* (New York: Penguin, 1982), chap. 2.

7. Work done by certain Christian philosophers known as "Reformed epistemologists" severely criticizes Clifford's evidentialism. See, for example, Alvin Plantinga, "Is Belief in God Rational?" in C. F. Delaney, ed., *Rationality and Religious Belief* (Notre Dame, Ind.: University of Notre Dame Press, 1979), pp. 7–27.

8. See especially Alvin Plantinga, *Warranted Christian Belief* (New York: Oxford University Press, 2000).

9. There is an interesting body of research to indicate that "threatening defense" is the best method for helping students cope with objections to their religious faith and worldview. Threatening defense involves exposing students to criticism of their faith and then helping them to work through them. See Nicholas Wolterstorff, *Educating for Responsible Action* (Grand Rapids, Mich.: Eerdmans, 1980), pp. 60–62.

10. Madeleine L'Engle, *A Wrinkle in Time* (New York: Dell, 1976), pp. 112–13.

11. Michael Cain, "Psychic Surrender: America's Creeping Paralysis," *Humanist* 43 (July–August, 1983): 5–11.

12. C. S. Lewis, *The Screwtape Letters* (New York: Macmillan, 1961), p. 8.

13. 2 Corinthians 10:4–5 (NRSV).

14. Henri de Lubac, *The Drama of Atheist Humanism* (New York: New American Library, 1963), p. 3

15. In his Father Brown stories, G. K. Chesterton provides a quaint illustration that intellect is not opposed to faith. Brown engineers the capture of the famous international criminal Flambeau, who had disguised himself as a priest in order to steal the Blue Cross from a conference in London. As Flambeau is being arrested by the police, he asks Brown how he knew he was an imposter. Brown tells Flambeau that, at breakfast that morning, he had unwittingly tipped his hand in attempting to seem like a

pious priest. "You attacked reason," said Father Brown. "It's bad theology." G. K. Chesterton, *The Complete Father Brown* (London: Penguin Books, 1963), p. 23.

16. A sampling of Christian intellectuals who faithfully conduct their scholarly vocation is found in Kelly Monroe, *Finding God At Harvard: Spiritual Journeys of Christian Thinkers* (Grand Rapids, Mich.: Zondervan, 1996).

17. Alvin Plantinga speaks of the benefit of the intellectual community at Calvin College, pointing out that their commonly understood intellectual heritage provided a basis for all discussions so that they did not have to "start at ground zero" every time they addressed some issue.

18. The revival of Catholic higher education in the early part of the twentieth century was intended to create a common culture. Two important aspects of that project were the revival of Thomism among Catholic thinkers, and the commitment to liberal arts (including versions of the Great Books program at the University of Chicago). For brief expositions of the thinking of Thomas Aquinas, see Ralph McInerny, *St. Thomas Aquinas* (Boston: G. K. Hall, 1977), and Etienne Gilson, *The Christian Philosophy of St. Thomas Aquinas* (New York: Random House, 1956).

19. Mark Noll, *The Scandal of the Evangelical Mind* (Grand Rapids, Mich.: Eerdmans, 1994), p. 44; see also Christopher Dawson, *The Formation of Christendom* (New York: Sheed and Ward, 1967), chap. 11, and David Knowles, *The Evolution of Medieval Thought* (New York: Random House, 1962).

20. Noll, *The Scandal of the Evangelical Mind*, p. 44.

21. Mark Noll, "The Earliest Protestants and the Reformation of Education," *Westminster Theological Journal* 43 (1980): 208–30.

22. Martin Luther, "Sermon on Keeping Children in School," in *Luther's Works*, American edition, vol. 6, ed. Robert C. Schultz (Philadelphia: Fortress Press, 1967), p. 211.

23. Susan E. Schreiner, *The Theater of His Glory: Nature and the Natural Order in the Thought of John Calvin* (Durham, N.C.: Labyrinth Press, 1991).

24. Noll, *The Scandal of the Evangelical Mind*, p. 3.

25. John Tracy Ellis, *American Catholics and the Intellectual Life* (Chicago: Heritage Foundations, 1956).

26. Neuhaus publishes the journal *First Things*. Bennett writes popular books recommending a return to classical learning and traditional

morality, such as *The Book of Virtues: A Treasury of Great Moral Stories* (New York: Simon and Schuster, 1993).

27. See the celebratory writings of the twentieth anniversary of the Society of Christian Philosophers in *Faith and Philosophy* 15, no. 2 (April 1998). On the rise of philosophy of religion in the twentieth century see Charles Talliaferro, "A Hundred Years with the Giants and the Gods: Christians and Twentieth-Century Philosophy," *Christian Scholars Review* 29, no. 4 (Summer 2000): 695–712. See also Thomas Morris, ed., *God and the Philosophers* (New York: Oxford University Press, 1994), and Kelly Clark, ed., *Philosophers Who Believe* (Downers Grove, Ill.: InterVarsity Press, 1993).

28. William E. Hull, "Toward Samford as a Christian University— Occasional Papers of the Provost," Samford University, Birmingham, Ala., July 15, 1990, pp. 5–6.

29. Romans 12:2 (NRSV).

30. George Marsden, *The Outrageous Idea of Christian Scholarship* (New York: Oxford University Press, 1997), p. 4.

31. Of course, the great theme of the analogy of being (*analogia entis*) is found in Aquinas. For a modern treatment, see E. L. Mascall, *Existence and Analogy* (Hamden, Conn.: Archon Books, 1967).

32. Augustine, *The Confessions* (New York: Oxford University Press, 1998), p. 208.

33. Norman Pittenger, *Life as Eucharist* (Grand Rapids, Mich.: Eerdmans, 1973).

34. Harry Blamires, *The Christian Mind* (Ann Arbor, Mich.: Servant Books, 1963), p. 156.

35. Bernard of Clairvaux, *On Loving God*, trans. Robert Walton (Kalamazoo, Mich.: Cistercian Publications, 1973), p. 94.

36. "To be, to exist" and "to be true" are equivalent. This is an integral theme in the work of St. Thomas Aquinas, who writes, "all things are true and no things are false (*omnis res est vera et nulla res est falsa*)," *Disputed Questions on Truth* I, 10.

37. St. Thomas goes on to argue that the human ability to know truth displays, first, the feature of dwelling most intensively within oneself and, second, being able to grasp the universe. This means that human beings have a very high degree of selfness and a very high degree of relatedness to all other things. Any definition of "spirit" must account for these two aspects.

38. Jeremiah 17:9 (KJV).

39. "[God] destroys both the blameless and the wicked" (Job 9:22 NRSV). It is fascinating to see Jesus empathize with suffering and not consider it punishment for sin. "And his disciples asked him, saying, Master, who did sin, this man, or his parents, that he was born blind? Jesus answered, Neither hath this man sinned, nor his parents: but that the works of God should be made manifest in him" (John 9:2–3 NRSV).

40. Matthew 22:34–40 (NRSV).

41. Romans 12:1 (NRSV).

42. Dallas Willard, *The Spirit of the Disciplines* (San Francisco: HarperSanFrancisco, 1988), p. 70.

43. Elton Trueblood, *The Incendiary Fellowship* (New York: Harper and Row, 1967), p. 118.

44. Dietrich Bonhoeffer, *Life Together* (San Francisco: HarperSanFrancisco, 1954), p. 30.

45. Matthew 5:13–16 (NRSV).

46. Robert Briner, *Roaring Lambs* (Grand Rapids, Mich.: Zondervan, 1993).

47. Robert Bellah et al., *Habits of the Heart* (Berkeley: University of California Press, 1985). See especially p. 295.

48. Richard J. Mouw, *Uncommon Decency: Christian Civility in an Uncivil World* (Downers Grove, Ill.: InterVarsity Press, 1992).

49. Second Vatican Council, "Pastoral Constitution on the Church in the Modern World," no. 1, in *Documents of Vatican II*, ed. Austin P. Flannery (Grand Rapids, Mich.: Eerdmans, 1975), p. 903.

50. Alvin Plantinga, "Advice to Christian Philosophers" (with a special, new preface for Christian thinkers from different disciplines), at www.faithandphilosophy.com. The original article appeared in *Faith and Philosophy* 1, no. 3 (1984): 253–71.

51. See B. F. Skinner, *Beyond Freedom and Dignity* (New York: Bantam, 1971) and *About Behaviorism* (New York: Vintage Books, 1976).

52. For example, see Michael Martin, *Atheism: A Philosophical Justification* (Philadelphia: Temple University Press, 1990). The academic journal *Philo*, published by the Council for Secular Humanism, was founded in 1998 to continue the contemporary discussion of the grounds for atheism.

Suggested Reading

Adler, Mortimer J. *The Paideia Proposal: An Educational Manifesto.* New York: Macmillan, 1982.

——. *Reforming Education: The Opening of the American Mind.* New York: Macmillan, 1988.

Barzun, Jacques. *The American University.* Chicago: University of Chicago Press, 1993.

Blaimires, Harry. *The Christian Mind: How Should a Christian Think?* 1st American edition. Ann Arbor, Mich.: Servant Books, 1978; 1st ed., 1963.

Bloom, Allan. *The Closing of the American Mind: How Higher Education Has Failed Democracy and Impoverished the Souls of Today's Students.* New York: Simon and Schuster, 1987.

Bok, Derek. *Higher Learning.* Cambridge, Mass: Harvard University Press, 1986.

Brann, Eva T. H. *Paradoxes of Education in a Republic.* Chicago and London: University of Chicago Press, 1979.

Buckley, Michael J. *The Catholic University as Promise and Project: Reflections in a Jesuit Idiom.* Washington, D.C.: Georgetown University Press, 1998.

Burtchaell, James Tunstead. *The Dying of the Light: The Disengagement of Colleges and Universities from Their Christian Churches.* Grand Rapids, Mich., and Cambridge: Eerdmans, 1998.

Dawson, Christopher. *The Crisis of Western Education.* New York: Sheed and Ward, 1961.

Derrick, Christopher. *Escape from Skepticism: Liberal Education As If Truth Mattered.* San Francisco: Ignatius Press, 2001.

Dewey, John. *Democracy and Education.* New York: Macmillan, 1916.

Ditmanson, Harold H., Howard V. Hong, and Warren A. Quanbeck, eds. *Christian Faith and the Liberal Arts.* Minneapolis: Augsburg Publishing House, 1960.

Dockery, David S., and David P. Gushee. *The Future of Christian Higher Education*. Nashville, Tenn: Broadman and Holman Publishers, 1999.

Donovan, George F. *Vatican Council II: Its Challenge to Education*. Washington, D.C.: The Catholic University of America Press, 1967.

D'Souza, Dinesh. *Illiberal Education: The Politics of Race and Sex on Campus*. New York: Free Press, 1991.

Ferré, Nels F. S. *Christian Faith and Higher Education*. New York: Harper and Brothers, 1954.

Fuller, Edmund, ed. *The Christian Idea of Education*. New Haven, Conn.: Yale University Press, 1957.

Garber, Steven. *The Fabric of Faithfulness: Weaving Together Belief and Behavior during the University Years*. Downers Grove, Ill.: InterVarsity Press, 1996.

Gleason, Philip. *Contending with Modernity: Catholic Higher Education in the Twentieth Century*. New York: Oxford University Press, 1995.

Grant, Mary, and Thomas Hunt. *Catholic School Education in the United States: Development and Current Concerns*. New York: Garland Publishing, 1992.

Greene, Maxine. *Education, Freedom, and Possibility*. New York: Teachers College Press, 1975.

Greene, Maxine, et al. *The Master Teacher Concept: Five Perspectives*. Austin, Tex.: Research and Development Center for Teacher Education, 1984.

Healy, June M. *Endangered Minds: Why Our Children Don't Think*. New York: Simon and Schuster, 1990.

Hesburgh, Theodore M., ed. *The Challenge and Promise of a Catholic University*. Notre Dame, Ind., and London: University of Notre Dame Press, 1994.

Hirsch, E. D., Jr. *Cultural Literacy: What Every American Needs to Know*. Boston: Houghton Mifflin, 1987.

Holmes, Arthur F. *All Truth Is God's Truth*. Grand Rapids, Mich.: Eerdmans, 1977.

———. *Building the Christian Academy*. Grand Rapids, Mich.: Eerdmans, 2001.

———. *The Idea of a Christian College*. Grand Rapids, Mich.: Eerdmans, 1975.

Hook, Sidney, ed. *In Defense of Academic Freedom*. New York: Bobbs-Merrill, Pegasus, 1971.

Hughes, Richard T., and William B. Adrian. *Models for Christian Higher Education*. Grand Rapids, Mich., and Cambridge: Eerdmans, 1997.

Hutchins, Robert M. *The Higher Learning in America.* New Haven, Conn.: Yale University Press, 1936.

John Paul II. *Fides et Ratio.* Boston: Pauline Books, 1999.

——. *Ex Corde Ecclesiae: On Catholic Universities.* Washington, D. C.: United States Catholic Conference, 1990.

Kirk, Russell. *Decadence and Renewal in the Higher Learning.* South Bend, Ind.: Gateway Editions, 1978.

Langan, John, S.J., and Leo J. O'Donovan. *Catholic Universities in Church and Society: A Dialogue on Ex Corde Ecclesiae.* Washington, D.C.: Georgetown University Press, 1993.

Malik, Charles. *A Christian Critique of the University.* Downers Grove, Ill: InterVarsity Press, 1982.

Mannoia, V. James, Jr. *Christian Liberal Arts: An Education that Goes Beyond.* Lanham, Mass.: Rowman and Littlefield, 2000.

Maritain, Jacques. *Education at the Crossroads.* Westford, Mass.: Murray Printing Company, 1978; 1st printing with Yale University Press, 1943.

Marsden, George. *The Outrageous Idea of Christian Scholarship.* New York: Oxford University Press, 1997.

——. *The Soul of the American University: From Protestant Establishment to Established Nonbelief.* New York: Oxford University Press, 1994.

Marsden, George M., and Bradley J. Longfield, eds. *The Secularization of the Academy.* New York: Oxford University Press, 1992.

Martin, Jane Roland. *Coming of Age in Academe: Rekindling Women's Hopes and Reforming the Academy.* New York: Routledge, 2000.

Neuhaus, Richard John, ed. *Democracy and the Renewal of Public Education.* Grand Rapids, Mich.: Eerdmans, 1986.

Newman, John Henry. *The Idea of a University.* San Francisco: Rinehart Press, 1960.

Niebuhr, H. R. *Christ and Culture.* New York: Harper, 1951.

Nisbet, Robert. *The Degradation of the Academic Dogma: The University in America 1945–1970.* New York: Basic Books, 1971.

Noddings, Nel, et al. *Justice and Caring: The Search for Common Ground in Education.* New York: Teachers College Press, 1999.

Noll, Mark A. *The Scandal of the Evangelical Mind.* Grand Rapids, Mich.: Eerdmans, 1994.

Oakley, Francis. *Community of Learning: The American College and the Liberal Arts Tradition.* New York: Oxford University Press, 1992.

O'Brien, David J. *From the Heart of the American Church: Catholic Higher Education and American Culture.* Maryknoll, N.Y.: Orbis Books, 1994.

Pelikan, Jaroslav. *Scholarship and Its Survival*. Princeton, N. J.: Carnegie Foundation for the Advancement of Teaching, 1983.

Pelikan, Jaroslav, et al. *Religion and the University*. Toronto: University of Toronto Press, 1964.

Pieper, Josef. *Leisure: The Basis of Culture*. New York: Random House, 1963.

———. *Living The Truth*. San Francisco: Ignatius Press, 1989.

Plantinga, Alvin. *The Twin Pillars of Christian Scholarship*. The Stob Lectures. Grand Rapids, Mich.: Calvin College, 1990.

Postman, Neil. *The End of Education: Redefining the Value of School*. New York: Vintage Books, 1995.

Schwehn, Mark. *Exiles from Eden: Religion and the Academic Vocation in America*. New York: Oxford University Press, 1993.

Sire, James W. *Discipleship of the Mind*. Downers Grove, Ill.: Inter-Varsity Press, 1990.

Sloan, Douglas. *Faith and Knowledge: Mainline Protestantism and American Higher Education*. Louisville, Ky.: Westminster/John Knox Press, 1994.

Sykes, Charles. *Dumbing Down Our Kids: Why America's Children Feel Good about Themselves but Can't Read, Write, or Add*. New York: St. Martin's Press, 1995.

Trueblood, D. Elton. *The Idea of a College*. New York: Harper and Brothers, 1959.

Van Doren, Mark. *Liberal Education*. Boston: Beacon Press, 1943.

Weaver, Richard M. *Ideas Have Consequences*. Chicago and London: University of Chicago Press, 1948.

Willimon, William H., and Thomas H. Naylor. *The Abandoned Generation: Rethinking Higher Education*. Grand Rapids, Mich.: Eerdmans, 1995.

Winter, David G., David C. McClelland, and Abigail J. Stewart. *A New Case for Liberal Arts*. San Francisco: Jossey-Bass, 1981.

Wise, Jessie, and Susan Wise Bauer. *The Well-Trained Mind*. New York: Norton, 1999.

Wolff, Robert Paul. *The Ideal of the University*. Boston: Beacon Press, 1969.

Wolterstorff, Nicholas. *Educating for Responsible Action*. Grand Rapids, Mich.: Eerdmans, 1980.

Index

ACLU, 143–44
actuality (Thomistic realism), 40–41
Adler, Mortimer
 curriculum, 117–19
 liberal education, 141
 multiculturalism, 177
 Thomistic realism, 41, 44
 Western canon, 170
aesthetics
 Christian perspective of, 106–7,
  122–23
 definition of, 15
 existentialism on, 67, 69, 70
 experimentalism on, 55, 58–59, 61
 idealism on, 22–23, 25, 224n.10
 naturalism on, 34–35
 postmodernism on, 83–84, 87–88,
  231n.57
 Thomistic realism on, 43–44, 45–46
analytic philosophy, 16, 72–79
Anglican Thirty-Nine Articles, 11
Apostles' Creed, 11, 12, 96, 221n.10
argumentation, 16, 201–2
Aristotle
 education, 1
 excellence pursuit, 193, 245n.1
 liberal education, 111, 237n.1
 moral education, 104, 147
 multiculturalism, 177
 normative philosophy, 77–78
art. *See* aesthetics

Asbury College, 130
the Atonement, 11
Austin, John, 74
axiology
 Christian perspective of, 103–7,
  119–23, 234nn.12, 14, 15,
  235nn.18–19
 definition of, 15
 education in, 142–50, 238n.12,
  239n.14, 240n.20
 existentialism on, 66–67, 69, 70
 experimentalism on, 54–55, 57–59,
  60–61
 idealism on, 21–23, 24–25,
  224nn.9, 10
 naturalism on, 30–31, 33–35, 37–38
 postmodernism on, 83–84, 86–88,
  231n.57
 Thomistic realism on, 42–44,
  45–46, 47

Bacon, Sir Francis, 28
Barth, Karl, 64
beauty. *See* aesthetics
behaviorism, 33, 38, 146–47
belief formation, 100–101,
 195–202, 233n.7, 246n.9
Bennett, William, 148, 177, 206
Berkeley, George, 20, 25–26
Bradley, F. H., 20
Broudy, Harry, 34

Buber, Martin, 64, 68
Buddha, 11–12

Calvin College, 130, 207, 247n.17
Camus, Albert, 64
canon, Western, 169–71, 174–78
career training and liberal education,
    111–12, 139–42
Catechism of the Catholic Church, 12
Chalcedon, 10
Chavez, Linda, 175–76
child learners, 178–83
Christianity
  academic freedom and, 167
  axiology and, 103–7, 119–23,
      234nn.12, 14, 15, 235nn.18–19
  characteristics of, 9–13, 203–12,
      221n.10, 247n.17
  cultural influence of, 215–20
  education related to, 107–9, 109–14,
      151–53, 182–83, 236n.35
  epistemology and, 100–103, 114–19,
      233n.7
  excellence pursuit in, 193–94,
      245n.1
  existentialism and, 64–65, 71–72
  experimentalism and, 62–63
  family of, 182–83, 244n.33
  idealism and, 22, 27
  integration with learning and, 95,
      132–39
  metaphysics and, 96–100, 112–13,
      233n.6
  moral education and, 143–45
  multiculturalism and, 171–74
  naturalism and, 30, 38–39
  philosophical analysis and, 78–79
  postmodernism and, 90–93, 232n.60
  and separation of church and state,
      157–62
  surrendering to God in, 212–15
  technology and, 189–91

Thomistic realism and, 41, 42,
    48–49
  truth pursuit in, 196–202, 210–11
the church
  community in, 214–15
  culture and, 216–19
  and state separation, 107–9, 157–62
Clifford, W. K., 195–97
College of the Holy Cross, 130
colleges of liberal education, 129–32
community in the church, 214–15
computers and education, 183–91,
    244n.35, 245n.42
Constantinople I, 10
Constantinople II, 10
Constantinople III, 10
creational metaphysics, 96–100,
    233n.6
cultural influence of Christians,
    215–20
curriculum
  Christianity and, 109–14, 117–19,
      236n.35
  existentialism in, 67–69
  experimentalism in, 55–59, 61–62,
      228n.12
  idealism in, 23–25, 26–27
  naturalism in, 31–36
  pedagogy and, 150–55
  philosophical analysis and, 74–78
  postmodernism in, 84–88
  Thomistic realism in, 44–46, 47–48,
      226n.44
  See also education

Darwin, Charles, 28
Dawkins, Richard, 28
Derrida, Jacques, 80, 82–83, 204
de Saussure, Ferdinand, 80, 230n.46
Descartes, René, 51, 86, 227n.1
descriptive philosophy, 16–17
determinism, 28–29, 36–37